PROFESSOR CAT JARMAN FSA is th[e]
Kings: The Vikings from Scandinavia t[o]
archaeologist and field archaeologist s
and Rapa Nui. In her work, she uses forensic ......
analysis, carbon dating and DNA analysis on human remains to
untangle the experiences of past people from broader historical
narratives. She co-hosts the podcast *The Rabbit Hole Detectives* with
Richard Coles and Charles Spencer and is a broadcaster who regularly contributes to TV documentaries as a presenter and historical
consultant.

A *TIMES* HISTORY BOOK OF THE YEAR

'Beguiling . . . I adored [*River Kings*] so felt like a young boy on
Christmas morning when I first opened *The Bone Chests* . . .
Jarman's investigation has something of a Dan Brown quest to
it . . . she's a diligent historian and a superb writer'
The Times

'This is the best kind of popular history, retelling the story of early
medieval England with an equally good grasp of textual sources,
archaeology and forensic analysis, and a love of Winchester'
Ronald Hutton

'Through their story, we can recapture the spirit of the Anglo-
Saxon age and, as Jarman writes, learn about the "past lives of
people who were a little bit like us, who lived, loved, and left an
imprint on the generations that came after them", and who in
their vexing anonymity encourage us to find out more'
Literary Review

'An engaging account of England's pre-Conquest monarchs,
from famous figures such as Alfred the Great to long-forgotten
kings Cynegils and Centwine'
i News

Also by Cat Jarman

River Kings: The Vikings from Scandinavia to the Silk Roads

THE BONE CHESTS

Unlocking the Secrets of the Anglo-Saxons

CAT JARMAN

WILLIAM COLLINS

William Collins
An imprint of HarperCollins*Publishers*
1 London Bridge Street
London SE1 9GF

WilliamCollinsBooks.com

HarperCollins*Publishers*
Macken House
39/40 Mayor Street Upper
Dublin 1
DO1 C9W8
Ireland

First published in Great Britain in 2023 by William Collins
This William Collins paperback edition published in 2024

1

ISBN 978-0-00-844731-1

Chest illustrations by Joe McClaren
Set in Adobe Garamond Pro by Jouve (UK), Milton Keynes

Printed and bound in Great Britain by CPI Group (UK) Ltd, Croydon

For Oscar and Sebastian

CONTENTS

CHEST I: KINGDOMS

CHEST II: THREATS

THE LOST CHESTS: MEMORY

CHEST III: PEACE

CHEST IV: SUCCESSION

CHEST V: CONQUEST

CHEST VI: IDENTITY

THE BONE CHESTS

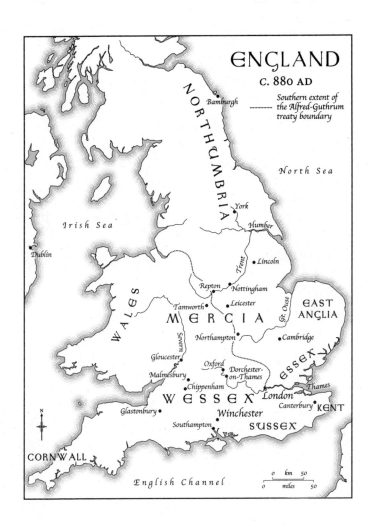

ENGLAND

C. 880 AD

········· Southern extent of
the Alfred-Guthrum
treaty boundary

North Sea

Irish Sea

NORTHUMBRIA

Bamburgh

York

Humber

Dublin

Lincoln

Trent

Repton
Nottingham
Tamworth
Leicester

MERCIA

Gt. Ouse

EAST
ANGLIA

Northampton
Cambridge

Severn

Gloucester
Oxford
Malmesbury
Dorchester-
on-Thames
Chippenham

WALES

ESSEX

Thames

WESSEX
London

Glastonbury
Winchester
Canterbury
KENT

Southampton
SUSSEX

CORNWALL

English Channel

0   km   50
0   miles   50

PLAN OF WINCHESTER CATHEDRAL

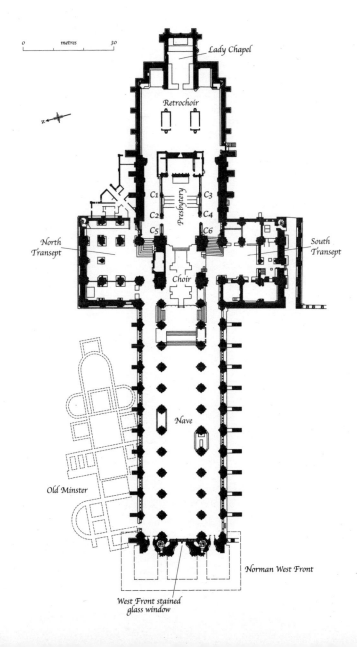

0   metres   30

Lady Chapel

Retrochoir

N

C1   C3
C2   C4

Presbytery

C5   C6

North Transept

South Transept

Choir

Nave

Old Minster

Norman West Front

West Front stained glass window

AUTHOR'S NOTE

The Winchester mortuary chests and the remains they contain have fascinated visitors to the cathedral for centuries. My intention with this book is to tell the stories of the chests and of the tumultuous times that they, and the people interred within, have found themselves in. Another theme of the book has been to consider why the kingdom of Wessex, and Winchester in particular, took on such significance in the history of England in the early medieval period. For this reason, the emphasis of the book is very much on the south and south-west of England, to the occasional negligence of the rest of the country.

I've taken the liberty of inventing a numbering system for the chests, placing them – vaguely – in chronological order, for simplicity and for narrative purposes. For discussions on the history of the chests and their contents, and the interpretations of who may *really* be inside them, I have relied on the excellent work by Martin Biddle and Birthe Kjølbye-Biddle (2005, 2016), Barbara Yorke (2021) and John Crook (2022) (see the select bibliography for full details). I'm especially indebted to John's analysis, which takes into account the preliminary results of the Mortuary Chests Project, a research project led by a team of archaeologists from the University of Bristol in collaboration with Winchester Cathedral that began in 2012.

While I have no personal involvement in the project, the team released partial results in May 2019, through a series of press releases and media statements. Further details of the results were also shared in the 'Kings and Scribes' exhibition in Winchester Cathedral, which opened in 2019 and is, at the time of writing, still open to visitors. The details incorporated in *The Bone Chests* are taken from those sources. As that project is still ongoing, their initial conclusions may well change – a normal part of the archaeological process!

Each section of this book opens with a narrative based on real people who have interacted with the chests over the course of history. While their thoughts and sentiments are by necessity imagined, the facts are taken from historical sources.

Ultimately, this is a story of past people and past lives, and of how their narratives are woven into what we refer to as history. It is a story of both the seekers and the sought, and the emphasis we place on physical remains and connections to the past – and not least, the power those remains have to shape our understanding of the present.

Wessex, July 2023

WINCHESTER, 1642

Wednesday, 14 December, between 9 and 10 a.m.

*I*n the early winter light, the city of Winchester is quiet. Inside the cathedral, the clergy are calmly going about their business, in this hour of the day set aside for administration. The looming threat to their community has not escaped them and the atmosphere is tense: two days ago, at noon on Monday, 12 December, Sir William Waller's Parliamentarian soldiers entered the city. The country has descended into civil war, a conflict that has divided all levels of society between those who support the king, Charles I, and those who are for Parliament. Power and religion lie at the heart of the conflict, leaving religious institutions in danger. The clergy can only put their faith in God's ability to keep them safe.

By now they know that their prayers are sorely needed. After passing through the gates of the city, the troops snatched horses belonging to the cathedral's estate; verbal threats were enough to seize them. Later that night they broke into the clergy's houses and the following day was filled with looting of the town at large – it would only be a matter of time before the cathedral fell victim too. So, on this Wednesday morning, there is little hope of defence when, in a sudden attack, invaders force their way into the six-hundred-year-old stone building through its great west door. The assault the soldiers have planned is more than just looting. Instead, it is a statement, their intent clear as they storm through the doors with colours flying, drums beating and torches lit. Some even ride their horses down the central nave of the *vast cathedral, with its arcade of arches either side, all the way to the choir, stopping only at the altar. Here the destruction begins in full force: the altar itself is broken apart and the wood carried to a nearby alehouse, along with prayer books and hymnals, torn from their shelves, later to be burned to ashes. The precious organ is smashed, the carved and carefully decorated Old and New Testament stonework flanking the stalls of the choir shattered. With the holiest centre of the cathedral defaced, the soldiers turn to their next target: the mortal remains of the ancient, venerated dead.*

The cathedral is filled with tombs, statues and memorials, and the soldiers are thorough. Monuments are wrecked and defaced in acts of wanton vandalism, in order to send a clear message. Finally, they turn their attention to the top of the finely carved stone screens that surround the central presbytery, the cathedral's beating heart, where religious ceremonies have been performed for nearly seven centuries. There, on a ledge, sit ten neatly spaced wooden chests, five on each side; placed up high to save them from 'rude and profane hands' by Richard Fox, the 57th Bishop of the See, in the 1520s. Cnut, Emma, William Rufus, Egbert and numerous other West Saxon kings lie within the chests; as do venerated ancient bishops. On this day in December, the soldiers clamber up the stone arches of the screens to reach their goal, the nimblest among them scurrying up the columns. When they get to the top, cheers and roars of success ring through the din.

Unceremoniously, the sacred chests are ripped open. Inside, bones reverently collected and curated by Fox and his predecessors are callously rifled through. But this is not enough. On the north side of the choir, the soldiers throw down the chests, smashing their contents onto the hard stone floor.

Yet this is a step too far for some of the onlookers. Voices cry out, compelling them to stop, and soon the Parliamentarian commanders take action, restraining their men from throwing down the rest of the chests. Still, the damage is done. The bones of the ancient kings of Wessex lie scattered on the floor of the cathedral, where they are deliberately trampled upon. The remaining chests may be saved but these bones will not be. As the destruction of the building resumes, observers watch in shock as the soldiers pick up the bones and hurl them at the beautifully crafted stained-glass windows that adorn the cathedral. The sacred remains of kings, queens, bishops and saints are used as missiles, shattering the artworks until nothing more than fragments are left on the floor below. Before the soldiers finally leave, they take with them items of silver and gold, anything they can find that is of value and portable: everything that is not, they have defaced or destroyed. The residents of Winchester can but watch as the troops ride through the streets carrying their spoils, some of them even dressed in the priests' vestments. The desecration of the cathedral is complete, and their message delivered.

It is only hours later, recovering from their terror, that the cathedral clergy begin to pick through the detritus of the onslaught, attempting to return what remains of those sacred bones to a safe place once again.

*I*n the southern corridor of the cathedral, a group of people has assembled. Half of them are clad, top to toe, in white paper overalls, with plastic goggles covering their eyes, masks over their mouths and nitrile gloves protecting their hands. For the first time in decades, the six mortuary chests that sit on top of the cathedral choir screens will be opened and their contents forensically analysed, using the latest scientific methods. A metal scaffold has been erected along the length of the stone choir, with a platform running around the narrow ledge where the chests now sit. The gentle voice of the cathedral's vice-dean travels across the space as he prays for the success of the project and in memory of the deceased. Two members of the forensic team carefully climb the ladder, the sound of metal against stone echoing around the quiet cathedral. When they reach the platform, they move to either side of the central chest, the one inscribed with the name of the eleventh-century king Edmund Ironside. Gently holding on to its sides, they lift the elaborately carved, painted lid and place it on the platform where they stand. Inside the chest, another, simple and unadorned wooden chest is revealed. Using the handles on its short ends, they lift this out too and put it on the platform. Here more members of the team wait with rolls of tin foil; gingerly, they wrap the chest to seal it, securing it with tape, taking every precaution to make sure the contents within are not contaminated. From the ground, a red mechanical cherry-picker slowly lifts a wide pallet towards them; they place the inner chest safely on the pallet and it is lowered to the ground. The process is carefully repeated with the remaining chests, each of them *labelled before they are taken, one by one, to the far eastern end of the building. Here the Lady Chapel beyond the retrochoir, one of three smaller spaces usually reserved for quiet worship, has been turned into a temporary laboratory. The bones in the chests cannot leave the cathedral, their home for more than nine hundred years.*

Inside the chapel, the team of anthropologists gets to work. The first chest is lifted onto a central table and the tin foil gently removed. Raising the lid, they see bones lying neatly laid out inside, clearly those of several individuals. Before a single bone is touched, the chests are photographed and drawn by hand in intricate detail, so that the exact position of each individual item is known and recorded. Afterwards, the bones are removed one by one and placed in a labelled bag ready to be described, documented, measured and identified. The team's aim: to catalogue and analyse the remains in an attempt to confirm whether, as they proclaim, the chests really contain the bones of the men and women who, in the space of five hundred years, witnessed and orchestrated the creation of England, fuelled and fortified by the actions of invading and settling Vikings and their descendants.

CHEST I

KINGDOMS

Cynegils d. 643
Æthelwulf d. 858

JUNE 2019

I *walk down the side aisle of Winchester Cathedral on a blustery and wet summer's day, jostling for space with locals and tourists taking shelter from the weather. A choir is practising for an evening performance, while a guide points out the tomb of Jane Austen to a group of Americans; a red rose lies wilting on the slab of her grave set into the floor beneath us. Walking across to the centre of the nave, I look up, taking in the vast scale of the stone structure. Winchester Cathedral was once the longest church north of the Alps: when first built, it measured a full 162 metres from end to end.*

The current cathedral, like most of its kind, is a patchwork of architectural iterations that only a trained eye can tease apart; each generation has added its enhancements to the eleventh-century structure commissioned by the new Norman elite, as led by the newcomer William the Conqueror. At the time the cathedral formed part of the Normans' extensive architectural reform of the nation's churches, a symbol of their desire to make an indelible, physical mark on his new territory. Before London began to play a leading political role around the turn of the eleventh century, Winchester had been highly significant for centuries: a key political and religious centre, first in the kingdom of Wessex, then in the fledgling country of England.

I turn to look towards the broad western front of the cathedral, with its three doorways and vast stained-glass window above, nine frames, or lights, wide. The frontage itself dates to the fourteenth century, its construction having been completed after the Black Death temporarily interrupted progress in the 1340s.

From a distance, there is nothing unusual about the window. The brightly coloured glass set within lead framing seems typical of its kind, and it's only when you walk up close that you notice that each of the fifty-three separate lights is a mosaic, made up of unevenly sized fragments: occasionally you can see a figure, a head or even a coat of arms, but mostly the glazing is more of an abstract composition. Here you get a glimpse of what the medieval visitor would have seen: an ornate depiction of the life of Christ, with apostles and prophets alongside him. The window is one of the few reminders left of the cathedral's fate during the Civil War, its original having suffered terribly in the Parliamentarian attack of 1642. After the onslaught all the glass that could be salvaged was diligently collected and kept, until a new mosaic was created some time after 1660.

Although they may be subtle, echoes of the past are all around me in this space. If you look carefully enough, you will no doubt find every century represented, with its religion, history, politics and sentiments, either through the architecture or more directly through the names, graves and actions of people whose lives were entwined with Winchester's past.

Today, I've come here specifically to see the mortuary chests. Turning my back to the window, I walk down the central nave again and just before the north and south transepts could take me either to the left or right, I reach the presbytery and the choir (or quire). A carved wooden screen divides the choir from the nave, separating clergy from worshippers. This is the oldest of the medieval choirs in England to survive largely intact: its elaborately carved wooden screens and furniture depicting foliage and figures, including so-called green men and a falconer, among many figures of a non-biblical nature. Up a few steps, the space is bounded at the other end by the Great Screen rising behind the high altar, an exceptionally intricate stone carved screen originally installed at the bequest of Cardinal Beaufort, one of Winchester's fifteenth-century bishops. The stone edifice centres on the figure of the crucified Christ, with tiers of statues all around representing the Company of Heaven. The current statues are just over a hundred years old, the originals having been systematically removed and destroyed in the reforms that took place in 1547: in acts of iconoclasm, devout Protestants demolished depictions of religious figures lest they encourage idolatry.

Today, however, with all this lavish craftmanship on display, it is easy to miss the bone chests. On either side of the presbytery are further stone screens separating it from the aisles to north and south. If you look up, you see a ledge several metres up, and here, in each of the six stone arches, a carved, painted and decorated wooden chest has been placed. Those six chests are the last to survive. Of the original ten that were commissioned in the 1520s by Bishop Fox, six were smashed by the Parliamentarians and four remain; the final two are replacements made around 1661.

The chests' history is an extraordinary and at times tragic tale; their story like something out of a Dan Brown novel. The bones within have survived – just – more than a millennium's worth of remarkable events, including the raid that left bones scattered and commingled on the cathedral floor. Each chest has a painted, Latin inscription, giving the names of the people allegedly interred within: people who made an indelible mark on the country's history. Thanks to these mortuary chests, Winchester is the only location in England where so many pre-conquest royals have been buried together in one place.

As I move closer and study each in turn, I see names that I recognise well: William Rufus – son of the Norman conqueror, notoriously described as 'the evil king who indulged unashamedly in unspeakable debauchery'. There's Eadred, a tenth-century king who expelled the Norwegian ruler Eric Bloodaxe and brought Northumbria under final English control; King Cynewulf, an eighth-century ruler who secured West Saxon independence on the eve of the first Viking attacks. Cnut the Great, the Viking ruler responsible for England's neglected invasion, is here too: he is the oft-forgotten king who for nineteen years included England in his Scandinavian empire. Remarkably, a woman is listed among the names as well: Queen Emma, wife first of King Æthelred the Unready, then of Cnut. The daughter of the Duke of Normandy, a powerful queen and mother of kings, who ultimately helped her great-nephew William the Conqueror stake his claim to the country. Ironically, Ælfwine, a bishop famously accused of having an illicit affair with Emma, is named here too.

Yet when you dig into the history of these chests, it is clear that the list of names cannot tell the full story. Written records dating back centuries before the chests were made tell of other names, whose remains may also have become jumbled up inside: more kings and several bishops. By the time of the Norman conquest in the eleventh century, Winchester had become the burial place for the rulers of England, with more recorded in this single place than anywhere else. But why here?

I walk out of the presbytery and into the northern aisle, to take a closer look at the chest in the far corner, inscribed with two names. One, I know well: Æthelwulf, the father of Alfred the Great, who laid the foundations for his son's immense success. The other I am less familiar with: Cynegils, who died in 648, at a time when there was no cathedral here and not even an England.

A church – likely its first – was built in the city in the seventh century, during the rule of Cenwealh, Cynegils' son. Emerging from the ruins of a former Roman town, that church was built during Winchester's fledgling years before it emerged as a major religious and political centre only a few centuries later. The church, later to transform into a minster – a church that was the focal point of a monastic community – then a cathedral, was the jewel in its crown; the city, for a while, the nucleus of the country.

As I stand in the aisle that bustles with tourists, I'm struck by how few people stop to look up at the chests and how, among those few who do glance up, so few seem to appreciate their importance. Are they, I ask myself, really as significant as I think they are? Are such *old bones still relevant in the twenty-first century? There is so much we don't know about these chests' histories: we're not even sure if the remains within have anything to do with those who are named on the outside. But perhaps, by untangling the bones, we might get closer to understanding not just who they were but also, why their remains have been preserved, and how their unique life stories fit into broader historical narratives – not least, the creation of England, and the stories we have told about that in the succeeding centuries. But to do so, we need to go back to where this all really began: the story of the kingdom of Wessex.*

KINGDOMS

I n 611, according to the *Anglo-Saxon Chronicle*, a king by the name of Cynegils succeeded to the throne in Wessex. In the time since the fall of the Roman empire two centuries earlier, what we now recognise as England had begun to materialise as a series of separate units, one of which was Wessex, the kingdom of the West Saxons, where Winchester is located. The realms' borders would wax and wane tumultuously over the centuries until England, as a *country*, began to take shape in the tenth century.

Yet the starting point for these kingdoms following the collapse of Roman rule is still unclear to us. After four centuries of Roman prosperity, in which Britain saw enormous growth in the number of towns, in industry, in agricultural productivity, and significant social and cultural change, the fall of Rome had an abrupt impact. By the end of the fourth century, towns and villas start to be abandoned across Britannia; coins are no longer minted; the production of pottery ceases. Cities such as the once prospering Londinium turn into veritable ghost towns. Life changes for the inhabitants of Britain: with the regular Roman army and members of the civil service either withdrawn or no longer paid in cash, the industries that propped up the economy become unsustainable and subsistence farming returns.

There were a few exceptions. Recent discoveries have challenged the view of an entirely desolate country: at the well-known Roman villa at Chedworth in Gloucestershire, a mosaic has been radiocarbon dated to the middle of the fifth century, well after the production of such crafts was thought to have ceased. It seems some of the people in the south-west were still living in luxury. Overall, however, the change was sudden and severe. Continental sources describe pagan raiders on the shores of Gaul, across the English Channel, in the fifth century and other sources depict the Britons being ravaged by Pictish and Irish attacks from the north. Then, if the sixth-century writer Gildas is to be believed, the real tragedy begins: the Saxons arrive on British shores and bring considerable misery in their wake. Gildas' tract, known as *On the Ruin and Conquest of Britain* (*De excidio et conquestu Britanniae*), states that the Saxons arrived as mercenaries to help fight against attackers from the north and west but later revolted against their allies.

A version of Gildas' narrative features in most subsequent early English writers' accounts of their history, taking his words more or less at face value. Somewhere from this point on, then, that origin story, the *adventus Saxonum,* became an indelible part of English history. But is the story true? Perhaps the most influential early English historian is a monk known as the Venerable Bede, who wrote the *Ecclesiastical History of the English People* in the eighth century. Living in Jarrow, Northumbria, Bede worked on his history of England for several years before its completion in 731 or shortly thereafter. It has proved one of the most influential and significant early medieval historic accounts ever since and it is, indeed, one of our most valuable sources for this period of English history. In it, Bede elaborates on the arrival of the Saxons, describing the three powerful Germanic tribes – Angles, Saxons and Jutes – that would later become the English people. In the year 449, according to Bede, the Angles or Saxons were invited to come to Britain by a king named Vortigern: they arrived in three longships and were granted lands in the east of the island on the condition that they protected it. However, Bede continues, this disguised their real intention. Instead of guarding the new territory, the newcomers sent word home summoning substantial new forces, which arrived with the aim of subduing the land of the Britons.

Bede's account is now understood to be deeply problematic: the idea of Germanic settlers arriving with fully formed identities relating to the continental tribes from which they originated is much too simplistic. For one thing, although some other groups were mentioned, Bede failed to mention groups such as the Franks, who are known to have come across the English Channel. More importantly, all the evidence now points to a situation in which *identities* were far more complex; those early migrants were a melting pot of people and origins. Writing several centuries after the time he describes, Bede was more likely reflecting a desire to explain the emergence of the strong identities that he understood from his own time, to give them a legitimacy by drawing them back into a past that was largely imagined.

There is now widespread agreement that these accounts are at best incomplete and at worst mythical and entirely fanciful. Similarly, the manuscripts of the *Anglo-Saxon Chronicle*, which provide a year-by-year account of events going back to the Roman invasions, began to be compiled from the end of the ninth century in the court of King Alfred, with the deliberate intention of creating a unified identity and a legitimisation of the Wessex ruling house.

As origin stories, they must therefore be taken with a pinch of salt. If we look to the archaeological evidence, however, we see this: there are, indeed, correlations between material culture in parts of England and that on the continent. Yet on the whole, in the late fifth century, identities and origins were clearly mixed and multi-faceted. By the time we reach 600, however, the situation had changed considerably and larger, regional identities had been formed, a key aspect of which was the creation of elites:

newly minted high-status families operating within social networks where material culture, gift exchange and marriage were all key components.

Identities were, in particular, expressed through the costumes of women. In Norfolk and on either side of the Humber, for instance, starting around 475, well-dressed women wore distinctive metal wrist-clasps sewn to the ends of their sleeves. The clasps hooked together a particular type of cuff, indicating that these women were wearing long-sleeved undergarments of a type known to be fashionable in western Norway. This implies that a certain number of Norwegian women – likely men too – had migrated and within a short space of time the fashion had spread and been widely adapted. Similar trends sprang up elsewhere: in Kent especially, inspiration could be drawn from fashions across the Channel, from the territory of the Franks. Within a few generations, such trends began to solidify into regional social markers. Jewellery and material culture, of course, formed only a small part of a much larger set of practices that altogether composed patterns of sameness and difference; patterns that were recognised as markers of identity. However, how the actual *kingdoms* that we later recognise came into being still requires some thought. There are two main views on this. The first suggests the idea of continuity, with kingdoms developing from the territories that existed in Roman Britain and areas like the Roman *civitas* – which had been a form of local government administration – being taken over by new warrior bands. The other view considers the process as being something entirely new, with no continuity and new kingdoms instead forming from the coalescence of smaller units, completely detached from pre-existing territories. There are certainly cases where one or the other makes sense, but it is hard to prove anything either way. However, numerous seventh-century kingdoms appear to map onto the Romano-British *civitates* and in some parts of the country, place names also suggest continuity: the name Devon relates in some way to the Dumnonii and Cornwall to the Cornovii.

The question of to what extent migration was involved in the making of what later became England remains contentious; some still argue that this *Englishness* was an entirely internal innovation while for others Bede's perspective – or something very much like it – is considered the gold standard.

Various scientific methods have been used over the years in attempts to answer this question of migration and understand the relationship between incoming Saxons and native Britons. These have included cranial measurements (phrenology) – a method that fell out of favour after its extensive use in racial stereotyping in the lead-up to the Second World War – and attempts at detecting race in skeletal material. Height and stature, for example: large-scale studies of cemeteries have shown that so-called Anglo-Saxon weapon burials often contained the remains of taller men. These wealthy graves, holding men with one or more weapons, were believed to be those of 'Saxons', whereas graves without weapons were more likely to be 'Britons'. However, there is no such way of detecting race or ethnicity. Height differences may well be genetically determined but equally, nutrition and access to a good diet will have a significant impact as well.

A DNA study recently tried to resolve the question of the size and type of migration events in Britain's history through the use of modern genetic samples. The study involved analysing the DNA of people alive today, on a large scale, as variations in genetic markers can reflect the movement of people in the past. The work claimed to show clear evidence in England of Saxon migrations, but with only a limited proportion of Saxon ancestry: the researchers estimated the maximum to be 50 per cent in central and southern England, and more likely in the range of 10–40 per cent. Yet this study has drawn criticism for a number of reasons, not least because it is difficult to untangle precisely *when* genetic changes took place in the past. Migrations from southern Scandinavia to England during the Viking Age, for example, would have seen people with the same genetic background arrive only a few hundred years later.

A more accurate result could come from the study of ancient DNA, the direct analysis of people alive at the time. There is great potential here, as around ten thousand graves from the earliest years of the medieval period have been recovered. In 2022, a team published the results of a large-scale, genome-wide ancient DNA analysis of 278 individuals from England dating to the early medieval period. The dataset was compared to DNA from skeletal remains from elsewhere in north-western Europe, as well as modern DNA, in order to investigate the extent of migration into England. The results were very clear: there had been a high degree of mobility, with up to 76 per cent of ancestry in eastern England deriving from the continental North Sea zone, from a migration that included both men and women of higher and lower status, identified from their gravegoods or other burial markers; in other words, people from all parts of society. There were, however, also individuals with little or no continental northern European (CNE) ancestry. Because the team could also identify family relationships, they found clear evidence, in several cemeteries, of mixing between ancestry groups. In one case, for instance, they showed that a family with several generations of CNE ancestry had integrated with a woman of ancestry they defined as 'Western British and Irish' (WBI), and had subsequent children with mixed CNE and WBI ancestry.

But while the team found high levels of migration throughout the sites they studied, there were variations between them; clearly no single pattern could fit all of England. The research showed, for example, more evidence of migration in cemeteries in south-eastern England than elsewhere, something that also fits with the archaeological evidence. When they compared the English dataset with those of other sites in Europe, it became clear that the likely origins of most migrants were to be found in the region that stretches from Denmark, south-western Sweden and northern Germany to the northern Netherlands. Intriguingly, however, they also found evidence of contact with Frankish territories, something that, again, matches the archaeology. The team was also surprised to discover that some of the migrations continued through the entire period, beginning very early on: some samples came from later Roman contexts. Elsewhere, sites like Sedgeford in Norfolk showed migration taking place as late as the eighth century, which has an impact on our understanding of the Viking Age migrations that began not long after.

Isotope analysis of human remains is another way of identifying first-generation migrants. We are, quite literally, what we eat, and our food and drink become the building blocks of all our tissues, from skin and bone to the enamel on our teeth that was formed during our childhood years. As we are constantly evolving organisms, our lunch today turns into the fuel of the cells that create the hair growing out of our scalps in a matter of days. This makes us walking diaries of our lives because what we consume carries with it subtle chemical signals that reflect not just the type of food we eat, but also where it was grown. All elements, such as carbon and oxygen, exist in different isotopes, which are simply atoms with different atomic weights. Variation in the ratios of these isotopes, however, can be specific to particular food types or environments, and those differences are passed up the food chain from soil to grain to wheat to bread to consumer. A loaf of bread made from wheat grown in Scotland will have a different isotopic signature to one from Frisia; drinking water imbibed in Norway will exhibit a different signature to that consumed in Wales. When our teeth are formed, those signatures are permanently locked into our enamel and can be measured when a skeleton is taken to a lab more than a millennium later. A recent large-scale study of cemeteries across England dating from the fifth to the eighth centuries also showed that migration took place throughout the entire period, both within Britain (especially from west to east) and from all regions of continental Europe, Scandinavia and even warmer areas like North Africa. Overall, the percentage of migrants appeared to be slightly lower than in the ancient DNA study. This could show us the longer-term perspective: descendants of migrants will have 'foreign' DNA but local isotope patterns.

The reality of the so-called Anglo-Saxon migrations, then, seems to be that there really was a high degree of mobility and migration across all levels of society and from a wide range of places, and they were not quite the very specific invasions the sources describe. Yet for centuries those migrations described in the *Chronicle* and by Bede have been seen as the key to England's history. 'It is with the landing of Hengest and his war-band at Ebbsfleet on the shores of the Isle of Thanet that English history begins,' wrote the historian John Richard Green in 1892. 'No spot in Britain can be so sacred to Englishmen as that which first felt the tread of English feet.' For Victorian historians such as Green, keen to pursue this noble origin story of the English, there were plenty of sources to go by. Importantly, the material that they relied upon, such as Bede's eighth-century account, had itself already been emphasising the key moments, groups and people that were venerated in Bede's own time.

The political landscape at this point in the post-Roman story is traditionally referred to as a heptarchy – a collection of seven kingdoms: East Anglia, Essex, Kent, Mercia, Northumbria, Sussex and Wessex. But this is almost certainly not the full picture. The idea that England was formed of these seven kingdoms is usually considered to have been conceived by the historian Henry of Huntingdon, when writing his book *Historia Anglorum* – the 'History of the English People' – in the twelfth century. Henry's narrative of England revolves around five great invasions, namely those of the Romans, the Picts and the Scots, the Angles and the Saxons, the Danes, and the Normans. He sees these as punishments that were inflicted on the people because of their lack of faith in God. For Henry, the unification of the English monarchy came about through the success of strong kings who ended up with large kingdoms after having defeated warring petty kings. Those he selected were the most prominent kingdoms found in documentary sources and some have gone as far as to suggest that Henry picked his own vision of Anglo-Saxon history. These were not the only kingdoms, but they were the ones that, towards the end of the period, became the major players.

Intriguingly, there has been a recent suggestion that the seven kingdoms also appear in a very unexpected source. In his *Book of Precious Records*, the tenth-century Persian historian Ibn Rusta records a passage derived from another Arabic writer by the name of Hārūn ibn Yaḥyā. The text describes how you could sail for three months from Rome to Burgundy, travel across mountains and ravines for a month to get to the land of the Franks, then overland until you got to the capital of Britain. This, he says, 'is a great city on the shore of the Western Ocean, ruled by seven kings'. The reference is difficult to interpret – was there actually a concept of a heptarchy already in existence, two centuries before this would be suggested by Huntingdon? And not only that, but also that this concept was known about as far away as Byzantium or Constantinople, where Ibn Rusta's source may have originated? While unprovable, it is certainly possible, although it is equally possible that the account refers to other subdivisions prevalent in the tenth century.

WESSEX'S FIRST CHRISTIAN KING

D espite all the problems with the sources, it appears that by the time Cynegils – that earliest king in the mortuary chests – came to power in 611, what would come to be known as Wessex was a regional, recognisable entity. The kingdom would not take on its best-known form until the eighth century and there are no maps or descriptions of the boundaries of its earliest version. An account of the formation of Wessex is given in the *Anglo-Saxon Chronicle*. The story goes that in the year 495, a Saxon by the name of Cerdic landed with his son somewhere on the south coast, where the two fought against the native Britons. A little while later, in 514, the West Saxons came to Britain with three ships, fighting against the Britons and putting them to flight. Further battles ensued until, in 519, a decisive victory enabled Cerdic to establish his superiority, and from this, the *Chronicle* states, came the origin of the Wessex lineage. Others had arrived on the scene too. The *Chronicle* notes that a certain Port and his two sons landed at Portesmupa (Portsmouth) and battled the Britons in the year 501. The Venerable Bede states that Jutes had established a province on the Isle of Wight that extended to the southern English mainland opposite. It has been suggested that this Jutish land could be that relating to Port and his sons. These individuals, then, were recorded as being among the founding fathers of the later kingdoms, to whom genealogies would be carefully crafted.

Cynegils' long rule was marked by warfare and rivalry, and many subsequent alliances with neighbouring Mercia. But the single event that was to define his reign – and is perhaps the reason why his name is one of the few that appear on the mortuary chests – is Wessex's conversion to Christianity.

The Roman empire had been officially Christian from the 360s onwards and this included Britain. Yet religion is rarely clear-cut:

while Roman Britain in general embraced Christianity, pockets of paganism survived; equally, after Rome's fall, the new religion had not entirely faded away. In fact, there remained strong regional differences and in western Britain, Christianity dominated. Eastern Britain told a different story: here the new religion had never quite taken as firm a root during Roman rule as it had in the west and as a consequence had little to cling to afterwards. Towards the end of the sixth century, however, missionaries were starting to take England's conversion to Christianity very seriously, especially in the pagan east.

Conversion proved key to the narrative written down by Bede. In 596, he tells us, Pope Gregory 'was inspired by God to send his servant Augustine with several other God-fearing monks to preach the word of God to the English nation'. In an account emphasising the paganism of the people of England, the delegation got only a short way along their journey before they became nervous: 'For they were appalled at the idea of going to a barbarous, fierce, and pagan nation, of whose very language they were ignorant.' They sent back Augustine, who was due to be consecrated bishop if the group were welcomed by the English, only for the Pope to respond that it was better not to have undertaken a high enterprise than to abandon it halfway: the group should buck up and get on their way. In the end, the mission proved successful. Landing on the Isle of Thanet, the group were given permission to preach in Kent and soon afterwards Augustine established his episcopal see in the city of Canterbury.

Yet the local success of Augustine's mission failed to lead to a general embrace of Christianity. It is difficult to judge what this meant in real terms, among the broader population. Even through archaeology, religion is very tricky to study and detect. Religious symbols such as crosses might give clues, but they don't help us determine how widely accepted a religion was. Burials are frequently used as a source of information, because funerary rites are often closely linked to religious beliefs. But even this is not clear-cut: while the rich pagan graves filled with gravegoods contrast sharply with simple Christian graves containing nothing but the body, this does not mean that unfurnished graves – that is, those without gravegoods – imply a deceased *Christian*.

Nonetheless, it seems clear that seventh-century Wessex was still pagan territory and Bede gives us the narrative of its conversion in 635, by none other than Cynegils. That year, Bede tells us, an Italian missionary named Bishop Birinus had promised Pope Honorius to take it on himself to reach 'those most inland and remote regions of the English, where no other teacher had been before him' – an area thought to be the Midlands. But Birinus never got that far, since soon after his arrival he entered the territory of the *Gewissae* (a group later to be named the West Saxons), who he found to be completely heathen. This, then, offered him a suitably needy audience and he decided to make it his focus, instead of seeking out more distant converts. We don't know the full circumstances around the event, but it is possible that Birinus made a beeline for the king's court in Oxfordshire in an attempt to convert Cynegils. Bede writes that when Cynegils agreed to be baptised, King Oswald of Northumbria – already a Christian – happened to be present to witness the conversion. He also explains that Oswald offered Cynegils an alliance by taking him as his godson, while Oswald married Cynegils' daughter Cyneburh. Afterwards the two kings jointly gave Bishop Birinus the city of Dorcic – Dorchester-on-Thames – for his episcopal see. Cynegils' son Cenwealh would also convert to Christianity a few years later, but not before an initial challenge: apparently, when Cenwealh succeeded to the throne on his father's death, he refused to accept the new religion. According to Bede, it took a war with neighbouring Mercia, which was under the rulership of King

Penda – incidentally a pagan – to convert Cenwealh. Originally married to Penda's sister, Cenwealh left her for another woman, who Bede leaves unnamed. This clearly did not go down well with Penda and drove him to war, causing Cenwealh to flee into exile in East Anglia: here, in the court of King Anna, he learned about and accepted Christianity, and was baptised.

We don't know exactly when Cynegils died but according to the *Anglo-Saxon Chronicle*, after his accession he held the kingdom for thirty-one years. This would place his death around 642, but we have no information about how he died or what happened to his body. The next we hear of his remains is the inscription on one of the mortuary chests. But how did he end up there? He would almost certainly have been buried somewhere else first, maybe Dorchester-on-Thames, because Winchester's heyday was yet to come, under the authority of his son Cenwealh.

OLD MINSTER – THE HEART
OF A FLEDGLING TOWN

'Oldminster ... became the very heart of the civilization of Wessex, and of England, and one of the foundation stones of the civilization of Western Europe.' These words, written by a former mayor of Winchester, are perhaps a little biased, but the point of view reflects the significance that Winchester would attain from an early point in the medieval period. By the late seventh century, the process was already underway.

The city dates its origins back to the Roman period, when it was known as Venta Belgarum. In its prime it had a walled centre: walls that later were to be rebuilt to contain its medieval city. The

Roman walls were punctuated by gates, with roads leading to other important centres: Northgate led to Silchester, Westgate to Sarum (Salisbury) and Southgate to Clausentum (Bitterne, near what would later become Southampton). Hence Venta's location was strategic, a place where many roadways met. This may explain why the town became such a bustling hub of trade and commerce and an administrative centre, as well as a meeting place for Romans and Britons from far afield. It had a good water supply and productive farmland nearby. Villas in the region had fine mosaic floors like those of houses in the city centre, showing how the town's wealth rolled out into the rich countryside.

By the fourth century, a list of Roman officers within the empire included someone in Venta who was in charge of the imperial weaving works there: a clear sign that the city was prosperous. There were large public buildings and its wealthy inhabitants dined on imported food and wine, using the finest ceramics and glass brought in from elsewhere in the empire. Yet sometime in the fifth century, in line with what was happening in the rest of Britain, the city declined. Its forum and streets gradually fell out of use and were lost, but archaeological evidence from the surrounding countryside suggests that it remained a focal point in the time that followed. Within the city walls too, there is some evidence of occupation in that early Saxon period: not much, but a few scattered artefacts – an amethyst pendant, vessel glass, some pieces of pottery and two spearheads among them – that reveal a presence.

The first written references to the city in the following period, however, are those we have already encountered, relating to Cynegils and, later, to his son Cenwealh. It seems likely that King Cenwealh built the first church around the year 650; one of the *Anglo-Saxon Chronicle* manuscripts claims he erected the minster there in St Peter's name in 648 and had it consecrated.

While there is no certainty as to the date, archaeological excavations have provided evidence that a church was constructed there around that time. This was the forerunner to and foundation of what became known from the beginning of the tenth century as Old Minster (or Oldminster), and was built just to the side of what is now Winchester's current, Norman cathedral. The church walls were laid on foundations made from broken and reused Roman tiles separated by courses of Roman rubble; material abandoned in the two centuries that had passed since the city's former glory. The style of the church, a cross-plan with a nave and narrower chambers to the east, north and south, was characteristic of those in northern Italy from the sixth century onwards. This, then, may reflect a link to Birinus and members of his Italian mission, as the sophistication of the architecture, the proportions and the technology needed to execute it clearly required in-depth knowledge.

Winchester, however, did not prove the initial focal point of Christianity in Wessex: that honour would be taken by Dorchester-on-Thames. It is unclear when the focus shifted westward, but it is possible it happened because of increasing pressure from neighbouring Mercia, as the border between the two kingdoms lay close by. According to Bede, Bishop Birinus was originally buried in Dorchester, but many years after his death his remains were translated to Winchester and laid to rest in the church he names as St Peter and St Paul. Bede also tells us that during the reign of Cenwealh, a new see was established in the city, after Cenwealh grew tired of Birinus' successor, a bishop from Gaul named Agilbert, because of his 'foreign speech'. The king, apparently, understood only Saxon. He invited another bishop by the name of Wini and divided the kingdom into two dioceses, giving Wini the city of Venta (or Wintancaestir) as his see in the year 660. Wini thereby became Winchester's first bishop. He was successful at first but for some unknown reason he too, like his predecessor, would feel the king's wrath and he was forced to flee to the central kingdom of Mercia, where he offered money in exchange for the bishopric of London in 656. This, however, did not prove a popular move because in the eyes of many of the clergy it amounted to simony: the practice, one of the greatest sins, of buying or selling spiritual or church benefits. As a result, Wini was shunned by many and condemned by Bede.

The church grew in significance as Winchester became more prominent. Yet whether it really had royal importance in the town from this early part of the seventh century is unclear: only one king is known to have been buried there in the seventh and eighth centuries, and grants of land received from the kings of Wessex in this period were not especially generous – which would suggest it was not a royal priority. Indeed, nearby lay another important economic centre: Hamwic, the predecessor to modern-day Southampton, only eighteen kilometres to the south, one of a number of *wics*, or emporia, that sprang up in the seventh and eighth centuries in strategic locations around the English Channel and the North Sea. With trade in the region lucrative, the *wics* were key, funnelling goods overseas and inland. This, some argue, suggests Hamwic represented the real centre of royal authority.

Coins may give us evidence in support of this, as Hamwic had a mint in the period between 725 and 775 while Winchester did not. The production of coins would not become widespread until later in the Early Middle Ages, so mints would almost certainly have been under royal control. Another sign of central control at Hamwic can be seen in its planning: an occupation that extended over a total of forty-seven hectares, with an arrangement of metalled roads and a grid pattern that seem to have been well maintained over time. Similar planning can be seen in Lundewic (London). No written evidence has been found that directly links a king to these towns but the extensive organisation that would have been needed to arrange the business of their administration would surely only have been possible for an elite entity like a king. In line with these developments, it seems likely that the seventh century was also the time when written records and contemporary annals started to be kept in Wessex.

On his death, Cenwealh was apparently buried in the church; according to one source, underneath the high altar.

A SUCCESSION OF RULERS

'Here Cenwalh passed away, and Seaxburh, his queen, ruled one year after him.' This short and innocuous-sounding entry in the *Anglo-Saxon Chronicle* for the year 672 is surprisingly remarkable: not for its wording, but for what it represents. Seaxburh is the only woman in this period to have ruled Wessex in her own right. In the West Saxon regnal list, she is the only woman to appear as a ruler – in a record that covers the 396 years up until Alfred's reign, from the time 'his ancestors had first conquered the West Saxons' land from the Britons'. The entry is not commented on as being something remarkable and Seaxburh's succession is treated in exactly the same way as that of any other ruler. But she clearly was unusual. In a patriarchal society, rulership remained men's territory.

We have very few details of Seaxburh and her life. Although not mentioned by name, she seems to be the second wife of Cenwealh recorded by Bede when describing how the king left his marriage to Penda's sister. Bede, however, claims that for ten years the kingdom was then ruled by a number of conflicting sub-kings, until Cædwalla subdued them all and reunited Wessex in around 685. It is perhaps not surprising that he left Seaxburh out of his story, not specifically because she was a woman, but because of what she represented: the story Bede tells of Cenwealh is a moral one, in part because the king was clearly not a good Christian, having been forced into exile by Penda after casting away his first wife and remarrying. Although not unusual at the time, this would have amounted to adultery in Bede's eyes. For him, the idea of the sin leading to dark times and a troubled succession would fit the narrative. An adulteress being rewarded with the throne, on the other hand, would not.

There is something else that is odd about Seaxburh's rule. The *Anglo-Saxon Chronicle* provides a genealogy and regnal list and in it a king named Æscwine succeeds in 674. Not only is there a missing year here – 673 – but the annal entry describes Æscwine's ancestry and his descendancy from the line of Cenwealh's great-uncle Ceolwulf. However, when Æscwine dies in 676, he is succeeded by Centwine, who was Cynegils' son and therefore Cenwealh's brother. This means that when Seaxburh took the throne, she did so despite the existence of a close male relative of the deceased king. We don't know the reason for this, but it might be that Centwine was elsewhere, or even too young; alternatively, her success might have been Seaxburh's own making. Another possibility is that Seaxburh herself came from a suitable, West Saxon lineage, although her name, with its *Seax* element, would have been more common among the East Saxons. In any case, her place as ruler left little to be commented on by the time of Bede's chronicle, suggesting that there had been nothing unusual or controversial about it. The first person to really remark on Seaxburh's attributes would be the chronicler William of Malmesbury, writing between the 1120s and 1140s. The queen, he said, 'exhaled more than female spirit' – (*plus quam femineos animos*) – suggesting that she exceeded the capabilities of ordinary women.

More usually, it was possible for women to rise to power in monastic life and especially in the role of abbess. Double house monasteries – with one community of men and another of women – were not uncommon. A description of that at Wimborne is given in the life of Leoba, an abbess in Francia until her death in 779:

> In olden times the kings of that nation had built two monasteries in the place, one for men, the other for women, both surrounded by strong and lofty walls and provided with all the necessities that prudence could devise. From the beginning of the foundation the rule firmly laid down for both was that no entrance should be allowed to a person of the other sex. No woman was permitted to go into the men's community, nor was any man allowed into the women's, except in the case of priests who had to celebrate Mass in their churches; even so, immediately after the function was ended the priest had to withdraw. Any woman who wished to renounce the world and enter the cloister did so on the understanding that she would never leave it. She could only come out if there was a reasonable cause and some great advantage accrued to the monastery. Furthermore, when it was necessary to conduct the business of the monastery and to send for something outside, the superior of the community spoke through a window and only from there did she make decisions and arrange what was needed.

Apart from this account, however, we have little knowledge of the Wessex monasteries in this period.

The decades after Cynegils' death were marked by a series of short-lived kings of whom the chroniclers have little remarkable to say. According to Bede, it was not just a single ruler after another, but a more complex situation with Wessex divided into a number of sub-kingdoms. It is unclear which is the true story. We know little of where these rulers were buried either, although the *Winchester Annals*, a set of thirteenth-century chronicles based in part on earlier annals by the Benedictine monk Richard of Devizes, state that both Æscwine and Centwine were buried in Winchester. Yet they make no mention of Seaxburh. Perhaps the question we should ask is: where else would her remains have been taken on her death?

A GROWING KINGDOM

The size and extent of Wessex at this time remain very uncertain as no boundaries have been recorded anywhere. But it is clear that disputes with the surrounding regions, and the kingdom of Mercia especially, continued. The only indication we have of the size of Wessex is an estimate provided in a document known as the Tribal Hidage. This much-disputed list exists as a copy dating to around the year 1000, but is thought to have originated in the seventh century. The document lists thirty-four peoples and tribes, along with the size of their territories measured in hides: this was a measure of land, which appears not to have had specific dimensions at this point but, rather, referred to the area capable of supporting one family, ploughing with one ox. In the Hidage the land of the West Saxons is by far the greatest in size, measuring 100,000 hides. It is likely that this is a later exaggeration but even so, seventh-century Wessex was certainly expanding. The king who was responsible for much of this is the Cædwalla who appears to have unified the kingdom again for a short rule of four years from 685. His success was consolidated by his successor Ine, who was king of Wessex from 688 until his resignation and move to Rome in 726: a reign of thirty-seven years.

Ine is best remembered for his law code, the first we know about from Wessex before the time of Alfred: for this reason, it is an important source of information on early West Saxon society and its legal and administrative system. Laws were nothing new. Both those already settled in Britain in the early medieval period and any incoming migrants would have had experience of legal systems, but it was only when Christianity was adopted that such laws were committed to writing. Few legal documents from the earliest period survive and most exist only in later copies. Yet when copies were made it would rarely be for the purpose of simply preserving a text for the future: instead, earlier codes were used for guidance or for some other purpose, such as to incorporate new legislation. So it can be hard to know how close the copied version was to its original and in some cases we know they were deliberately altered. Alfred the Great, who in the late ninth century compiled his own extensive and ambitious law codes, would expressly state that he adopted a policy of picking and choosing which former laws to keep. He ordered law codes to be collected, and 'to be written many of them which our forefathers observed, those which I liked; and many of those which I did not like, I rejected with the advice of my councillors, and ordered them to be differently observed'. Ine's law code would be one of those he decided to copy and would be included as a sort of appendix to his own.

Law codes typically include details of *wergilds* (literally meaning 'man-payment') – the amount that had to be paid in compensation for a crime, including the loss of life. Such amounts were set depending on your status in society. If convicted of a crime you would have to either pay the penalty or go through an ordeal. The latter could take two different forms, and it was the accuser who decided which you would undergo: the ordeal of water or of iron. For the water ordeal, there was a choice between cold water and hot water. In the former, the accused would be thrown into some convenient body of water, such as a pond or river, fastened to a rope. If he floated, he was guilty. In the hot water ordeal, the accused had to seize a stone from the bottom of a cauldron of boiling water. If the choice was an ordeal of iron, the accused had to carry a heated weight of iron a specific distance: in both this and the hot water ordeal, you were considered innocent if, after three days, your hand had healed – sometimes completely, but if your accuser was more lenient, it would be allowed to heal naturally without infection. These ordeals took place in the church and involved numerous elaborate rituals and variations. Depending on the severity of your crime, you might have to dip your hand into the water only down to your wrist; in more serious cases, you would have to immerse it all the way to the elbow. If the accused was a cleric, however, he might have to swallow a consecrated morsel that had been urged to choke a guilty party. Trial by ordeal would remain a common way to mete out justice until 1215, when the Pope prohibited priests from taking part, which effectively ended the practice.

Ine's seventy-six-clause laws deal with everything from how quickly a child must be baptised (within thirty days) and what happens if a slave or freeman works on a Sunday (fines, flogging or the forfeit of freedom) to the range of fines due if caught fighting (a sliding scale based on location and even whether drinking was involved and if one party 'bears it with patience'). They also outline the age of criminal responsibility for theft (ten) and a myriad of regulations relating to theft, slavery and other crimes, mostly for the purpose of specifying punishments. Some laws deal with outsiders: law 20, for instance, says 'If a man from a distance or foreigner goes through the wood off the track, and does not shout nor blow a horn, he is to be assumed to be a thief, to be either killed or redeemed.' Similarly, there are rules about traders operating outside ports or towns, in the country-side, suggesting trade was controlled at a higher level. This ties in well with the archaeological evidence from *wics* and the flour-ishing trading towns of the early eighth century: Ine has even been linked to the founding of Hamwic on the southern coast of the kingdom.

There are also laws relating to agriculture and what happens if one person's cattle eat up all of the crops and grass of a shared group of freemen. Finding pigs in your forest or mast-pasture (relating to the practice of letting pigs feed on fallen nuts and acorns) without your permission would attract a fine; related meas-ures specify the proper thickness of bacon as measured in fingers. Woodland came under protection, with specific punishments for felling or burning down trees: this would also be dependent on size, and it would be more expensive if you were caught cutting down a tree, for example, 'under which 30 swine could stand'. Punishments were more lenient for felling trees than for burning them down. Fire is a thief, Ine's laws proclaim, while the axe is merely an informer. Other laws deal with taxes and food rents, something that gives us an unusual insight into the food produc-tion and eating habits of the time. Law 70.1 specifies the food rent expected from ten hides: 10 vats of honey, 300 loaves, 12 'ambers' of Welsh ale, 30 of clear ale, 2 full-grown cows, or 10 wethers, 10 geese, 20 hens, 10 cheeses, a full amber of butter, 5 salmon, 20 pounds of fodder and 100 eels.

Apart from the insights these law codes give us into the legal system, they also tell us how embedded Christianity had become in Ine's kingship, only a few generations after the religion was introduced to Wessex. Yet the fact that some things had to be specified in law – such as the timeframe for infant baptism – could also suggest the religion was not entirely and securely lodged in the lives of the general population: a reminder that the picture we glean from texts will not always reflect the real-life situation.

Like those of so many others, Ine's rule was marked by a number of conflicts with neighbours. But the *Anglo-Saxon Chronicle* gives unusual insight into his wife Queen Æthelburh's involvement in politics. In 710, the *Chronicle* informs us, while her husband was away campaigning in Sussex, she destroyed the fortress in Taunton that he himself had built. The circumstances are obscure, but Henry of Huntingdon explains that it was done to chase out a young dissident by the name of Ealdberth; presumably Æthelburh came to her husband's assistance in his absence. According to William of Malmesbury, writing in the twelfth century, it was Æthelburh who convinced Ine, in 726, to abdicate and travel to Rome, where he eventually died. Her background is unclear, but a forged charter from Glastonbury records that she was the sister of King Æthelheard who succeeded Ine – so she herself may have been of notable ancestry.

Æthelheard was replaced by Cuthred, followed, briefly, by Sigeberht. All three kings were allegedly buried in Old Minster, but their burials have not been identified.

REDISCOVERY

'BRITON FINDS SITE OF SAXON CHURCH. Digging in Winchester Yields 7th Century Foundation Near Norman Cathedral. OTHER RUINS DETECTED. Medieval Manuscripts Gave Clues to Archaeologist for Locating "Minster"' . . .

Detective work by a British archaeologist has disclosed the buried foundations of one, and possibly two, large Saxon minsters, or churches.

New York Times, 22 August 1962

*I*n 1961, a decision was made to build a new hotel – the Wessex Hotel – in the centre of Winchester. Roger Quirk CB, a civil servant with an interest in early medieval archaeology, had recently published two reports proposing the location of both the Old and New Minster churches, the latter built at the start of the tenth century, which at that point were lost. The New Minster that had been planned by Alfred the Great and built by his son Edward the Elder, Quirk argued through written and topographical evidence, had once been situated precisely where the new hotel was to be erected, just to the north of the present cathedral. The town clerk and the Ministry of Works agreed to an archaeological excavation and Martin Biddle, an archaeologist who had already made a mark in the field with excavations at St Albans and Jericho, was dispatched to lead it.

The site of the proposed car park was the first to be examined and the archaeology turned out to be preserved beautifully. The area had been used as a cemetery from the Middle Ages until the 1860s, but beneath that, to a depth of more than three metres, the stratigraphy – layers of soils and deposits laid down over time – lay undisturbed, revealing evidence of the first Roman streets laid and relaid over decades, a tenth-century cemetery and, finally, a medieval building complex. These early excavations uncovered the extraordinarily rich past of the city and its development. The following year Biddle struck metaphorical gold: on the cathedral green, he found what would later prove to be the seventh-century high altar of Old Minster. The year after, this trench was extended and the remains of another building were revealed, which turned out to be the nave of New Minster, built *in the late ninth or early tenth century. The secure identification of the two buildings was made easier thanks to the reports of Quirk, who had dug out all the references to the two churches he could find. In the twelfth century, the historian William of Malmesbury had stated that 'the two churches lay so close together that a man could scarcely walk between them'. Biddle had found the minsters, he had rediscovered two of the most significant churches in England.*

With Wessex's conversion to Christianity, burial – at least of those in the higher echelons of society – became focused around churches. Serious consideration was now given to the final resting place of royal and other important figures and individuals of particular standing, such as kings, were assigned the most prominent locations. Sometimes the deceased would have already expressed a preferred place, but more often than not these decisions were taken by their descendants – often for political reasons.

Up until the mid-ninth century, practically all the kings in the West Saxon regnal list are noted as having been buried in Winchester's Old Minster. However, the excavations revealed only two graves in the seventh-century nave: the first, Grave 67, held the body of a man aged about twenty-five to thirty-five, buried with the remains of a gold-fringed cloth and headdress and garter-tags of niello. The headdress and prominent location could suggest a royal burial, but the date of the garter-tags pointed to someone who was buried in the ninth century. The second, Grave 68, was empty: all that remained were the fittings of an elaborate iron-bound coffin that had been broken apart when the body within was moved. Here, perhaps, was evidence of one of the many translations of bones that had taken place over time. Could the bones the coffin once contained now be among those in the mortuary chests? The only clue to the date of this burial was a coin that was found in the fill of the grave – in other words, in the soil that had been backfilled into the empty grave. It was a penny of King Edmund, Eadred's brother, who had ruled between 939 and 946. But why had one burial been moved and not the other? One likely explanation is that those graves had somehow been marked and recorded, and their occupants well known: a deliberate decision could then have been made on who should receive an alternative resting place.

So where did all the other burials go? It is very possible the majority were moved, but equally the area beyond the church was probably used. The southern section of Old Minster remains unexcavated, as it lies too close to the present cathedral: a fact that means it will likely never be examined.

CHEST II

THREATS

Cynewulf d. 786

Egbert d. 839

*B*ishop Henry of Blois walks slowly down the nave of the cathedral built under his grandfather, William the Conqueror. His robes and his characteristic long, flowing beard mark him out for the onlookers, who have gathered to witness the blessing of the bones of the ancient kings. The king, Henry II, who is the bishop's first cousin once removed, will shortly arrive to attend the ceremony. Having been Bishop of Winchester and Abbot of Glastonbury for almost thirty years, Henry of Blois is keen to make his own mark on the cathedral and today's ceremony is one element of a major scheme. Henry is no stranger to architectural work: as well as the ecclesiastical buildings he has commissioned, he has also built extensively for himself – palaces with elaborate and ingenious water features and spaces for exotic birds and wild animals. The bishop is an extraordinarily wealthy man: back in 1086, Domesday Book listed the value of the Glastonbury and Winchester estates at around £2,500, the equivalent wealth to that of a leading earl. Now Henry has set his mind to preserving the dignity and respect of England's former kings and bishops, whose bones have been carefully preserved in this cathedral for several centuries. Reminding the king and his contemporaries of Winchester's vital role in the country's history will not do any harm either.

For a long time Henry has been bothered by the way the ancient dead have been placed in different locations around the cathedral, after having been moved from Old Minster and the later addition New Minster. Some were interred in completely unfitting places and he needs to take urgent action. For some of them, he has commissioned separate tombs to be built but for most, lead sarcophagi have been made. Not only does the bishop know who these predecessors are and how they slot into the jigsaw of England's history, he knows the power they hold to reinforce the regime's precarious grasp on authority.

England has only just emerged from the Anarchy, a period of civil war and political unrest following a succession dispute after the only legitimate son of Henry I died in the 1120 White Ship disaster. The country's stability and peace, which Henry of Blois has worked hard to help ensure – not least through his abilities as an eloquent speaker and negotiator – are still under threat. With it: his own position. Only a few years ago, he played a prominent role in negotiating the treaty that would allow the current king to take the crown. The treaty was sealed right here in Winchester with a kiss between King Stephen and Henry II. Now, in a complex political climate, the bishop has just returned from a strategic retreat abroad made after his loyalties and actions had been questioned, and his current work on the cathedral is in part designed to emphasise the continuity of the monarchy. But these old bones hold a personal affection for Henry too. Throughout his life he has taken a great interest in history and antiquities, in holy relics and in artefacts. On his many trips to Rome, the contemporary author John of Salisbury wrote of him, Henry could be seen touring the antique shops, buying Roman statues that he had shipped home to England. On his death in several years' time, many of these statues and numerous other artefacts will be bequeathed to Winchester.

As he circles the great altar and inspects the lead sarcophagi placed in front of it, Henry thinks about the role of each king and bishop in the country's history. He has a very personal link to some – Queen Emma was his great-great-great aunt. Others' stories he has learned of through the work of his good friend, the monk and historian William of Malmesbury. A few decades ago, William wrote the greatest history of England known to date, basing his work on that of venerable writers like Bede and his own research into – and embellishment of – the *past. Henry runs his hand along the sarcophagus containing the bones of Cynewulf, the eighth-century king, and considers the centuries of external threats that he and his descendants had to contend with, especially from the north. While here in the south such terrors are now confined to the past, just a few years ago, as the 1150s began, Eysteinn Haraldsson, the king of Norway, launched an attack on Aberdeen before ravaging the north-eastern shores of England. Henry recognises the fragile nature of peace, and of kingship, but with his days of diplomacy behind him, his best bet now is to look to the past to reinforce the present.*

BORDERS

In 757, more than a century after the death of Cynegils, Cynewulf became king of the West Saxons. The size of Wessex's territory ebbed and flowed during his rule, as it had done for centuries past and would in the centuries to come. His ascent to power had not been straightforward, since in order to rule he had to drive out his predecessor, Sigeberht, a feat he had achieved by gaining the support of most of the leading men of Wessex. Right at the start of his reign, Cynewulf is recorded to have met with King Æthelbald of Mercia, at which point the Mercian king gave away land to the West Saxon monastery in Malmesbury, a location likely to have been in the border zone between the two kingdoms. This meeting may suggest some sort of recognition of Cynewulf's kingship, but it could also have represented a form of subjection to Mercian rule. This would not have been unusual, as Æthelbald frequently granted land to peripheral kingdoms and rulers – such as those of the Hwicce, a kingdom that survived until the end of the eighth century – and acknowledged their subordinate position.

Æthelbald proved a particularly successful Mercian king, at least for a while, whose future success had been prophesied by St Guthlac. Although Bede is typically silent on the Mercian kings, he mentions that in 731 Æthelbald had authority over 'all of the southern English'; soon after, a charter describes him as 'king of Britain'. The strength of his rule can also be seen in his coinage, which circulated widely throughout Mercia and Kent, and similar coins – without the image of the king in a helmet-crown – could be found in Wessex too. This demonstrates a close connection of some sort between the two kingdoms, yet Æthelbald's popularity was clearly not universal. An insight into his private life is preserved in a lengthy and seriously damning letter from the missionary Archbishop Boniface dating to 746 or 747. In it, Boniface – a Benedictine monk who worked to spread Christianity in mainland Europe – begins by praising the Mercian king for his good deeds, before approaching the topic of 'reports of an evil kind' that had reached his ears. Æthelbald, he has heard, has not taken a lawful wife as ordained by God: something he could be forgiven were it for the sake of abstinence and chastity. Rumour has it, however, that the latter was not the case and Æthelbald had, in fact, been governed by lust, having stained his reputation by the sin of lasciviousness and adultery. What was even worse, wrote a disgusted Boniface, the king had been fornicating in monasteries, defiling holy nuns and virgins consecrated to God. The rest of the letter sets out – at great length – the seriousness of these sins that, if true, will surely land the king in hell. Even the pagans, Boniface explains, take such matters seriously.

As more of an aside, Æthelbald is also accused of stealing revenues from the church and allowing his ealdormen – high-ranking royal officials – to use violence against monks and priests. A second letter is preserved alongside the first, addressed to the priest Herefrith, who was entrusted with delivering the message to Æthelbald. Rewarded with some incense and a linen cloth for his trouble, Herefrith was asked to read and explain the message, because Boniface had heard the king 'condescends on some occasions to listen to your [Herefrith's] advice to some extent'. The nature of Æthelbald's death suggests Boniface was not the only one to be discontented with the king: he was murdered in battle at Seckington by his very own warband. This murder, which took place less than a year after Cynewulf's accession, proved to be significant for the Wessex king's future success.

Cynewulf was clearly effective, as he would manage to retain his throne for an impressive and unusual thirty-one years. He was generous to the church, donating lands to monasteries. Controlling his kingdom's borders remained a key concern: it is recorded in the *Anglo-Saxon Chronicle* that he repeatedly fought the 'Britons' to the west of his kingdom and a charter mentions a war with the men of Cornwall, indicating that Cynewulf would have needed to protect his land to the west as well as to the north and east. However, the primary challenger during his reign was Æthelbald's successor Offa of Mercia, to whom he would have to concede much of his kingdom at various times.

Cynewulf faced internal threats too and we have a particularly detailed account of one from the *Chronicle*. For the eighth century, entries are typically very short, but a lengthy entry for the year 757 starts with Cynewulf's accession, before going on to discuss an event that took place over three decades later, which led to his death. The threat to his power came from an ætheling – a young man of noble, perhaps royal, birth – by the name of Cyneheard: the former king Sigeberht's brother. The story goes that Cyneheard learned that King Cynewulf was staying with a woman, usually interpreted to be his mistress, at a place called Meretun (likely at Marten in Wiltshire) with a small 'troupe'. Planning an ambush, Cyneheard and his men rode out to the manor, reaching the estate without being noticed by the king's men. But there their luck ran out, as they were spotted arriving by the king himself, who went to the door to fight off the attackers. On recognising Cyneheard, he rushed out and greatly wounded the ætheling, as the cries of his mistress finally brought the king's men to the fight. Cyneheard, still alive, tried to bribe his way to safety by offering the king's thegns 'money and life', but not one accepted. Instead, they chose to fight to their deaths. When word of the ambush got back to Cynewulf's estate the following day, his remaining thegns rushed to Meretun where they discovered to their dismay that their king lay dead too. Cyneheard was holed up in the stronghold and again offered bribes: money and land, if they would grant him the kingdom. But the *Chronicle* strongly emphasises the loyalty of the men, who all claimed they would never follow the slayer of their king.

Fighting ensued and eventually Cyneheard lay dead too. As another record states, the 'cruel slayer was himself killed without pity by Ealdorman Osric in vengeance for his lord'. The *Chronicle* briefly records that at his death Cynewulf was buried at Winchester and was succeeded by Beorhtric.

The detail given is curious for the *Chronicle*, especially the emphasis on loyalty and the role of the *witan* or *witenagemot,* the council of the king, in advising him. The entry stands out because of its length and style, and was clearly something that was inserted into the *Chronicle* after being composed separately: it has all the hallmarks of what would be expected in an account of heroic codes of behaviour. The men described here are so loyal to their lord that they would rather die in battle than surrender to the enemy's forces. More than anything, the episode is useful in enabling us to understand the feuds and rivalries between different branches of an eighth-century royal house.

NEW THREATS

In Beorhtric's reign, sometime between the years 786 and 802, a new enemy appeared on the southern shores of Wessex, one that would remain at the top of the political agenda in Wessex and beyond for the next three centuries. The event is recorded in the *Anglo-Saxon Chronicle*, which places it in the year 789: in the

reign of Beorhtric, it states, three ships of raiders arrived, the first
ships of Danish men to launch an attack on English shores. We
will never know if this truly was the first such raid, but it is the
earliest record of one, and pre-dates the better known attack on
Lindisfarne four years later. An account in the tenth-century chronicle of Æthelweard fills in more detail, including the information
that the raiders came from Hordaland in modern-day Norway. In
the written records, the term 'Danes' would become shorthand for
what we usually refer to as the Vikings: at other times the same
people are described simply as pagans. It is unlikely that the
chroniclers knew, or really cared about, their geographical origins.
In Æthelweard's telling, the raid took place on the island of Portland
on the coast of Dorset. When the ships appeared on the horizon,
he wrote, the royal reeve Beaduheard (a chief official acting on
behalf of the king) rode out to meet them. Beaduheard seems to
have assumed the ships' crews were merchants headed for the
nearby town of Dorchester, as he ordered them, in an authoritative
manner, to report to the royal residence. The arrivals responded
by brutally slaughtering him and the men who had accompanied
him to the shore.

The seemingly peaceful reception given to the ships by the reeve
is intriguing, as it suggests that similar ships could have been a
familiar sight: after all, the bustling trading town of Hamwic lay
only a short distance along the coast to the east. The assault is not
recorded by any other contemporary sources, and we don't know
if the raiders attacked the nearby town. In contrast, more details
exist of the infamous attack on the island monastery at Lindisfarne
in Northumbria on 6 June 793. The raid is known from numerous
accounts – some of them contemporary with the event itself. The
letters of Alcuin of York, a scholar at the court of Charlemagne,
for example, provide insightful details. Writing from across the
Channel, Alcuin was clearly highly distressed by the events on

Lindisfarne and his letters demonstrate the shockwaves this attack sent through north-western Europe. He wrote to Higbald, Bishop of Lindisfarne, at the same time berating the Northumbrians for the attack, which he suspected could have come about from their being bad Christians.

The entry on the Portland raid also states that it was the *first* such attack on English shores, something that appears to be an important point to the author. But why should this be the case, and why the addition of Portland? The *Anglo-Saxon Chronicle* would start to be compiled a century after these events in Wessex, at the court of Alfred the Great. At the time he was embroiled in bitter conflicts with the Vikings on a large scale: it may well have been important to him to demonstrate that the first Viking attacks had been directed at Wessex.

Remarkably, however, after the attack on Lindisfarne, no more raids are recorded in extant English sources until 835, during the reign of King Egbert: a gap of more than four decades. Does that mean the Vikings left England in peace? This is unlikely. Instead, an important point to remember is that the written sources are biased towards the south-west: the scribes who compiled the core texts of the *Anglo-Saxon Chronicle* were focused primarily on Wessex. Events in the north, for instance, are usually either off the radar or simply ignored, so even if they knew of such attacks, they may not have had reason to record them. Unfortunately, archaeology has been of little use to resolve the question, as it is practically impossible to identify or date specific raids except in extreme circumstances. Even at Lindisfarne, no physical proof of the attack remains. Several seasons of excavation work have located the early medieval monastic site but no tell-tale signs of the raid. As a matter of fact, research has shown that the community continued to thrive for decades afterwards, so the attack was clearly not the end. This could indicate that the raiders' aim was not complete devastation, but more a hunt for riches. Additionally, if the monastic community was allowed to survive, it would mean another lucrative attack could be made in the future.

Despite this lack of direct evidence, other sources do suggest England faced a wider threat from raids – presumably by Vikings – at the end of the eighth and the beginning of the ninth centuries. Alcuin wrote another letter in 797 addressed to the clergy and nobles of Kent. In it, he asks for the former archbishop to be reinstated in Canterbury but also for political unity to face the threat of attacks. 'Very great danger threatens this island and the people dwelling in it,' he writes. 'Behold a thing never before heard of, a pagan people is becoming accustomed to laying waste our shores with piratical robbery.' Such wording strongly suggests that raids were becoming commonplace. Other clues point to intense pirate activity. A number of documents refer to the need for protection against raids, including at Lyminge, a double monastery. As early as 792, a text records Offa of Mercia making a grant to churches in Kent, excusing them from their obligation of military service 'against seaborne pagans with migrating fleets'. This service explicitly included the building of fortifications against the pagans. The reference not just to fleets of raiders but also to defences shows that at least a year before the Lindisfarne attack, those threats were being taken seriously. Whether the danger was limited to the east coast of England is hard to tell.

An interesting question that has come to the forefront of research recently is how much contact there really was between England and Scandinavia before the first recorded attacks. Parts of Britain had been connected to Scandinavia for a considerable amount of time, the links of Norfolk and other parts of eastern England with western Norway through female dress ornaments being just one example, and the Jutes, of course, allegedly stemmed from Jutland in Denmark. Material culture elsewhere also hints at a similarity between art styles and suggests other links: the Anglo-Saxon helmet discovered at Sutton Hoo in East Anglia, for example, has close parallels at sites like Sigtuna in Sweden. Since at least 700 or so, the network of trading settlements known as *wics* had developed on both sides of the English Channel, up to the North Sea and across to the Baltic. It makes sense, therefore, to talk about a North Sea World from which Britain was certainly not cut off or isolated, and nor was Scandinavia. The earliest Anglo-Saxon coin found in Norway was discovered at Ervik on the western coast: it had been struck in Northumbria between 737 and 758. Similarly, evidence of early contact between Northumbria and Scandinavia has been found in a cemetery at Bamburgh: isotope analysis of burials there dating to between the seventh and ninth centuries revealed a large number of the dead had grown up in Scandinavia. Yet despite these earlier and seemingly peaceful contacts, the events of the end of the eighth century would change those connections for ever.

By the time we reach the beginning of the ninth century, there was extensive raiding activity in Ireland and across the English Channel in Francia. Both the Irish chronicles and the *Royal Frankish Annals* report battles and attacks: in Ireland, many were successfully thwarted, while Francia seemed less fortunate despite managing to fend some of them off. In his biography *Life of Charlemagne*, the ninth-century Frankish scholar and courtier Einhard wrote of continuous raids on the coasts of Gaul and Germany: Charlemagne apparently travelled up the Frankish coast to build a fleet and to set up guards, presumably for this very reason. In Flanders, thirteen pirate ships managed to set fire to dwellings and capture cattle before being driven away, while in 820 in Aquitaine raiders got away with a large amount of booty. In other words, these early records suggest that obtaining portable wealth and food for their crews were the Vikings' main objectives.

A curious account in the *Frankish Annals* reveals how the Vikings also used blackmail to achieve their aims. In an entry for the year 809, the *Annals* describe the kidnap of an English deacon by the name of Aldwulf, who had been captured and taken to Britain by pirates while escorting the exiled Northumbrian king Eardwulf on a visit to Charlemagne and the Pope in Rome. The pagans demanded ransom for his safe return and the *Annals* describe how this was provided by one of King Coenwulf of Mercia's men, after which Aldwulf was dispatched back to Rome. We don't know where in England the Vikings took their hostage to, or where the negotiations took place, but it was presumably somewhere in Mercia, perhaps on the eastern Kentish coast, as Kent was under Mercian control at the time. So by this point not only were pagan raiders a common threat, but strategies of blackmail and release formed part of their repertoire. There is also an intriguing possibility that they may have had temporary bases or even camps in England, seeing as they had somewhere in Mercia to bring Aldwulf back to. Even so, this early phase of Viking activity appears to have been focused largely on the procurement of riches, in hit-and-run attacks that saw them return to Scandinavia at the end of a raiding season, without much interference in internal politics or ambitions of conquest. Within half a century, however, that was to change drastically.

A NEW DYNASTY

In 802, Egbert succeeded to the throne and a new phase of West Saxon history began. While Egbert ruled, the Viking threat would come to the top of Wessex's and the rest of the country's political agenda. At the same time, one of Egbert's key achievements

would be his ability to secure the throne of Wessex for his descendants, leading to his grandson Alfred the Great's rule from 871.
Alfred's own descendants were to rule Wessex and, subsequently,
all of England, until 1013. For this reason, the chroniclers clearly
felt it important to establish his genealogy. In the *Anglo-Saxon
Chronicle* entry for 855, Egbert's lineage is spelled out and traced
back thirty-two generations and even beyond, to an ancestor who
was born on the Ark, which leads us back to Noah and eventually
to Adam. A vital part of the claim was to show that Egbert originated from the line of Cerdic, the legendary founder of the West
Saxon kingdom back in the sixth century. Demonstrating such
lineages was crucial, in order to express stability, continuity and
legitimacy to rule: the fact that the biological and historical accuracy
of these bloodlines included a fair bit of creative licence was not
so important. It seems that for the West Saxon rulers, this became
a matter of urgency in the ninth century. In reality, Egbert's family
may well have come from Kent.

Egbert came to power after the death of his predecessor Beorhtric.
A later entry in the *Anglo-Saxon Chronicle*, relating to Egbert's own
death in 839, states that for three years before his rule, or possibly
even more, Beorhtric and the Mercian king Offa had conspired
to drive Egbert out of England and into exile in Francia. Little
more detail of this aggression exists, but we do know something
about the alliance between Wessex and Mercia: Beorhtric was
married to Offa's daughter Eadburh, as mentioned in the *Chronicle*'s
entry for the year 789. That the marriage is mentioned and, in
particular, the bride's name is given is very unusual: the names of
rulers' wives rarely appear, showing how important the union was
for both sides and helping to explain the alliance between Offa
and Beorhtric. For the former, it gave access to a West Saxon king
who was dependent on him, while the latter gained a powerful
neighbouring ally. Succession may well have been the reason for

their attempt to drive Egbert out, because he could have posed a threat to any future sons of Beorhtric and grandsons of Offa. Egbert himself would also have been a danger to Beorhtric, both because he was a descendant of one of Ine's brothers and because his father Ealhmund had been recognised as a king in Kent.

Our most detailed source on the union between Beorhtric and Eadburh, and the events around the king's death, comes from much later: Asser, a ninth-century bishop who acted as a teacher and counsellor to Alfred the Great, included some curious stories about the queen, Eadburh, in his biography *Life of King Alfred*. After the wedding, he wrote, and as soon as she had won the king over and with that gained power through most of the kingdom, the new queen changed. She started to behave like a tyrant, says Asser, just like her father Offa had been. Eadburh demonstrably loathed all those her husband liked, acting despicably towards them, tricking and deceiving as many of them as she could. Those she could not manipulate, she poisoned. Eventually, Asser continues, while trying to poison a close friend of the king, she accidentally murdered her husband: Beorhtric died when he drank from a poisoned glass intended for his friend. Eadburh fled to Francia and the court of Charlemagne, taking countless treasures with her and offering some of these expensive gifts to the emperor. The story goes that Charlemagne, sympathetic to her predicament, gave her a choice: she could either marry him or his son. Eadburh replied that she would prefer his son, as he was considerably younger. Her answer clearly angered Charlemagne, who said that if he had been her choice, he would have given her his son in marriage. Now, thanks to this insult, she would have neither. Instead, the Frankish emperor gave her a large convent to preside over. But the life of an abbess did not suit Eadburh. The wicked queen continued living recklessly and was eventually 'caught in debauchery with a man of her own race', whereupon she was destined to live a life of poverty and misery until her death. It seems unlikely that the details of this story – or anything of it at all – are true but the telling of it a few generations later serves the purpose of discrediting the bloodline of Beorhtric's regime, if he and Eadburh had borne any children. Such offspring would have been threats to Egbert's own descendants. However, her need to escape to Francia is not implausible considering the animosity between Beorhtric and Egbert. In any case, Asser's reasons for mentioning the story a few generations later are revealing. In his retelling, he uses it to explain why West Saxon women could be the wives of kings, but could not be *queens*: he says this is something he heard from his elders, so the practice in his own time was merely a continuation of an age-old tradition.

There is surprisingly little information about the early years of Egbert's rule. In his first twenty years as king almost all that is recorded are his campaigns against the Cornish. But by 825 he is also battling against the Mercians: for much of his rule, as with his predecessors, disputes over this neighbouring territory are high on the list of priorities. In the year 828, at 2 a.m. on 25 December, there was a lunar eclipse, recorded in the *Anglo-Saxon Chronicle*. 'Here,' it says, 'the moon grew dark on Christmas night.' Next, we hear that Egbert succeeded in what others before him had not: he captured the kingdom of Mercia and 'all that was south of the Humber'. The *Chronicle* explains he was the eighth king to be *Bretwalda* – 'Wide Ruler', as the later manuscripts have it or, in the earliest of them, Manuscript A, *Brytenwalda*, which some translate as 'Britain-ruler'. Yet Egbert's triumph was not to last: a mere year later, Wiglaf, the former Mercian ruler, regained control of his kingdom.

The biggest threat to Egbert came from beyond the sea. When he took up his kingship, just under a decade after the infamous attack on Lindisfarne in 793, the Vikings were still a distant threat, but as the raids ramped up the burgeoning Viking problem reached crisis proportions. In 836, Egbert was thoroughly defeated by a band of raiders at Carhampton on the Somerset coast. In 838, an important entry in the *Anglo-Saxon Chronicle* asserts that an alliance was formed between the people of Cornwall and the Vikings, implying good lines of communication between the two sides. But two years on, Egbert led his troops into battle in Cornwall, successfully defeating the alliance.

When Egbert died in 839 of unknown causes, he was buried in Old Minster. By the time of his death, King Egbert of Wessex had established his domain as a powerful entity in Britain, extending his rule to include Kent, Surrey, Essex and Sussex. He has been described as the most successful of the West Saxon kings up to that point. So how did Egbert achieve so much more success than his predecessors? His considerable conquests of other territories would have given him plenty of wealth that he could use to purchase support. Any ruler in this period must have known how high a risk there was of usurpment by others with either a legitimate claim or simply a desire for kingship.

SETTING THE SCENE

When Egbert died, the West Saxon throne was inherited by his son, Æthelwulf, who had previously been sent by his father to take control of the kingdom of Kent. We know that in the year before his death, Egbert had already acknowledged his son as his heir at an assembly at Kingston-upon-Thames in Surrey. This arrangement was actually not common, and he became the first West Saxon ruler since 641 who was demonstrably succeeded by his son.

Æthelwulf was married to a woman by the name of Osburh, with whom he had five sons – Æthelbald, Æthelbert, Æthelstan, Æthelred and Alfred – and at least one daughter, Æthelswith. According to Asser's biography of Alfred, Osburh was descended from the royal house of the Jutes of Wight, allegedly founded by Stuf and Wihtgar, according to the origin story told in the *Anglo-Saxon Chronicle*. Interestingly, it has been pointed out that this Jutish heritage would have given Alfred an ancestral link to Danes from Jutland, which may have been useful for him when wanting to have his lordship recognised by Vikings: with this he could prove a Scandinavian connection.

Throughout his rule, the ongoing relationships with Kent and Mercia would be key to Æthelwulf's political career. He continued to hold Kent as a sub-kingdom and later on, in turn, he would place his son Æthelstan in charge, just as his father had placed Æthelwulf himself. Æthelwulf won favour in Kent by drawing nobles into his presence and keeping them as his loyal ealdormen, a common strategy for ensuring loyalty in Wessex too. An object discovered by chance in a cart rut in the small Wiltshire village of Laverstock in 1780 may well illustrate this: a gold finger-ring decorated in what is known as Trewhiddle style, decorated with niello. The ring features foliage designs and in the centre, two peacocks facing each other. Underneath this reads the name 'Æthelwulf'. A ring of this type could only have been associated with the king and may well have been a gift to a loyal follower.

The benefit of the close relationship with Kent was clearly mutual: even before his father died, the minster communities, which were significant institutions to contend with, had chosen Æthelwulf for protection and lordship. In turn, he had promised that they could choose who was to be head of their institution without any interference. But the alliance had another major benefit to the people of Kent too. In the year 839, the Viking threat was very real and the Kentish coast had borne the brunt of many of the attacks for quite some time. That year Æthelwulf made plans for a pilgrimage to Rome, something he had decided to do after news of a dream reached him. The dream, that of a priest, was troubling. In preparing for his trip, Æthelwulf sent legates to Louis the Pious, emperor of Francia, to request the freedom to travel through Louis' territory. The details of the dream have been preserved because the writer of the *Annals of St Bertin* included it in the entry for 839. In the dream, the account informs us, the priest was visited by a man who asked him to follow him to a strange land full of remarkable buildings and a church filled with boys reading. The boys read of the great sins and crimes of Christians and attempted to intercede for them. That particular year, for example, there had been an abundance of fruit, but because of the sins of the people, most of the crops had perished. More seriously, if the men did not quickly repent, something terrible would befall them: for three days and three nights, a great mist would cover the land. Out of the mist would sail the *homines pagani* – the Northmen – to randomly murder men and destroy property, with both fire and sword. The only way to escape this was by doing penance for their sins, in the form of prayers and fasts. It is interesting that Æthelwulf chose to share this dream – and the anxiety about Viking attacks – with Louis, and it suggests that a threat like this was well understood and something the other king would have empathised with.

In 850, a charter states that a landowner by the name of Ealburh gave food rent – a form of tax in kind – to the monastic community of St Augustine's in Canterbury, from her estate in Kent. As a way of saying thank you, the community was expected to sing Psalm 20 every day on her behalf in return. But if it proved impossible to pay rent because of heathen attacks, the estate could be excused, for up to three years, vividly demonstrating the very real and tangible threat to agricultural production from Viking raiders too. Clearly, it was not unheard of for crops to be destroyed or even stolen.

A lavish gospel book provides an insight into the activities of the Vikings and the response to them. The *Codex Aureus* was granted to Christ Church Canterbury by an ealdorman named Alfred and his wife Waerburg. While the book in itself is nice enough, it is the inscription inside that makes it unusual. Here it says that the couple *ransomed* the book from a heathen army in an act of piety, revealing another very deliberate tactic on behalf of the Vikings to blackmail their victims: a book like that would have had little or no value for a pagan audience but the local communities were so desperate to get it back that they were willing to pay for it. Ironically, the book is now owned by the National Library of Sweden.

The *Anglo-Saxon Chronicle* entry for 850 underlines the seriousness of the Viking threat. This year, it states, Æthelstan and Ealdorman Ealhhere struck a great raiding army at Sandwich in Kent, capturing nine ships and putting others to flight. This represented a turnaround for the West Saxons as several years previously, in 843, Æthelwulf had fought unsuccessfully against thirty-five shiploads of Danes at Carhampton in Somerset, by the Bristol Channel. But the Vikings were about to step their activities up a notch because the same year, it is recorded that for the first time the 'heathen men' overwintered in England, on the island of Thanet. By the following year, raids increased in severity, with an alleged 350 ships entering the mouth of the Thames and storming London and Canterbury. The Mercian king and his army, presumably based in London, were put to flight and the Vikings continued south across the Thames. Finally, they arrived at an unknown place named Oak Field, where Æthelwulf, helped by his son, fought them. The West Saxon army emerged victorious and 'made the greatest slaughter of a heathen raiding-army that we have heard tell of up to this present day'. Æthelwulf's successes would even be famed overseas, as in about 852, a letter from an abbot in Francia by the name of Lupus congratulates the king on his victories against the pagans. Lupus offers support in the future in the form of prayers, as long as Æthelwulf sends him a gift of lead for his monastery roof in return.

But other threats had to be dealt with as well as that of the Vikings. In 853, King Burgred of Mercia asked for Æthelwulf's help in bringing the Welsh back into subjection, something they did together with success. It is perhaps not a coincidence that in precisely the same year, Æthelwulf's daughter Æthelswith married the Mercian king, cementing the alliance between the two rulers.

By this time most of the area south of the Thames, including the whole of Berkshire, belonged to Wessex and later the king would extend his reach to what is now Cornwall. Yet it was Wessex, and especially Winchester where his father was buried, that lay close to Æthelwulf's heart.

That same year the king appears to have begun furthering plans for his sons' futures. Alfred, his youngest son, had been born in or around 849 on the royal estate at Wantage in Berkshire. When the boy was around five or six, Æthelwulf took him on the first of two pilgrimages to visit the Pope in Rome, where he would consecrate him as king and sponsor him at confirmation. The journey to Rome was arduous, not least for a very young boy, and there were several routes the pair could have chosen from. The first involved waterborne travel, on the River Rhône from Lyon to Marseille, and then across the Mediterranean to the port of Ostia just outside Rome. This way, however, could be perilous because of the threat of piracy and seemed less favoured. More popular was the overland route, stopping off at monasteries and hospices, many founded specifically for the purpose of housing pilgrims. The traveller from England would start at the mouth of the Seine, then move across Francia towards Lausanne and the Alps, crossing via the Great St Bernard Pass – one of the most ancient passes through the Western Alps, where a hospice was in existence from the early ninth century. From there the journey continued into Lombardy, Tuscany and central Italy until finally reaching Rome.

Alfred would be sent a second time a few years later and on one of his visits may have been accompanied by his brother Æthelred. Æthelwulf may have been motivated to send his younger sons on these trips because of the risk to them posed by their older brothers. The wills of Æthelwulf and Alfred make it quite clear that the king intended Æthelbald, his oldest son, to inherit Wessex, and Æthelbert Kent. But by invoking the authority of the Pope, he gave the two younger sons a greater chance at becoming kings too, of a smaller kingdom that might be separated out, or if the others died heirless, or even in the case of sibling rivalry. Some of the Carolingian heirs had fallen victim to the latter, facing a threat of being tonsured, that is, invested as a monk into religious service to block them from taking the throne. In the biography of Alfred by Asser, it says that Æthelwulf specifically drafted his will so that his sons wouldn't quarrel.

Around this time Æthelstan appears to have died, his last known activity a victory in a naval raid against a Viking fleet at Sandwich in the year 851. But while the eventual burial locations of Æthelwulf and his remaining three sons are all recorded, nothing is known of Æthelstan. An intriguing possibility is that he was the man buried in Grave 67 at the Old Minster site excavated by Martin Biddle. The gravegoods and burial location both imply that this was someone of a very high, and possibly royal status; and the age at death and the ninth-century date for the grave would fit Æthelstan.

In 855, Æthelwulf decided to make another pilgrimage. In advance, he asked Charles the Bald, who at the time was king of the Western Franks, for permission to travel through his kingdom. This was granted and on arrival Æthelwulf received a warm welcome from Charles, who provided him with an imposing escort to allow him to journey safely to his destination. With him to Rome, the West Saxon king brought lavish gifts for St Peter: according to the biographer of Pope Benedict III, they included 'a fine gold crown weighing 4 lb . . . one sword bound with fine gold; four silver-gilt Saxon bowls; one all-silk white shirt with roundels, with gold-studding; and two large gold-interwoven veils'.

On his return via Francia the next summer, however, as the *Annals of St Bertin* explain, Æthelwulf became betrothed to Judith, Charles's eldest daughter. What had happened to his first wife Osburh, at this point, is unclear: she may have died or Æthelwulf may simply have rejected her, as she is never heard of again. After a three-month stay in the Frankish court, on 1 October the two were married in the palace of Verberie in what is now northern France in a ceremony carried out by Hincmar, the Archbishop of Rheims. The archbishop consecrated Judith and placed a diadem on her head, after which the union was sealed by exchange of royal gear and gifts. But what is especially notable is that the *Annals* explain that once they were formally married, Æthelwulf conferred on Judith the title of queen, something, it says, that 'was not customary before then to him or to his people'.

This fact is reiterated a few decades later, in the biography of Æthelwulf's son Alfred by Asser, when he says that 'the people of the West Saxons do not suffer a queen to sit next to the king, nor do they even permit her to be called a queen but only wife of the king'. In a beautiful demonstration of this, Asser, in his biography, does not even mention his subject's wife, Ealhswith, by name. This, then, is one of the main reasons why so few women in the West Saxon royal line have been destined for fame. The knowledge may also have been the reason why Charles the Bald wanted to make sure his daughter was consecrated as queen, so that she was sent off to a foreign land with a little more security as to her status. At the time of her marriage, Judith was likely as young as twelve, which was then the legal age of maturity for women in Francia. Æthelwulf, in contrast, was probably in his fifties and already had five sons, two of them adults, from his first marriage. All of this put Judith in a precarious position and much of her future would depend on her ability to bear her new husband offspring. For these reasons, her anointment as queen must have been especially important to Charles. As this was a religious ceremony, the church could enact its particular magic on her fate, making guarantees for her future fertility.

The ceremony itself also made a mark. The text spoken that day by Hincmar in consecrating Judith as a queen is called an *ordo*, and the words it included are partially preserved. It is special because this was the first *ordo* recorded for queen-making: there were several in existence for the consecration of a king, but none for a queen. The so-called *Judith-ordo,* therefore, is significant. It seems that Hincmar took material he had for the consecration of kings – perhaps even some from Wessex – and compiled his own formula suitable for Judith. The *ordo* starts with a marriage blessing, including a prayer for Judith's chastity, a prayer that she is worthy of her dowry, a prayer recalling good wives of the Old Testament, and the fertility blessing. The consecration and coronation prayer follow. In fact, the words that were spoken that day were so significant that some of them were used when Queen Elizabeth II was crowned in 1953.

In the ninth century, the only West Saxon women who had any real impact on politics, leaving their mark on history, were the wives of Mercian rulers. After Alfred's sister Æthelswith married Burgred of Mercia, she witnessed charters with the title *regina* and made grants both in her own name and alongside her husband. Even the *Anglo-Saxon Chronicle* refers to her as *cwen* – 'queen'. Incidentally, the same title was used to refer to Judith. Another Mercian queen to make a mark would be Æthelflaed, Alfred's eldest daughter, whom we will hear of later. The distinctive position of women in Mercia is also demonstrated by the fact that Cynetryth, the wife of Offa, is the first woman, and one of only two, in early medieval north-western Europe to have had coins issued in her own name. Cynetryth's coins are pennies that were minted as versions of those made for her husband, with her name followed by 'Regina M' – placing her as the queen of Mercia. The coins also show her image, making them the earliest depictions of a queen from England. It is thought the coins were either inspired by others minted for the contemporary Byzantine empress Irene or, alternatively, that they were made as imitations of coins depicting later Roman emperors. After all, Offa used imagery on his coins that showed him as a Roman emperor. Cynetryth also attested charters and held joint lordship with her husband over the Mercian monasteries. It has very recently been discovered that Charlemagne copied Offa's example by having coins minted in his wife Fastrada's name too: this came to light in 2023, when a study published details of a single such coin acquired by a museum in Aachen. These two coins are important because they demonstrate the power these two rulers were prepared to share with their wives.

The alliance between Wessex and Francia formed with this marriage was a significant one: Æthelwulf now had a prestigious ruler as his father-in-law (even though Charles was probably younger than him at the time), and likely increased support against the Viking attacks that were plaguing the kingdoms of both sides of the English Channel with increasing severity. In Francia, the threat was ongoing: substantial warbands marauded along both the Seine and the Loire. Support from overseas may well have been of benefit to Charles as well, and he was likely impressed by the successes Æthelwulf had shown against the Vikings only a few years before.

However, tensions were brewing at home. While Æthelwulf was still overseas, word of his Carolingian marriage apparently provoked a rebellion. Æthelbald, his eldest son, rose in revolt and attempted to strip Æthelwulf of his kingship, concerned about the threat of further siblings in his claim to the kingdom. Peace was negotiated – the so-called eastern districts stayed with Æthelwulf and the western districts were ruled by Æthelbald – but it meant that the king was forced to accept what was essentially a demotion.

Judith and Æthelwulf did not have any children, a fact that may have made the new queen's position harder. Only two years after they married, Æthelwulf died, on 13 January 858. No details of the circumstances exist but his body was buried at Steyning in Sussex, before being moved to Winchester at an unknown point.

The close hand with which both Æthelwulf and his father before him had taken control of Kent may be related to the fact that Egbert's background was essentially Kentish, as his father – Æthelwulf's grandfather – had been among the last of the independent kings of Kent.

By the time of his death, Æthelwulf had paved the way for Alfred to become a legendary king whose actions would lay the foundations of a fledgling England.

THE REMAINS

*R*eassembling commingled remains is a difficult task. Inside the *chests, it is immediately apparent that the bones are in complete disarray. When they have all been taken out and inventoried, the team has a collection of more than 1,300 fragments, ranging from entire skulls and long bones to vertebrae and finger bones. Among the remains lie occasional animal bones, including the vertebra of a sheep; to the untrained eye, similar enough to pass for that of a human.*

In order to try to identify individuals from a collection like this, it is necessary to separate the bones into unique skeletons, which is no easy task. Each fragment has to be carefully analysed to see if it can be matched to any of the others. Size is a good starting point: long bones, for instance, are typically easy to match up by length and thickness. Smaller bones and fragments are more challenging. Where age can be estimated, this can be of help, as can certain pathologies – evidence of injury and disease – that affect more than one bone. Osteoarthritis, for instance, leaves tell-tale signs on the surface of the joints. Other clues, when you study a collection like this, come from the colour and texture of each bone. Many of the deceased may have been buried in the ground initially, perhaps in the cemetery at Old Minster, before their remains were moved to the chests: the colour of the surrounding soil would have left its mark on the porous bone. For others, the corpse may have been placed in a stone or lead coffin, where the unique atmospheric conditions would have affected the bones' appearance too.

Eventually, by matching the separate bones, the team announces that they have at least twenty-three partial skeletons spread between the chests; far more than the names of those that have been recorded. This raises an intriguing question: who are the rest of them? And how did they end up in the chests? The records we have from Winchester show clearly that there were numerous earlier burials, and also earlier mortuary chests. But why did only some of the most celebrated kings and bishops end up in the current chests, and what happened to others – those, such as Alfred, who made such an impression not just on the history of Winchester, but on the country's communal memory?

THE LOST CHESTS

MEMORY

*A*s *Bishop Richard Fox watches the men climb down the rickety wooden ladders for the last time, he allows himself a moment of reflection. What were their lives like, those men and women whose bones now have a new resting place? He hopes the new mortuary chests he commissioned for their remains will help preserve their memory. The ten wooden chests fit perfectly on the stone screens he recently had made for either side of the presbytery. The screens are magnificent and have already created a stir. He had them designed in the 'all'antica' style – the mode of the ancients – a trend he picked up from the continent and brought back to England. Winchester is the perfect place to experiment and, like its bishops before him, Fox is a wealthy man indeed, able to invest in major refurbishments. The screens sit within arcades that were created in the early fourteenth century, two hundred years before his time, when the older Romanesque apse at the east end of the cathedral was also replaced. Back then a row of niches was created in another screen at the back of the presbytery. Each niche had a pair of statuettes placed within, with Jesus and Mary in the central position. 'The bodies of saints lie here buried in peace,' an inscription says, 'through whose merits many miracles shine forth.' The niches were of help to Fox when he made the new chests because they also listed names: the term 'saints' seemed loosely applied, as the names inscribed were those of thirteen kings, Queen Emma and two bishops. When Fox began his work, the old chests were in a somewhat sorry state. Some of the lead chests had deteriorated badly, although others, made of timber in the previous century, were in better condition: finely painted, with decoration including the faces of those buried inside. But* while some of those timber chests bore names, this had given Fox something of a headache: the names didn't quite match the remains inside. This was not news to him, however. He has trawled through the history books and cathedral records and found an explanation by the fifteenth-century historian Thomas Rudborne. When Henry of Blois gathered the bones into the lead sarcophagi, Rudborne wrote, 'it was not known who were kings, and who were bishops, since names were not written on the tombs.' For this reason, he wrote, Henry had placed them all in lead sarcophagi, 'kings with bishops and bishops with kings, all completely mixed up'.

Nevertheless, Fox divided the bones up as well as he could, and had the names painted on the outsides for all to read. Does it really matter, he wonders to himself, if we know exactly whose bones were whose? Surely, preserving what remains and, not least, their memory is by far the most significant thing; their names have been saved for posterity.

Memory is important to Fox and he has taken steps to ensure that his own life, and those of others he has worked for, will also be preserved here, intertwined with the ancient dead. He tilts his head back to take in the timber vault above the presbytery and the chests, with its painted bosses set within it. He completed this almost twenty years ago. He sees his own personal badge with the pelican pecking at its breast, alongside the arms of his numerous bishoprics. Beside them are the symbols of the kings, Henry VII and Henry VIII, as well as the Bosworth thorn bush sprouting Tudor roses. There is also the symbol for Catherine of Aragon, whose journey to London he personally organised. Little does he know that in just over a decade those very people represented high above him will be the cause of a cataclysmic rift in the church that will endanger the cathedral's saintly remains.

Glancing back down at the mortuary chests, he ponders their longevity. Will they still be there in five hundred years' time? What has happened to all the other eminent kings and queens whose bones are now lost — will they still matter in the future?

THE SONS OF ÆTHELWULF

Æthelwulf had made clear in his will what he wished to happen upon his death, something that was essential with so many sons able to inherit his kingdom and his estate. Æthelbert was to keep the eastern portion of the kingdom that he had already ruled for a while and the family possessions in western Wessex were to be divided among whichever of the remaining three sons lived the longest. In 858, it was Æthelbald who succeeded to the west of the kingdom as both Alfred and Æthelred were too young.

Left a widow with no children, Judith found herself in a difficult position, aged no more than about fifteen. However, her fate was to keep her in Wessex because the year his father died, Æthelbald, her stepson, married her. His decision was apparently met with outrage, at least if we are to believe Asser's biography, which records that the wedding took place 'against God's prohibition and Christian dignity, and also contrary to the practice of all pagans' and that it incurred 'great disgrace from all who heard it'. However, it seems the practice of stepmother marriage was not entirely unheard of elsewhere in Britain and in continental Europe. It was clearly of benefit to Æthelbald, as he would in essence take on the alliance with Francia that his father had made before him. But for Judith, this situation would prove unlucky too. Again the marriage remained childless and her new husband died another two years later, making her position in Wessex highly insecure. Selling everything she had acquired, she returned to her father, Charles, who took her in and kept her protected in a way befitting a queen. However, Judith seems not to have been too happy with the new situation and in 862 fled from her father with a count named Baldwin and married him. Charles the Bald was furious. The eloping couple sought support from both the Pope and neighbouring kingdoms, and even, apparently, received an offer of refuge from a Viking ruler in Frisia. Eventually, Charles forgave her, and the couple settled in Flanders, producing two sons: one of whom would end up marrying Alfred's daughter Ælfthryth.

The cause of Æthelbald's death is unknown, but it is not implausible that he died in battle. All we know is that he was buried in Sherborne. From this point on, his brother Æthelbert ruled, not just the eastern parts, but the entire kingdom of Wessex: the Viking threat to Wessex, and even to Winchester, his alone to face. Only a few years after Æthelbald's death, an attack on the town came, and is described by Asser: a great Viking army arrived from the sea and laid waste the city, managing to obtain 'immense booty' before returning to their ships. On their way back the raiders were opposed by ealdormen from both Hampshire and Berkshire, who took up the fight. The Vikings, apparently, were 'cut down everywhere' and eventually took flight 'like women'.

Æthelbert remained in charge of Wessex until his death in the autumn of 865 and his rule has been described as one of great peace and harmony, at least internally. But that same year of his death, when his younger brother Æthelred took the throne, yet another new threat loomed on the horizon, one that would indelibly mark the future of not just Wessex, but the entire country.

ARRIVAL OF THE GREAT HEATHEN ARMY

In the year 865, according to the *Anglo-Saxon Chronicle*, something changed in the dynamics of the Viking presence in England. That year, the same year that Æthelbert, son of Æthelwulf, died, 'a great raiding-army came to the land of the English'. The army took up winter quarters in East Anglia, and were provided with horses by the East Anglians, who they apparently made peace with. The nature of this 'peace' is not known, but it likely worked heavily in the invaders' favour. East Anglia was ruled by Edmund, who may well have seen the benefits of giving the newcomers what they wanted. Earlier that year another raiding army had arrived at Thanet in Kent and the inhabitants had promised them money in return for peace, but the raiders didn't keep their side of the bargain: having secured safe access, they left their camp one night and raided across the east of the region. According to Asser, they knew they could obtain more money by secret plunder than by peace.

The army appears to have been different from others that came before it, at least in terms of how it was treated in the sources and also in its unprecedented success in the following years. Its size may have been one reason: we have no definite understanding of how big it was but the description of it as 'great' implies it was of an unusual size. Yet even the understanding of the normal size of an army, or '*here*', is mixed. The only clue we have is found in Ine's seventh-century law codes, where up to 7 men are known as 'thieves', from 7 to 35 men are a 'band', and anything above that is an 'army'.

Over the next few years, this Great Army – or Great Heathen Army, as it became known – moved into the different kingdoms in what seems like a deliberate strategy of setting up winter quarters each year before moving on. After that first winter in East Anglia, the army headed across the mouth of the Humber towards York, in the kingdom of Northumbria. That year Northumbria was harrowed by civil war. The people had deposed the former King Osberht and taken another in his place: Ælla, who the *Chronicle* states had no hereditary right, and this caused political disruption.

The *Chronicle* and the almost contemporary account of Asser, the biographer of Alfred, both record that eventually the two kings united to fight the enemy, gathering a large force and attacking them inside and outside York's fortified walls. A slightly later source, Symeon of Durham's twelfth-century *Tract on the Church of Durham*, adds details: he claims the Great Army had captured the city on 1 November, 'filling everything with blood and lamentation', using swords and fire, as Symeon graphically describes, to destroy monasteries and churches and leave nothing behind except the roofless walls. If the date is correct, this was All Saints' Day: a major Christian feast day. Attacking on such a day would have caused an enormous amount of disruption, a common Viking tactic and a successful one: York found itself under the Great Army's control. The Northumbrian kings' attempt to recapture the city, according to Symeon, would not come until 21 March 867. On that day the two kings and their armies, joined by eight nobles, burst into the city and fought stubbornly on both sides of the walls. The surprise attack initially 'terrified' the invaders, but they soon responded in kind, with fierce and savage fighting on both sides, and the battle ended in much bloodshed, especially on the side of the Northumbrians. By the finish, both kings, Osberht and Ælla, lay dead and the entire kingdom remained with the Scandinavians.

The fall of York is known from numerous accounts in English, Irish and Welsh sources. But the battle was also remembered across the sea, by the Scandinavians, and from the eleventh century it features in a number of accounts there as well. The first of these is a poem dating to the 1020s or 1030s by a skald – a poet of heroic deeds and events – named Sigvatr Þórðarson. Interestingly, this particular skald was writing an encomium to King Cnut, who by then had conquered England, and reciting this event would have been a deliberate way of demonstrating the long history of successful Scandinavian conquest. Along with several other eleventh-century writers, he names the leader of the Viking force as Ivar, one of the sons of the legendary Ragnar Lothbrok. The death of Ælla was, according to Sigvatr, a very personal attack, and he describes how Ivar 'had Ælla's back cut with an eagle'. The same account appears in the saga of Ragnar Lothbrok, further describing the blood-eagle ritual: a gruesome form of torture by which the ribs are severed from the spine and the lungs pulled through the victim's back to form wings, like those of an eagle. This method of execution was allegedly performed on others too, throughout the Viking Age, if the Old Norse sources are to be believed: although some have it as a less gruesome act, merely the carving of the symbol of an eagle into the victim's back. Horrifying either way, although new research has shown that the blood-eagle ritual was certainly possible, anatomically speaking, and may have fitted well into the fragments we know of the Viking Age military society in which ritualised torture was par for the course, there is no evidence that this was actually more than a literary device.

The fall of York is important because it was the first time an entire kingdom had come into Viking hands; hands that would, over the next decade or so, be the threat that catalysed the shaping of England. York would also remain the focus of the entire Scandinavian kingdom in the north of England until the death of Eric Bloodaxe in 954, which would mark the end of almost a century of their control.

After their success in Northumbria, the Great Army headed for Mercia and towards the end of 867, took winter quarters in Nottingham. As a result, pressure mounted on the Mercian King Burgred and he clearly decided to capitalise on his former alliances with Wessex, as his councillors asked Æthelred and his brother Alfred to help defeat the Vikings. The two agreed and travelled with their army into Mercia and up to Nottingham, arriving, Asser explains, single-mindedly seeking battle. But the Vikings had different plans. Defended by a stronghold, they refused to fight and the West Saxon army was unable to breach the wall, leaving them with no choice but to negotiate peace and return home to Wessex. We don't know the terms of this agreement, but the Great Army made no further foray into Mercia afterwards. Instead, they headed back to York, where they stayed for a whole year. For a time, at least, the West Saxon-Mercian alliance proved successful. The following year, the Viking army headed back to East Anglia, overwintering in Thetford, although the precise location of their camp has never been found. Whatever agreement the Vikings had come to with King Edmund a few years earlier had clearly either been broken or was no longer relevant, as the East Anglian king battled fiercely against them. On 20 November 869, Edmund's life came to an end in a manner that was to resonate for centuries to come.

THE DEATH OF ST EDMUND

The story of King Edmund's death in 869 was reported in the *Anglo-Saxon Chronicle* and in Asser's biography, but throughout the Middle Ages the tale was elaborated on to the extent that it is difficult to know what really happened and, crucially, why. According to Asser, Edmund was killed on the battlefield with a large number of his men, leaving the entire kingdom of East Anglia in the hands of the Vikings. The *Chronicle* is less clear, suggesting the battle was won first and the king killed later. A later manuscript of the *Chronicle*, Manuscript E produced in Peterborough, adds that after their victory the army not only conquered all the surrounding land, they also 'did for all the monasteries to which they came'. 'At the same time,' it continues, 'they came to Peterborough: burnt and demolished, killed abbot and monks and all that they found there, brought it about so that what was earlier very rich was as it were nothing.' This is actually the first reference to a wider campaign of targeting religious institutions such as churches and monasteries, something much expanded on in later sources. The impact on the monasteries is backed up by archaeological sources, which show no evidence of monastic activity between the 870s and 970s: at the same time, no manuscripts survive from the period, and the line of succession of the East Anglian bishops was broken. The Great Army clearly disrupted not just politics but also religion.

The more famous account of Edmund's death is provided by a Benedictine monk, Abbo of Fleury, who made a visit to England in 985, originally intending to head a new monastic school at Ramsey in Cambridgeshire. While in England he visited the aged Archbishop of Canterbury, Dunstan, who told Abbo the full story of Edmund's death, one he had heard many years earlier at the court of King Æthelstan (reign 924–939). At the court, perhaps in Winchester, a 'decrepit old man' had appeared in front of the king to tell the story. The man said that he had been Edmund's armour bearer when he died, so at least fifty-five years before his visit to Æthelstan, and he had been there to witness the death of the king with his own eyes. On his return to Ramsey, Abbo was urged by his fellow monks to write the story down and send a copy back to the archbishop: this is what survives today. Abbo's account is compelling but also rather fantastical. He explains that the army, led by Inguar (Ivar), arrives in East Anglia by sea following an attack on Northumbria in 869. In the coastal town they interrogate the locals to find out where King Edmund is, killing all of the men in the region to prevent him from mustering an army. They locate Edmund at a royal estate and send an emissary with their demands: to have his ancient treasures, his hereditary wealth, and for Edmund in the future to reign under Ivar. Edmund takes advice from a bishop, who advises him to accept the demands. He refuses. He says he will die for his country and for his people and declares he will rule under no one but God. Yet in his response to the Vikings' messenger, he says he will agree to rule under Ivar if the latter agrees to convert to Christianity. Before this message is fully delivered, Ivar arrives and takes Edmund prisoner, clearly too impatient to listen. Edmund's death is gruesome. First he is bound in chains, beaten and taunted by the Vikings. Then he is tied to a tree and whipped. Throughout, King Edmund calls out ceaselessly to Christ with a broken voice. This only infuriates his captors who begin to use him for target practice, piercing his body with arrows, inflicting wound upon wound until he is barely able to draw breath. Finally, when only a few vestiges of life remain in the Christian king's body, he is wrenched from the tree and made to stretch out his head, 'which had ever been drawn by the royal diadem'. He is promptly decapitated. In a final act of disrespect, the Danes throw his head into the forest in order to deny him any hope of a Christian burial.

According to the story, they succeeded, almost. Some years later, when peace was restored, Abbo writes that the East Anglians were able to find Edmund's body, just not his head. They put together a search party and eventually a voice cried out, 'Here, here, here!' Following the sound, the searchers found Edmund's head between the paws of a monstrous wolf, embracing it gently in protection. This was the first miracle that led Edmund to sainthood.

While Abbo's account has some reliable elements to it, he makes a long series of errors and seems completely ignorant of the movements of the Great Army as reported in the *Anglo-Saxon Chronicle*. Many parts of the tale are clearly literary embellishments and deliberate biblical allegories: the wolf, for instance, can be compared to the lions that spared the prophet Daniel and the story of the bishop's advice that Edmund rejected has a parallel in the Book of Job. The wolf may be rooted in East Anglian folklore and its identity in local legend: the Wuffing dynasty, thought to have ruled between the sixth and the mid-eighth centuries, had long used this animal as its symbol, making it a fitting protector of the kingdom's very last ruler.

The year following the fall of East Anglia was marked by a number of battles. It very quickly became clear that the Vikings had set their sights on Wessex. A particularly descriptive account is given for the year 870, with several battles near Reading, giving us an unusual insight into the military structure of the raiders. The first battle took place at a site called Englefield – which Asser calls the 'Plain of the Angles': the victory went to the West Saxons. Four days later, a second battle was fought in Reading, this time led jointly by King Æthelred and Alfred, along with a large army. Now, both sides suffered massive losses but the Vikings 'had possession of the place of slaughter'. Finally, after another four days, the armies met again at Ashdown, in an enormous battle where many thousands ended up killed. The Viking army was divided into two bands: one led by the kings Bagsecg and Halfdan and the other, by their jarls, or chiefs. By the end of the day, Bagsecg and several jarls lay dead on the battlefield. However, Asser gives more detail, implying that the Vikings' eventual defeat – forced to flee by the West Saxons – proved a close call. Copying their enemies' division of force into two, Alfred and Æthelred headed to them separately but the king was delayed as he insisted on remaining in his tent at prayer, refusing to leave until the priest had finished mass. His Christian faith was so important, he said, that he would 'not forsake divine service for that of men'. However, the victory did not end the Viking threat. Yet another battle took place at Merton two months later – a location yet to be identified but that might have been the same *Meretun* where Cynewulf and Cyneheard were both killed in 786. In total, the *Chronicle* states that nine battles were fought against the Great Army in the kingdom south of the Thames: these are described as *folcgefeoht*, typically translated as 'national fights'. After the Battle of Reading, the Great Army was bolstered by the arrival of a Great Summer Army. By the end of the year, the Vikings made peace with the West Saxons: this may well have involved a bribe, with the English paying them off to stay away. After all, this had been tried before in Kent, when the raiding army overwintered in Thanet in 865 – an agreement the raiders promptly broke.

After Easter in 871, King Æthelred died, possibly as a result of wounds received on the battlefield. His son Æthelwold was still a child, so Alfred, the youngest of Æthelwulf's five sons, succeeded to the throne. He was forced to guarantee property rights for his nephews, something that would later have implications for the relationship between them and Alfred's own sons.

CAT AND MOUSE

After the hectic battles of 871, for the next two winters the Great Army focused on Mercian territory, by taking winter quarters first in London and the following year at Torksey in Lindsey. In both places, their overwintering took place after an agreement, making 'peace' with the Mercians.

In 873, the Great Army got on the move again from their base in Torksey, this time heading for the jewel in the crown of the Mercian kingdom: the monastery in Repton. At the time Repton was a hugely wealthy and prospering monastic institution. Located on the River Trent, it had been founded at least as early as the seventh century, as described in Felix's *Life of Guthlac*, a saint who spent two years there under the guidance of an abbess.

Today remnants of that early monastery remain under the church of St Wystan, which is built on top of a crypt that was once either a shrine or a mausoleum dating to the eighth century. Repton was the known burial place of several significant kings of the Mercian royal house: a suitable target for a force intent on capturing yet another kingdom. The *Anglo-Saxon Chronicle* gives us a very brief account. In this year of 873, it says, the army moved from Lindsey to Repton, taking up winter quarters, driving King Burgred across the sea into exile and conquering all that land. There is no mention of a battle, and it appears that Burgred fled without a fight: knowledge of the fate that befell other kings, such as Edmund, may well have been on his mind. The Mercian king travelled to Rome with his wife Æthelswith, daughter of Æthelwulf, never to return. He died in the city and was buried in St Mary's church in the English quarter, an area near St Peter's, with a hostel and a church, inhabited by a group of English ecclesiastics, pilgrims and other travellers. Pilgrimages to Rome from England were relatively frequent among clergy, nobles and even common people.

Until recently, Repton was the only Great Army winter camp that had been identified through archaeological excavations. In the 1970s and 1980s, investigations around the Anglo-Saxon church of St Wystan revealed extensive evidence of a Scandinavian presence. The excavators, Martin Biddle and Birthe Kjølbye-Biddle, identified what they suggested was a defensive ditched enclosure, although the interpretation of this is now uncertain. More significant was the discovery of a number of Scandinavian graves around the church. The most famous is the so-called Repton warrior, Grave 511, a man with several severe injuries, including a deep axe wound into his left femur – thigh bone –that almost certainly cut off his penis and left testicle: those who buried him made sure he was made complete again for the afterlife by leaving a boar's tusk between his legs. He was also buried with a Scandinavian-style sword at his side and a Thor's hammer pendant around his neck. A second grave, containing the body of a younger man, was placed beside him and the two were covered by a joint rectangular stone setting that included deliberately broken-up pieces of a finely carved Anglo-Saxon stone sculpture. Recently, ancient DNA analysis of these two men showed that there was a direct, first-degree relationship between them, proving that they were father and son. Isotope analysis of the tooth enamel suggested they grew up in a location very similar to each other, likely in southern Scandinavia, possibly Denmark. These graves are some of the very few certain Scandinavian burials known from the whole of England, and the only ones that can be associated with written evidence of the Great Army.

Yet these individual graves did not provide the most spectacular evidence for the Viking presence in Repton. In 1982, the archaeologists excavated a large mound in the garden of the vicarage next-door to the church. The mound had previously been dug into by antiquarians in the seventeenth and nineteenth centuries, with reports of a vast assemblage of bones and even the burial of a giant, nine foot tall. While the existence of this giant could not be proven, in the 1980s the team discovered a spectacular assemblage: a two-roomed building, possibly a chapel or mausoleum, that had been cut down to just the lowest stretch of the walls. From the outside, steps led down into the ruined building and in the innermost room, a layer of red sand had been placed on the floor. On top of this lay the commingled remains of nearly three hundred skeletons. Although the antiquarian investigations had disturbed the group, the team could clearly see that in places the bones had been stacked by type, as a neat pile of thigh bones still remained in one corner. This mass burial, then, was actually a carefully curated charnel of bones, as the dead had previously been interred elsewhere, then exhumed and moved to a communal grave. Artefacts provided a suggested date: five coins found among the deposit could be dated to between 872 and 875, while fragments of Scandinavian-style weapons and long-distance imported artefacts like a carnelian bead suggested connections to the Viking world. The elaborately constructed mound over the top of the deposit indicated the same: by the late ninth century, mound burial of any kind had gone completely out of fashion in Christian kingdoms like Mercia, but it was still a very common practice in Scandinavia. After correcting for the effects of diets high in seafood, which can make dates seem too early, the radiocarbon dates from the bones showed they were consistent with a date in the ninth century. As a result, Repton may be the only real evidence we have of the people who formed part of the Great Army.

For decades the site was also the only Viking winter camp to have been archaeologically identified, and its supposed fortified enclosure offered a blueprint for searching for encampments elsewhere. That was all to change in 2013, when the Viking camp at Torksey was discovered. Torksey, however, was of a very different nature to Repton. The site was located through the identification of metal-detected artefacts of types that it had become apparent could only be associated with the Vikings, and the Great Army more specifically. These included large numbers of small lead gaming pieces; Islamic dirham coins obtained through trade with eastern networks; 'hacksilver' – pieces of precious metal cut up to be used for payment; and weights of types known to be of Scandinavian origin. Eventually, the discoveries at Torksey led to a whole new way of identifying the movements of the Great Army through the English landscape. It is particularly intriguing that the Torksey evidence bears no signs of conflict, and that the Scandinavian presence there appears to have acted as a catalyst for later industry and settlement in the area. The process of 'making peace with the Mercians' may therefore be seen to have been an agreement that suited both sides well.

The last thing we know of this winter's events is that the Vikings installed Ceolwulf, who is described in the *Chronicle* as 'a foolish king's thegn', to rule Mercia, promising loyalty and giving them hostages. Ceolwulf is usually interpreted as a puppet king, who vowed that the kingdom should be ready for the Scandinavians whenever they might want it, as would he himself, along with anyone who would follow him, at the service of the raiding army. The description in the *Chronicle* is derogatory and implies disloyalty by Ceolwulf.

Repton appears to be a turning point for the Great Army. At the end of the winter, the force, led by four kings, split in two: possibly, although none of the sources confirm this, separating off the summer force that had arrived in 870. One part, under the leadership of Halfdan, headed north into Northumbria, getting embroiled in battles with the Picts and the Strathclyde Britons. The following year, Halfdan divided up land and settled: the *Chronicle* states that he and his men proceeded to plough and provide for themselves. The other part of the force, led by the three kings Guthrum, Oscytel and Anund, had clearly not given up on Wessex. They promptly headed south, in what can only be described as a game of cat and mouse with Alfred over the following five years. Yet this was apparently not the only Scandinavian force that Alfred had to contend with. The next winter, while Guthrum and his army settled in Cambridge for a year, Alfred went out to sea with a ship-army to fight seven shiploads of enemies. Soon after this, he had to deal with an attack at Wareham in Dorset: this time he did so through negotiation. According to the *Chronicle*, that raiding army granted him their most distinguished men as hostages, and they swore him oaths on what is described as 'the sacred ring' – something they had apparently never agreed to do to any other nation – agreeing to go quickly from the kingdom.

Finally, Alfred and the remnants of the Great Army met in what is often considered to be their most decisive battle, at Ethandun – and it is the story of this battle that has so thoroughly fixed Alfred in the general public's mind and in England's history. The battle and the treaty that was to follow have become so important that Alfred's victory – where he once and for all 'defeated the Vikings' – features on the syllabus of the 'Life in the UK' theory test taken by anyone wanting to apply to become a British citizen.

In the winter of 878, after the Twelfth Night (that is, early January), Guthrum and his men attacked the royal estate at Chippenham, where they overwintered, ravaging across Wessex. Alfred, who had been staying in Chippenham at the time, fled south-west across the Somerset marshes, allegedly taking shelter at the house of a swineherd for a few days. The days were filled with reflection and prayer for the king, waiting for God – through his servant St Neot – to send him a divine means of driving the Vikings out of his kingdom. One day when the swineherd was out, Alfred was left alone with his wife, who was busy baking cakes or loaves of bread. Leaving the loaves on the hearth, the swineherd's wife turned away, expecting Alfred, who was warming himself by the fire, to keep an eye on them for her: however, he was so lost in his thoughts that he didn't notice them burning. The woman berated him, not realising she was talking to the king, but Alfred apologised and promised to turn the remaining loaves for her. The moral of the story is usually interpreted to show how fervently Alfred wanted to rescue his kingdom; his devotion to God; and also that he was such a trustworthy man that he could safely be left alone with the swineherd's wife. But – as we'll see – while Alfred may have held the Vikings back from Wessex, it would be far from correct to claim they were *defeated*. The story of the cakes may not be true, but we do know that Alfred sent out a call for men from across the kingdom to join him, mustering at a place known as Egbert's Stone in Wiltshire in the seventh week after Easter. Finally, the two sides met in battle at the site of Ethandun, thought to be what is now the village of Edington in Wiltshire. Here Alfred had the upper hand. He chased Guthrum's men back to their 'fortress' (probably Chippenham) and besieged them for fourteen days; with all their supplies cut off, they eventually admitted defeat and agreed to a truce. Guthrum agreed, along with forty of his men, to be baptised, something that took place in an elaborate ceremony three weeks later. During the ceremony, the parties exchanged precious gifts and Guthrum was given the baptismal name 'Athelstan': a West Saxon royal family name, which may indicate the high status offered to him. Afterwards the Viking army spent a year at Cirencester before finally leaving Wessex and returning to East Anglia, where they settled and divided up land.

At some point after this, and before Guthrum died in 890, Alfred and Guthrum also came to a legal agreement. We know this because it survives in written form, but without a date attached. In the treaty, the two parties gave formal recognition to territory between them, explicitly spelling out that free men among the English had legal protection if they ventured into Guthrum's land, and vice versa. This treaty is often understood as a border agreement between England and what later becomes known as the Danelaw, the territory under Danish rule, but that is inaccurate. There *is* a boundary described in the treaty, but the word Danelaw doesn't come into use until much later. The boundary that the two parties agreed on starts along the course of the Thames, then runs up the River Lee to its source; from thereon it moves to Bedford; then up the River Ouse until it reaches the Roman road Watling Street, near modern-day Milton Keynes, although it isn't clear what happens beyond that point. This certainly wasn't a permanent boundary or one that would later define areas of Scandinavian settlement: we can see that from place names because while most Scandinavian place names are found to the north and east of this boundary line, they also spill across it. So what did the treaty really mean? It certainly seems to have been a formal division, separating Guthrum's East Anglian stronghold from those areas that belonged to Alfred. It may even be that it was created to facilitate coexistence between two quite different political, administrative and ideological worldviews. Intriguingly, the treaty's wording specifies that it was made 'both for the living and those yet unborn' – hinting that both parties thought of this as a long-term arrangement: the Vikings were there to stay.

Although later traditions like to see Edington and the subsequent treaty as the ultimate victory for Alfred, this was far from the truth. Treaties like this one were clearly not always respected. In 885, the *Anglo-Saxon Chronicle* tells us that the raiding army in East Anglia broke the peace with King Alfred. The West Saxons were no better, as that same year Alfred had already sent an army into Guthrum's territory. The battle did, however, reflect an important change, as from this point on the Vikings' attentions would begin to turn away from Wessex back to territories they already held in their power – at least for a while.

After Guthrum was pushed back from Wessex, the 880s proved a decade of relative peace for Alfred, with few external attacks. Internal politics, however, remained on his agenda, and especially important was the restoration of London in 886. At the time the city was within Mercia and had most likely been in Viking control since 877. It was important because of its location, and especially because of the Thames: a highway that could take invading ships from the coast at the Thames estuary far inland into Mercian territory. The threat was clearly felt by Alfred, especially after a Viking fleet assembled, ready to attack, at Benfleet on the coast in 885. While that particular fleet seemed unsuccessful, Alfred made a bold move and launched an attack on London in 886, besieging and capturing the city and subsequently restoring its defences. Control of London was entrusted to the Mercian ealdorman Æthelred, who soon after married Alfred's daughter Æthelflaed. The aftermath of this event is significant: the *Chronicle* says that 'all the English people that were not under subjection to the Danes submitted to him'. This is likely to have included people from several different kingdoms and in fact Asser uses the phrase 'all the Angles and the Saxons'. From this point in time, too, certain charters describe Alfred as 'king of the Angles and of the Saxons' and 'king of the Anglo-Saxons' – something that implies an authority far beyond just that of Wessex, and one that was cemented with a common adversary in mind.

Alfred had managed to keep the relationship with Mercia in good standing for some time, which is evident in the issue of shared coinage with King Burgred, his brother-in-law, before he was chased away by the Great Army. Yet what happened after Ceolwulf, the so-called puppet king, was put into place is confusing. By 883, a charter shows that Alfred had somehow managed to gain recognition as overlord of Mercia. While the *Chronicle*'s description of Ceolwulf's rule gives a West Saxon view that is highly derogatory, the reality may have been different. He may have been more independent from Viking influence than is suggested. We know that Ceolwulf issued charters in his own name and that he even minted coins. Intriguingly, the latter suggests a much closer interaction with Alfred and Wessex than the written accounts would have us believe, while recent new finds have forced a rethink as to just how important Ceolwulf might have been and may even suggest that Alfred deliberately attempted to erase him from history.

HIDDEN EVIDENCE

In November 2019, at the Crown Court in Worcester, three men were sentenced to a combined jail term of more than twenty-three years for a crime they had committed four years earlier. Two of the men, George Powell and Layton Davies, were metal detectorists, who in the spring of 2015 had discovered a hugely significant hoard of coins and artefacts near Leominster in Herefordshire – a hoard that would later be valued at more than £5 million. Its significance, we know now, is enormous: it contained coins that shed unprecedented light on the relationship between Alfred, Ceolwulf and the Vikings – and consequently the relationship between the kingdoms of Wessex and Mercia – in the years that would prove to be instrumental for the formation of England as a single nation. Yet because of Powell and Davies' actions, the vast majority of those coins are now lost. The hoard, estimated to originally have contained more than three hundred coins, alongside several unique gold and silver artefacts, fell under the definition of treasure according to the 1996 Treasure Act: this means that it should have been reported to the local coroner within fourteen days of its discovery, as it was the property of the Crown. Instead, Powell and Davies kept the find secret and began trying to sell the items on the private market, contacting antiques dealers around the country and offering the artefacts for sale. The plan seems to have been unsuccessful. Several of these dealers later reported to have turned the pair away, advising them – although they clearly already knew – that they had a duty by law to report their finds to the authorities. Consequently, Powell and Davies turned to an acquaintance, Simon Wicks, another detectorist and minor dealer with a criminal past, who agreed to act as an intermediary. Coins were handed over during a clandestine meeting, lasting only a few minutes, at a motorway service station along the M4.

Despite the secrecy, rumours began to circulate in the metal detecting community about the hoard and these soon came to the attention of the local finds liaison officer, Peter Reavill. Peter contacted Powell and Davies, warning them of the severe consequences if they really had illegitimately hidden a hoard. Just a few days later, the two decided to declare four gold items and two coins, claiming the latter had been dispersed, meaning they would not meet the definition of a 'hoard'. They denied the existence of the remaining coins, but Peter was not convinced. What followed over the next few months is like something out of a police drama show.

Sometime in July that year, the British Museum received a tip-off that a substantial hoard had been found in the area of the Welsh borders, advising the authorities to make inquiries among local dealers. They were also advised to contact Dix Noonan Webb, a prominent auction house in London's Mayfair, which specialises in coins. It turned out that a month earlier Wicks had deposited with them nine of the coins he had received from the Hereford hoard and in late July another seven. The coins had been accepted by medieval coin specialist Jim Brown, who at the trial admitted he realised they must all have come from a single hoard. Nevertheless, the link between the coins and Wicks, Powell and Davies was now clear. The police seized the coins from the dealers and ordered full searches of the three men's homes. Numerous artefacts were confiscated and sent to the British Museum for investigation; many of these had been deliberately concealed. Speaking about the searches sometime later, Superintendent Edd Williams from West Mercia Police reported that they had even found a coin hidden inside the handle of a magnifying glass. The men's mobile phones were also confiscated. From these the police force was able not only to reconstruct the trio's extensive contacts but also establish Powell and Davies' presence in the area the hoard was discovered at precisely the right date and time, something the two had vehemently denied when questioned. Perhaps most importantly, the police could also recover deleted mobile phone images which, although grainy and blurred, revealed the hoard as it had been when first discovered. Some of the photos were so detailed that investigators were able to recognise coins Wicks had attempted to sell, while also proving that the story the pair gave to Peter Reavill, about having found only two dispersed coins, had been completely fictitious.

Still, Powell and Davies refused to cooperate with the police and in particular declined to reveal their exact findspot. Yet along with the recovered photos, two other images showed the landscape surrounding the field, no doubt so that the detectorists could return to the spot to search for further treasure in the future. The information was enough for county archaeologist Tim Hoverd, who knew the Herefordshire landscape inside out, to identify the exact field in question. A team of archaeologists was brought in to investigate the area, but it was clear that there was no more evidence to be found. A ground-penetrating radar survey suggested that the hoard had not been buried in a settlement or cemetery, making it more likely to have been loot buried in the context of Viking raids.

This is exactly what the identification of the objects suggests as well. In addition to the coins, the objects Powell and Davies reported included a silver ingot, a gold finger-ring with niello inlay, a gold arm-ring with a clasp in the shape of a serpent or beast biting its tail, and a rock-crystal sphere encased in an exquisite and delicate gold frame, made to be suspended like a pendant. The rings both fit ninth-century, high-quality craftmanship from England, while the sphere dates to the sixth or seventh century, and is of a type known both from eastern England and the Frankish empire. The ingot is of precisely the type the Vikings used as currency and although only one was reported, the photos show several more in the original hoard.

Among the thirty coins that have been recovered to date, one was a Frankish silver penny of Louis the Pious and another an Islamic dirham dating to the early eighth century. Both were coins that could not have been used as legal tender in England, but types that were valued among the Scandinavians for their high-quality silver content. The remaining recovered coins were all Anglo-Saxon, one of them a unique kind that was only issued for a very brief time in 879, giving us a *terminus post quem* – a 'date after which' the hoard must have been buried. It is also these coins that are so revealing about the relationship between Ceolwulf and Alfred, and the kingdoms they ruled over.

Remarkably, a similar hoard was discovered that same year in a field near Watlington in South Oxfordshire by metal detectorist James Mather, at a site that once lay on the border of Mercia and Wessex. The Thames flows only a few miles to the south, connecting the area all the way down to London and the North Sea, while an ancient trackway passes nearby. Initially finding a small bar of silver, then a number of pennies, James reported his hoard and a subsequent excavation revealed almost 250 silver objects. The hoard was pretty similar to other Viking hoards, containing a combination of silver arm-rings, hacksilver, silver ingots and coins. There were around two hundred complete silver coins, and among them, coins that could date it to a very narrow period of time at the end of the 870s. The coins included issues of both Alfred and Ceolwulf, along with two of Æthelred, who was Archbishop of Canterbury from 870 to 879, as well as two Frankish silver pennies. Thirteen of those coins were also of the so-called 'two emperors' type. Previously, only two examples of these coins had been published, so to find this many together was highly significant.

The Watlington and Hereford hoards are remarkably similar and were likely both placed in the ground around the same time. And between them the new evidence they provide of the relationship between Alfred and Ceolwulf is staggering – especially important is that in the Hereford hoard are coins from several different moneyers, something that tells us they were issued widely, not just commemorating a special event. There must have been a very significant alliance and one that lasted several years. Why, then, does Ceolwulf disappear after 878, and why is he described so negatively in the *Chronicle*? The relationship between Ceolwulf and the Vikings is also confusing, as the *Chronicle* entry suggests he remained loyal to *them* rather than Alfred, which is not what the coins suggest. Did something happen that caused the West Saxons to later want to erase him from history? In any case, in these last years of the 870s and early 880s, Alfred clearly took decisive measures to manage the relationship between Wessex and the surrounding kingdoms, and especially the Scandinavians: keeping his friends close and his enemies closer.

SETTLEMENT

The name Danelaw has become synonymous with north-eastern England and Scandinavian territory and is typically related to the Alfred–Guthrum treaty. But the term itself doesn't actually appear until just after 1000, when we find it in legal documents that describe regions under *Dena lage* ('law of the Danes') in opposition to those under *Ængla lage* ('law of the English'). Nevertheless, it is clear that there were differences in laws between the territories that were already in existence before the eleventh century. There were also administrative differences: in the Danelaw, shires – regional areas – were divided up into *wapentakes* (from Old Norse *vápnatak*) rather than into *hundreds*, and taxes were calculated in *carucates* (an area that could be ploughed by six oxen) rather than *hides*. Even so, the documents we have available to us make it clear that although the Danelaw areas had their own special legal positions, they were still thought to be legal provinces within the English kingdom. The Danelaw was never a fully coherent political unit, but certainly by the time of Alfred's death in 899, the *Chronicle* describes his (English) territory as that which was 'not under Danish control'.

What this also means is that by the late ninth century, there was a substantial settled Scandinavian population in England. Yet we have never quite been able to determine how big this population really was at any given point in time. The extent of Viking-controlled land would seem to imply a sizeable number of migrants, but it is difficult to identify them. The written records are devoid of figures: in fact, the only numbers we have relating to the Vikings are counts of the number of ships appearing on the horizon or, occasionally, numbers of dead on a battlefield. And it is hard to tell if these are realistic; they will have been estimates at best and exaggerations at worst.

Typically, one of the best estimates for the number of settlers has been the distribution of Scandinavian place names. Plots of these show a clear distribution in the north, Midlands and east of England, while the territory of Wessex is almost devoid of them, something that matches the historical narrative. Yet whether you can really equate place names with groups of cultural settlers is unclear. Archaeologically, we have no way of identifying Scandinavian settlements as there are no distinct building types or village patterns to uncover. Graves, too, can be tricky to distinguish as those of incoming migrants. Just as with the earlier Germanic settlers in the centuries after the Roman period, gravegoods are not reliable markers and in any case it seems that the custom of burying people in that way soon went out of fashion. While DNA and isotope evidence has been helpful in a few individual graves, like that of the Repton warrior, this has not been the case on a wider scale across the country. A large-scale study of modern DNA – that is, analysing the ancestry of people living in the country today to estimate movements in the past – gave divided results. The study set out to look at population movement in Britain over perhaps as much as ten thousand years, with a particular aim of identifying local and historical migration patterns. When observing the so-called 'Anglo-Saxon migrations', the study found a significant but small contribution of migrant DNA: it accounted for 10–40 per cent of ancestry, which is in marked contrast to the more recent ancient DNA study that estimated the figure at up to 76 per cent in certain regions. What's even more interesting is the evaluation of Scandinavian migrations: the modern DNA study's authors suggested that there had been 'no obvious genetic signature of the Danish Vikings, who controlled large parts of England . . . from the ninth century'. This result came as a surprise because it was completely at odds with the contemporary under-standing of Viking Age migration. Later, other researchers pointed out that the genetic differences between the ninth-century migrants and those who had migrated from southern Scandinavia in the three centuries before would be minute. Reworking the calculations to take this into account, the researchers found that there had, after all, been a substantial number of settlers from Scandinavia.

ALFRED'S LIFE AND LEGACY

The facts about Alfred's life must be carefully excavated from the legends and myths surrounding him, but this is no easy job. Much in the same way that someone's life today can be observed through social media, his has been presented to us in curated snippets that present a particular image for a particular reason, some of them contemporary with his life, many others created in the 1,100 years that have passed since his death.

Much of Alfred's fame was of his own making: he worked hard during his lifetime to ensure his legacy was recorded and spelled out. The West Saxon court and religious institutions were prolific producers of texts. Some of the most significant documents we have in reconstructing the history of the period were commissioned by Alfred. Among the books that he may have had translated into Old English was Gregory the Great's *Liber Regulae Pastoralis*, or *Pastoral Care*, but perhaps the most influential of the works that came out of Alfred's court was the *Anglo-Saxon Chronicle*. While on the surface, it may appear to be an attempt at an objective reporting of historical events, this, as we have seen, is far from the truth: it had a very particular ideological purpose. What we refer to as the *Anglo-Saxon Chronicle* consists of collated texts and one, the so-called Common Stock (material dating up to 891, common to most of the different versions), was clearly the product of Alfred's court. This text has two obvious aims: to constitute part of his educational reform and to create a common national identity for the English nation that was then in its infancy.

The early annals in the *Chronicle* were selected specifically to provide authority for Alfred through his alleged bloodline, that of Cerdic, and would provide the same for his descendants. We don't know how much Alfred himself was involved in creating the *Chronicle*, although the same political perspective was fundamental to those who were in his scholarly circle.

In 1574, the first printed edition of a manuscript known as the *Life of King Alfred* was published. The manuscript was based on an original attributed to Asser, the Welsh bishop who acted as his teacher and counsellor. That copy was likely written down some-time around the year 1000 and ended up in the possession of the

antiquary John Leland in the 1540s. Leland must have obtained it
from a religious house after the dissolution of the monasteries and
eventually it ended up in the hands of Matthew Parker, the master
of Corpus Christi College, Cambridge: it was he who was responsible for the printed edition. However, the original medieval account,
which ultimately found its way into the spectacular private manuscript collection of Robert Cotton, was destroyed in a fire on 23
October 1731, along with vast numbers of other irreplaceable texts.
Because the original is lost, our only version of Asser's text is that of
Parker. Unfortunately for us, as was common at the time, Parker
did not produce a straightforward copy of Asser's *Life* but instead,
interspersed it with what he considered improvements. These
included other stories he was certain were authored by Asser too
but had been separated from the original text by mistake. Most
famously, Parker added parts of the *Annals of St Neot's*, which he
mistakenly believed Asser to have written, including the now
infamous story of Alfred and the cakes.

At various places in the *Life of King Alfred*, Asser quotes from
the *Vita Karoli*, also known as the *Life of Charlemagne*, a ninth-
century text written by Charlemagne's courtier Einhard within a
few years of the Frankish emperor's death. The *Vita Karoli* has
been said to have *created* Charlemagne, or at the very least been
extraordinarily influential in presenting him in a way that could
be read as a model for rulership. This, then, must have been a
fitting example for Asser to use for his own work. Asser's *Life* falls
roughly into two parts, the first Alfred's life up to the year 887,
based mainly on the *Anglo-Saxon Chronicle* with some additional
extras. After that it seems that the text comes more directly from
Asser's associations with Alfred: this is because in 887 Alfred learned
how to read Latin. The nature of Asser's account changes; he no
longer has to stick to mundane translations of events in the
Chronicle. Instead, what follows is a rather long and rambling

narrative of achievements and activities, as well as a characterisation of Alfred's rule, the way he organised his affairs, how he encouraged religion and a description of his interest in justice and the pursuit of wisdom.

For some reason, the *Life* ends quite abruptly in 893, several years before Alfred's death. It looks as if it was never quite completed and that what we have is more like a draft: there is no description of Alfred's successes against the Vikings in the 890s or any elaboration on his death, even though Asser outlived the king by at least a decade.

Interestingly, it appears that this account was written primarily for a Welsh audience and it has been argued that this was in order to reassure the Welsh that they had submitted to a king they could consider as wise, just, effective and, above all, Christian. In this sense, Asser was acting more or less as a publicist for Alfred, in ways one could easily imagine a modern-day politician might want before an election to ensure his or her image was as well-presented as it could be.

Regardless of the bias of the sources, many of the facts of Alfred's life can be reconstructed. In 868, he married Ealhswith, daughter of Æthelred Mucel and his wife Eadburh, who according to Asser was of royal Mercian lineage. We know surprisingly little about Ealhswith, a fact that is no doubt due, in part, to the low status a queen had in ninth-century Wessex. Even Asser, while mentioning her in passing, never gives her name: it is highly unlikely he didn't know it, so leaving it out must have been a deliberate choice. Alfred and Ealhswith had five children who survived to adulthood. There were three daughters, the eldest of which was Æthelflaed, who later married Æthelred, ruler of the Mercians, and would rise to fame for her political and military prowess; the second daughter Æthelgifu became abbess at Shaftesbury; and Ælfthryth married Baldwin II of Flanders – the son of Judith from her marriage with Baldwin I. Alfred's two sons were Edward and Æthelweard.

We know that for most of his life Alfred was plagued by illness. According to Asser, his suffering started at his wedding, when he was hit by a sudden and severe pain unknown to physicians; this was to last from his twentieth year up to his fortieth and beyond, without remission. Alfred even alludes to his sickness in his own writings, and Elias, the patriarch of Jerusalem, sent him medical advice: remedies for alleviating constipation, diarrhoea and pain in the spleen. Asser also, however, gives a different account: he explains that in his adolescence, Alfred developed *ficus*, a condition usually translated as haemorrhoids or piles, after praying to God to give him a minor ailment in order to curb his carnal desires that must surely have displeased the Almighty. Tolerating illness, Alfred apparently believed, would strengthen his ability to lead a religiously devout life. After a while, however, this proved too much and he prayed to have the piles replaced by a different, but less visible (albeit not too serious) condition. Alfred's prayers were immediately answered and the piles spontaneously disappeared. Some have speculated that the *ficus*, and his desire to curb his sexual desires, was caused by homosexual activity. Many, however, believe that Alfred suffered from Crohn's disease, a painful and debilitating long-term inflammatory bowel condition, although this posthumous diagnosis is still debated.

Throughout his rule, the threat of Viking attacks continued, so Alfred introduced a number of reforms to defend Wessex. Chief among these was his network of fortifications known as *burhs,* spread across the kingdom. The Old English word simply means defended site and is the root of the later term 'borough'. Alfred's *burhs* were located along major rivers or significant roads, conveniently placed to control access, providing him with a secure bulwark against invaders. Defended sites, of course, were nothing new. We can find place names that include the element 'burh' going back several hundred years, sometimes describing early monasteries such as those at Glastonbury and Malmesbury. Even before Alfred's rule, in the period around 825–50, defence had become a priority for wic sites because of increased Viking raids. The marauders themselves used fortifications in their campaigns, especially the Great Army: numerous records in the *Chronicle* attest to this. The same was the case for the defenders.

Yet Alfred's *burhs* formed part of a specific scheme to fortify strategic locations, one that was later to be continued by his daughter Æthelflaed and her husband in Mercia, as well as his son Edward the Elder. A document known as the Burghal Hidage, which probably dates to the early tenth century, is especially useful for understanding these sites. It lists thirty-three places and the number of hides associated with each of them, plus a set of calculations that explains how many hides were needed to man known lengths of wall. For an acre's breadth of wall, it says, sixteen hides are required to both establish and defend it. If each hide was represented by one man, each section of wall known as a pole could be furnished with four men. This meant that a furlong required 160 hides. The urban planning of Winchester formed an important element of the scheme.

Either during Alfred's rule, or just before, the area inside the former Roman walls of Winchester was planned to contain a new grid of streets. Through its centre, between the east and west gates, ran the high street, with parallel back streets providing easy access for goods. On a north–south axis lay eighteen streets that catered for the growing population. The grid pattern can still be seen today and the high street highlighted the town's commercial importance. It may even be that the emphasis on walls and protection provided a shrewd incentive to keep people *in*, rather than living in the surrounding countryside, and thereby aided the city's economic development.

What inspired Alfred to carry out these initiatives is unclear, but there are parallels on the continent in the defensive measures carried out by the Frankish king Charles the Bald in the 860s. This may well have given the West Saxon king inspiration.

Around this time, Winchester acquired new, royally inspired functions. The trading base at Hamwic had been under significant threat from Viking raids, just like similar trading settlements around the English Channel. While Winchester had been the target of a major attack in 860, a few decades later we see the first real indication that the town was truly Alfred's centre: the *Anglo-Saxon Chronicle* entry for 896 explains that after his forces dealt with an attack on Viking ships that were operating out of the Isle of Wight, the captured Vikings were brought to the king in Winchester, where he ordered them to be hanged. There is also a record of a town reeve during that year, the first mention of such an official in the city, and it seems that Alfred began minting coins there at about the same time. Winchester, in Alfred's hands, was prospering and rapidly enhancing its royal status.

As would become apparent later, however, these developments were accompanied by growing tensions between the kings and the bishops. The latter may well have resented the considerable financial burden all of Alfred's new plans and improvements brought with them. Nevertheless, the town also became an important religious centre. Alfred's queen Ealhswith founded the nunnery of Nunnaminster there, possibly as a future retreat for her own widowhood.

ALFRED ORDERED ME TO BE MADE

In 1693, a farmer ploughing his field near Athelney Abbey in Somerset brought up a spectacular golden object from the soil. The artefact is now known as the Alfred Jewel, as it is inscribed with the words AELFRED MEC HEHT GEWYRCAN – 'Alfred ordered me to be made'. Measuring around six centimetres in length, the jewel has a tear-shaped golden frame shaped around a rock crystal, with a figurative design in enamel of a person wearing a green tunic, holding unknown objects in each hand. The pointed end of the jewel is shaped as an animal's head, with a hollow tube or socket protruding from its mouth and a rivet fitting: there may once have been a longer, thin rod fixed onto the end. Art-historical comparisons and the find location, in what had been important West Saxon land, make a date of the late ninth century and the Alfred in question our Alfred the Great very likely. Now most interpret the jewel to be what is known as an *aestel*, or pointer, used to follow a text while reading. In the preface to his translation of Pope Gregory's *Pastoral Care*, Alfred specifically states that he intended to send copies of the book to each bishopric in his kingdom and that with these books, he would include an aestel.

This interpretation of the object fits well with our understanding of the importance of both literacy and Christianity to Alfred. During his reign, the king initiated an unprecedented programme of spiritual and cultural revival. The preface to *Pastoral Care* sets out his reasoning: learning had once flourished in the country but in recent times had declined to the extent that very few could read and understand Latin and the sharing of wisdom had become largely neglected. To Alfred, this was a serious matter. It had long been widely believed that the threat of the Vikings was God's punishment for a people who had not truly followed their Christian calling: this way of thinking can be seen as far back as Alcuin's admonishments of the Northumbrians after the attack on Lindisfarne in 793. The threats to their people could be compared to the biblical plagues and scourges inflicted on the Children of Israel by God. To please God, and thereby to repel the Vikings, good Christians had a duty to keep up such things as standards of Latin.

To achieve his aims, Alfred established a court of scholars similar to that of Charlemagne in Francia. One of these, whom Alfred recruited himself, was Asser, who at the time was a monk at St David's in Wales.

The king also set up a school based at his royal court, a place where, as Asser states, even children of lesser birth were educated (although it is unlikely this meant it extended to every level of society). One important consequence of Alfred's programme was that the English language received such a boost that it became the major language used for prose literature, as opposed to Latin. The programme also had a huge impact on the development of literature, not least because of the vast number of works that were being translated. As well as restoring the intellectual standing of the kingdom, it aimed to replenish libraries looted and burned by the Vikings.

But while the identity so strongly emphasised by Alfred's scholars is an *English* one, it also allowed for local identities that reflected the various kingdoms' heroic forefathers while, wisely, seeking to show how they were all linked and related: members of one large family. It just so happened that the most eminent of these families belonged to the rulers of Wessex.

It was the Scandinavian newcomers who had started to firmly take root in England that Alfred needed to confront: he had to define the group that ruled against them. In fact, a chronicler in the reign of his son Edward would write that Alfred 'was king of all of the *Angelcynn* except for those under Danish dominion'. It was, in other words, in the face of this enemy that the group he ruled and reigned over came to be defined. And it was just as important for Alfred to motivate his people to continue fighting and to remain loyal to the West Saxon royal house. He could achieve this by recording the successes of his predecessors and circulating these widely in an increasingly literary society.

There are plenty of events that the *Chronicle* leaves out. While his successes against the Vikings are spelled out in detail, very little is shared about the reigns of Alfred's three brothers who ruled before him. Similarly, there is no mention of the rebellion that prevented his father Æthelwulf from resuming his kingship when returning from Rome in 856. These omissions would have been deliberate: not a good idea to remind his people of possible failures, or that a coup of that kind was possible.

The word *Angelcynn* – which essentially came to mean 'English' – needs some explaining. It arrived via a Latin term, originally used by Gregory the Great and adopted by Bede in his *Ecclesiastical History*, namely *gens Anglorum*. *Angelcynn* was first found in a Mercian charter from the 850s and it appears to have been used to describe a distinction between foreigners and those of English origin. But it is not until the late ninth century that it seems to have been in more common use, and in very deliberate contexts: those that fitted Alfred's wider ideology, of creating a joint identity and to promote learning, including the translation and compilation of books whose wisdom he urged his bishops to assist him in teaching to 'all the freeborn young men now among the Angelcynn'. This, in Alfred's mind, would help to restore Christianity among the English aristocracy, something that he felt had declined in part because of the lack of understanding of Latin in fact, a problem so serious that God had sent the Vikings to punish them.

The link to Christianity is crucial. Alfred very deliberately used biblical history as an allegory for his own nation, recalling forms of law-giving from the Old Testament in the shaping of his own state. In fact, Bede before him had compared the *gens Anglorum* to the new Israel, whereas Alfred went as far as to claim to be restoring a state that had previously existed, bringing together diverse people under one single Christian law. It was important for him to push this idea of a common history, especially because of the centuries of competition between Mercia and Wessex. With the external threat from the Vikings being so serious, emphasising a common past helped to create a unified identity in the present.

On 26 October 899, Alfred died, of unknown causes, aged around fifty, leading to a brief succession dispute, in which his son Edward the Elder – seemingly his choice to inherit his kingdom – was challenged by Alfred's nephew Æthelwold, the son of Æthelred. Although Edward was successful, the conflict with his cousin would have ramifications a few years down the line, and the bones of his ancestors were to play a key part.

A NEW MINSTER

In 901, two years after his father's death, Alfred's eldest son Edward established a new monastic foundation in Winchester, located immediately north of the existing church. Edward's new monastery became known as New Minster, promptly giving the old church the name 'Old Minster', as both churches were the foci of monastic communities. It seems that New Minster was intended to provide a burial place for Edward's family, for his mother and father and their descendants. The project was clearly a strong statement by Edward, and is described in a contemporary record that details the acquisition of new land to the north of Old Minster, including part of the old church's cemetery, in order to allow the new church to be built within a yard of its predecessor.

The new church was spectacular: its plan was an aisled basilica similar to the church that Charlemagne had built at St Denis, which would later become the burial place of the kings of France. However, despite the arrival of the new-build, Old Minster continued to be used. The community reacted strongly. Not only had they lost their royal burial site, with its accompanying prestige, but the new church was clearly intended to be larger: archaeological evidence indicates that New Minster occupied double the area of Old Minster. In response, over the next few years new wings were built on the sides of Old Minster and later several new chapels.

Bad feelings between the kings and bishops of Winchester – and therefore the Old Minster community – had begun back in the late ninth century. Both Egbert and Æthelwulf had been close to the then bishop, Swithun. It was with the help of the clergy that Egbert's family had been able to establish itself as the only branch of the royal house from which the future kings could be chosen, so it had been in their benefit to nurture a positive relationship. But things had begun to change when the sons of Æthelwulf came to power. The coup staged by Æthelbald while Æthelwulf was away on pilgrimage clearly shifted the dynamics. After his death, Æthelwulf's sons tried to prevent Old Minster from getting some of the estates he had left it in his will, and the choice of Sherborne, not Old Minster, for Æthelbald's and Æthelbert's burials would be another sign that Old Minster had fallen out of favour. By appropriating land for his new church, Edward would be known at Old Minster as *rex avidus* – a greedy king. Importantly, King Edward moved the remains of Alfred into his new church, which took some funds away from Old Minster: Alfred's burial church had been left fifty pounds in his will, and this money is likely to have moved to New Minster along with the body. The translation of Alfred's remains would have been a spectacular event witnessed not just by the clergy, but by the whole population of Winchester.

Edward may have been keen to assert another change too: to emphasise his, and before him his father's, political reach, moving away from that of his grandfather and great-grandfather. While Egbert and Æthelwulf's West Saxon kingdom had been powerful and extensive, it was Alfred, and by extension Edward, whose rule reached towards something much bigger. Or, in the words of one historian: 'The Old Minster was the foundation of the kings of Wessex: the New Minster that of the kings of England.' Seen in this light, the close proximity of the two churches was a deliberate statement, as was the translation of only Alfred's bones and none of those of Edward's older ancestors.

The movement of those bones is crucial if we are to understand what Edward was trying to do. By taking his father's bones away from the clergy, he not only avoided having to compete with the bishops for control over his ancestors' legacy, but he could also use his possession of them to assert his political power.

If we understand graves, and in particular royal and high-status graves, as memorial devices, designed to be read by the living, showcasing the deceased's identity and position through his or her funeral and tomb (or at least the identity the living chose to repre-sent), Edward's handling of his father's remains helped him to keep Alfred's legacy relevant and in people's minds. In fact, it appears that Alfred had done the same to his father's remains: the body of Æthelwulf, who had originally been buried in Steyning, Sussex, was later moved to Old Minster.

There is also a parallel in Edward's actions with the use and translation of saints' bones, a practice that was common throughout the early medieval period. Saints' relics did not just have religious and often miraculous power – they, too, could be used for political purposes.

A curious incident shows how Edward seems to have treated his father's remains with similar reverence to those of a saint. A document produced around the year 920, only decades after Alfred's death, and known as the Fonthill letter, recounts the case of a thief named Helmstan. He had committed some serious theft during Alfred's lifetime, but managed to avoid punishment after the intervention of his godfather, who seemed to know the king. However, the incorrigible Helmstan went back to stealing not long after, and this time he had less luck: with Alfred now dead, his godfather could no longer defend him so his property at Fonthill was confiscated and Edward made him an outlaw – essentially a death sentence. What's curious about the story is that Helmstan managed to escape punishment by having his outlawry removed and his property returned after he visited Alfred's body and brought a 'seal' to his godfather, which the latter gave to Edward. It is difficult to understand what happened here, but it has been suggested that Helmstan claimed sanctuary at Alfred's grave. This was something that featured in laws at the time, whereby fugitives could pay a fee to a consecrated church and receive a period of respite or a reduced sentence. The highest protection would normally be given at the site of a saint's relics. In other words, by granting a pardon after a visit to Alfred's tomb, Edward appears to have treated his father's remains on the same level as those of a saint. The new burial place, away from Old Minster filled with centuries of other kings and saints, would have given Alfred the worthy focus he deserved.

Why was it so important for Edward to assert his power and legitimacy in this way? As the eldest son of Alfred, the former king, he had succeeded to the throne, but others were keen to stake their claim to power too. Immediately after Edward took over, his cousin Æthelwold, son of his uncle Æthelred, rebelled. Æthelwold seized Wimborne, where his father was buried, and Christchurch. He stayed at Wimborne along with his men and a nun they had kidnapped, vowing that he would either live there or die there. This may be the chronicler's literary flourish, using a heroic tone for stylistic effect, but nonetheless, Edward rose to the challenge and arrived with an army. In response, Æthelwold made what was probably a wise choice of abandoning his rebellion and riding away in the night. Next, he cunningly decided to escape to Vikings who had settled in Northumbria, where he was welcomed with open arms and received as a king.

In the following years, Æthelwold made further attempts to take Wessex, leading eventually, in 902, to his death in a battle at 'the Holme', an unknown location. Here, alongside his Viking allies, Æthelwold fought against an army composed largely of men from Kent. Among others who died that day was the Kentish ealdorman Sigehelm, whose daughter Eadgifu would later marry Edward.

Æthelwold's choice of Wimborne, the site of his father's burial, as a place to make a stand echoes the significance that Edward himself placed on Alfred's tomb. It seems as though Æthelwold may have tried to legitimise *his* claim by emphasising his West Saxon royal roots: what Edward did, with the building of New Minster, was to show that he was part of something even bigger, namely an all-encompassing nation. His father, after all, had been the first to have named himself as *rex Anglorum et Saxonum* in his charters, a title Edward himself used in one of his earliest grants to New Minster, even though the disputes over the succession meant there was far less unity than in his father's time.

A few hundred years later, different tales were circulating as to the reason for Alfred's translation: the canons of Winchester Cathedral, for example, declared that Alfred's ghost caused so much trouble in Old Minster that his son had no choice but to move him to a new church.

ÆTHELFLAED – LADY OF THE MERCIANS

Conflict with the Vikings continued throughout Edward's reign. He also substantially expanded his father's project of building fortifications, improving and rebuilding those that needed it and commissioning others. The conquest of the territories settled by the Vikings also loomed large on the agenda: at this point, large parts of the north and east of the country, including much of the central kingdom of Mercia, were still in Scandinavian hands.

The Mercians turned out to be important allies for Edward. Sometime in the 880s, his sister Æthelflaed had married Æthelred, lord of the Mercians, and she came to play a crucial part in early tenth-century politics. The marriage between the two had been a key symbol of the collaboration of the kingdoms; Æthelflaed herself was part-Mercian through her mother's side. Showing herself to be an equal to her husband, she became heavily involved in rebuilding parts of Mercia that had recently been recovered. By 911, when Æthelred succumbed to illness and died, she had proven her military and political prowess to such a degree that the Mercians chose her as sole ruler. Over the following years, she founded towns and churches, commanded military operations and forged alliances to help further her cause.

This was a time of intense conflict over the Danelaw, and border areas between English- and Danish-controlled territory became key battle grounds. Not only did Edward have to contend with the Danes in the Midlands, but there were also Scandinavian forces from the Irish Sea region and York to deal with. Æthelflaed, like Edward, followed the highly successful strategy of building fortifications, in the continuation of the work of their father, and they used the *burhs* – created to administer military units, coordinate supplies and even foster trade – both to defend from attacks and to launch offensives. In the spring of 917, for example, Edward had ordered a fort to be built at Towcester in what is now Northamptonshire, a location chosen specifically to block an advance from the town of Northampton, a little further to the north and one of the Vikings' strongholds. In the summer that followed, Vikings from Northampton and Leicester stormed the new fort, but could not penetrate its defences. Further north-west, Æthelflaed took the Danish town of Derby while another army captured the Viking fort at Tempsford, in the process killing what would be the last Danish king of East Anglia. By the end of 917, this joint campaign between Æthelflaed and Edward had been so successful that they had seen the submission of all the Danish armies south of the Humber. This included, eventually, the so-called 'Five Boroughs' – the main administrative centres of Derby, Leicester, Lincoln, Nottingham and Stamford – that had been under Viking control for decades. However, in the middle of this campaign, on 14 June 918, Æthelflaed died in Tamworth, aged in her late forties. Her body was taken to Gloucester, where she was buried alongside her husband, and where almost a decade earlier she had moved the relics of St Oswald – a Northumbrian hero-king, coincidentally the godfather of Cynegils – from the East Midlands.

At her death, Æthelflaed left behind an adult daughter, Ælfwynn, who seems to have been the intended heir to Mercia. But Edward had other ideas. He must have seen Ælfwynn as a threat because he placed her under West Saxon control and six months later deprived her of all her lands and deported her to Wessex, thereby taking control of the kingdom. Writing about Edward in its entry for 918, the *Anglo-Saxon Chronicle* concludes that 'all the people who settled in Mercia, both Danish and English, submitted to him'. If it is true that Ælfwynn was briefly in charge of Mercia before Edward took over, that would make this the only time a woman succeeded another female ruler to one of the early English kingdoms. Yet the real impact of these years could be seen in the fact that before long Edward had also taken political control of the Danelaw, in essence making him the first king of all of England. He died on 17 July 924 near Chester, possibly after a battle, and was buried in the New Minster he had created for his family. When he died, he left a large family: he had married three times and had a total of fourteen children. Of these, four of the sons were to become kings after him and five of the daughters would marry into European noble houses.

KING OF THE WHOLE OF BRITAIN

U pon the death of Edward in 924, his kingdom, so recently expanded from that of Wessex to that of a nation, split into separate parts again for a short time. His eldest son Athelstan, according to the so-called *Mercian Register*, a set of tenth-century annals, was appointed king of Mercia while his half-brother Ælfweard succeeded to Wessex. Ælfweard, however, died just sixteen days later and was buried in New Minster alongside his father. This, then, paved the way for Athelstan to rule over Wessex too, but his take-over was not straightforward, as the reports of tensions and political difficulties in Wessex attest. It may be that Athelstan was seen as an outsider in Winchester, as he had been educated and trained for rulership at the Mercian court of his aunt, Æthelflaed.

Nonetheless, the kingdom Athelstan inherited was larger than any a West Saxon king had ruled before him, and he clearly had his mind set on expansion. While Edward had success in subjugating the southern parts of the Danelaw, north of Mercia the kingdom of the Northumbrians was in Scandinavian hands, ruled from York by the Viking king Sihtric, who had once been king of Dublin. The

Scandinavians had been in control over much of northern England since the ninth century, and the Irish Sea region had also been under Scandinavian control since early raids in the late eighth century were followed by more substantial attacks and settlements in the ninth. The region included what became the town of Dublin, and there were close links both in trade and politics between Dublin, York and the Scandinavian homelands. In the tenth century, the Irish Sea connections remained important. Now, Sihtric's control over the northern and eastern parts of England was extensive, and a number of different coin types were minted in his name, some from as far south as Lincoln. Athelstan must have been acutely aware of the threat the Scandinavians in the north could pose to his kingdom and this must be why, only a short time after his accession, he forged a treaty with Sihtric in 926 at Tamworth, the former Mercian capital. In securing this alliance, Sihtric was baptised and married one of Athelstan's sisters, Edith, cementing the relationship between the two kingdoms. Sihtric's commitment to Christianity appears to have been pretty loose, however. According to a twelfth-century source, he reverted to paganism and rejected his wife not long afterwards. That religion was a complex issue among the Scandinavians in Northumbria at the time is clear. At this point none of the Scandinavian countries were yet Christianised and in York dual allegiances can be seen in a series of coins minted there in the 920s; they are known as the St Peter's coins because many of them do, quite literally, state on the obverse that they are 'St Peter's money'. The coins have a sword on one side, and some also depict a Thor's hammer.

The alliance with Northumbria, in any case, represented a success for Athelstan. When Sihtric died the following year, in the first half of 927, Athelstan promptly made a grab for the kingdom of Northumbria, claiming legitimacy because of the former alliance. This momentous occasion marked the first time a king had held the region along with the southern territories, in what was now fast becoming the country of England.

It was also the first time a West Saxon king had held a territory bordering the Scots and even if Athelstan's conquest of Northumbria was successful, it would be precarious: the region had been under Scandinavian rule for a long time. Consequently, and to fully secure his border, Athelstan met with the rulers of the neighbouring kingdoms on 12 July 927 at Eamont near Penrith. Those he met that day were the leaders of the West Welsh, the Scots, the people of Gwent and the ruler of Bamburgh, all of whom made pledges and oaths, showing their respect for the new England gathered by Athelstan. According to the chronicler William of Malmesbury, around the same time Athelstan made sure to raze a fortress that had been built by the Vikings at York, 'in order to leave disloyalty no place of refuge'.

It certainly seems likely that this was a tumultuous time for the Scandinavians in the region, as the evidence from a hoard discovered in 2007 suggests. The Vale of York hoard was found by a father-and-son metal-detecting team, Andrew and David Whelan, in a field near Harrogate in Yorkshire. A silver cup had been buried in the ground and when conservators at the British Museum carefully excavated its contents, they found a spectacular collection of objects, including a gold arm-ring, sixty-seven pieces of silver in the shape of fragments of arm-rings and hacksilver, along with more than six hundred coins. These included not only several Islamic coins, demonstrating the extensive eastern trading links that had been in place at the time, but also many rare coins of Athelstan. In fact, one of these had first been minted around 928. Overall, it seems likely that the hoard was buried for safekeeping in a period of turmoil following Athelstan's takeover, quite possibly by a wealthy Viking leader.

For the first time since the Great Army's conquest of York in 865, the supremacy of the Vikings in Northumbria had taken a turn for the worse and, as one historian put it, Athelstan's reign 'marked a major stumbling block to the ambitions of viking-kings in England'.

During his rule, Athelstan made a concerted effort to extend his influence even outside the boundaries of Britain, through gifts and alliances, including the marriages of his sisters: as well as the union of Edith with Sihtric, he was instrumental in setting up the marriage between his half-sister, also named Edith (Eadgyth), and Otto, Duke of Saxony and later crowned emperor by the Pope. Athelstan involved himself politically across the English Channel, too, by helping his nephew, Louis d'Outremer, attack the Flemish coast in 939, and he appears to have taken in Bretons fleeing from Viking attacks.

Intriguingly, tradition has it that he fostered Hakon, the son of the Norwegian king Harald Fairhair, thereby creating alliances with other Scandinavian groups. Although there are no contemporary sources to corroborate this, in both sagas and other twelfth-century accounts, Hakon has the nickname *Adalsteinsfostri* – 'Athelstan's fosterling'. William of Malmesbury reported that at one point Athelstan received a magnificent longship from Harald, complete with a golden beak and purple sails. We have no way of knowing if this story is really true, but it is not entirely implausible. In any case, it demonstrates the complexity of the relationship between Athelstan and different groups of Scandinavians: those in Britain and Ireland, and those back in the Scandinavian homelands. This was never a simple story of the English versus the Vikings, but rather of individual rulers and factions competing against one another.

What is also important to understand is that the appearance of written sources like these in the Middle Ages, in which the relationships between the Scandinavians and the early English rulers are emphasised, served specific purposes. Some of the people mentioned, such as Harald Fairhair, would have been immensely important in the Scandinavian homelands, in building the new nation-states that traced their origins to the end of the Viking Age. Norway, Sweden and Denmark would all emerge as separate and unified kingdoms around the turn of the millennium. Sagas and other narratives served to create collective origin stories: Harald Fairhair, for instance, is portrayed in the sagas as the first king of Norway, whose descendants include the country's current royal family. Even today, the website of the Norwegian royals lists their genealogy going all the way back to Fairhair, although the sources are sketchy on the details of his rule and many even doubt his existence. In medieval traditions, Harald had an important part to play in the settlement of many of the Scandinavian colonies overseas, including Britain, Ireland, Normandy and Iceland: many were said to have originated because Norwegians had to flee Harald's harsh rule at home.

Athelstan seems to have been particularly interested in collecting relics. He may have inherited some from his grandfather Alfred and purchased others from abroad, and he gave many of them to the church.

In addition to Athelstan's control over the north, he gained overlordship of the Welsh, effectively extending his kingdom to the west too. His achievements were reflected in the titles he used to describe his rulership. At the beginning of his reign, he followed his father's and grandfather's example of styling himself 'king of the Anglo-Saxons'. Following his success in 927, his style became more grandiose: documents title him as either *rex Anglorum* ('king of the English'), *rex totius Britanniae* ('king of the whole of Britain'), or even the very elaborate description *nodante dei gratia basileos Anglorum et eque totius Brittannie orbis curagulus* ('by grace of God king of the English and equally guardian of the whole orb of Britain'). More simply, on coins, he went by *rex totius Britanniae*.

Athelstan died on 27 October 939 in Gloucester but he was not buried in Winchester, as his father and brother had been. Instead, he was laid to rest at Malmesbury Abbey.

FINDING EADGYTH

I n 2008, a large sarcophagus in the medieval cathedral in Magdeburg, Germany, was opened. A team of archaeologists looked on as its heavy stone lid was lifted and moved aside with a hoist, revealing, for the first time in centuries, what was inside. Immediately, the team saw a lead coffin bearing an inscription:

EDIT REGINE CINERES HIC
SARCOPHAGVS HABET . . .

('This sarcophagus contains the remains of Queen Edith . . .')

Later they discovered that inside this coffin, a delicate silk fabric enveloped a bundle of bones: the partial skeleton of a woman.

The body they found that day had been interred in the stone sarcophagus in 1510 and was allegedly the remains of Eadgyth – also known as Edith, wife of Emperor Otto the Great. Eadgyth had died unexpectedly in the year 946 aged around thirty-six. Records show that in the centuries after her death, her bones had been moved at least three times before ending up in the lead coffin in Magdeburg; each time they had been treated with utmost reverence, both because Queen Eadgyth had been a beloved character in her own time and also because she represented a significant alliance between two major European royal families. She was one of two daughters of Edward the Elder with his second wife Ælfflæd and also the granddaughter of Alfred the Great. Her marriage to

Otto was initiated by her brother Athelstan, seemingly as an aspect of what can only be seen as his foreign policy. An alliance between the powerful German emperor and the princess of a noble Saxon family was clearly of benefit to both sides. For this reason, in the autumn of 929, five years into Athelstan's rule, Eadgyth and her younger sister Eadgifu were sent to the continent in the company of Bishop Cenwald of Worcester. The two were sent together so that Otto could choose his preferred wife: the choice fell on Eadgyth – apparently, it was love at first sight. The two married soon after and Eadgyth secured her future by giving birth to a son and heir, and later to a daughter.

While we don't know much about her life in the years that followed, it appears that when she died Eadgyth was considered a popular queen. The tenth-century canoness and poet Hrotsvitha of Gandersheim described Eadgyth as brave, stubborn and capable, and a woman who was 'of pure noble countenance, graceful character, and truly royal appearance'. Even more, Hrotsvitha stated that 'she was so very highly regarded in her own country that public opinion unanimously rated her the best woman who existed at that time in England'.

But were those bones in the lead coffin really hers? The first analysis was carried out by an osteologist, who revealed that the skeleton was indeed that of a single person, and of a woman aged between thirty and forty: both facts a match for Eadgyth. There were abnormalities on the head of one of her femurs, something often seen in horse riders. This would be fitting for a tenth-century noblewoman, as would the fact that carbon and nitrogen isotope analysis indicated that she had eaten a diet rich in proteins and especially fish. Textiles found within the lead coffin were dated to the right period. DNA analysis would be of little use, as even if ancient DNA could be successfully extracted – not a given in 2008 – the team had no relatives to compare it to. Instead, they turned to strontium and oxygen

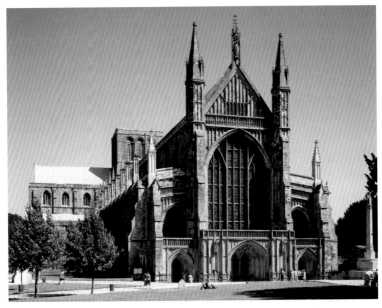

Winchester Cathedral, western front

Presbytery with four of the chests on top of the stone screens

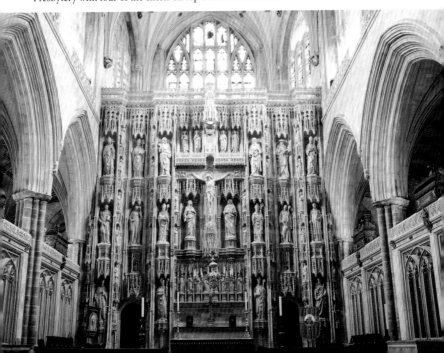

Chest One:
Cynegils and
Æthelwulf

Chest Two:
Cynewulf and Egbert

Chest Three:
Eadred

Chest Four:
Edmund

Chest Five:
Wini, Cnut, Ælfwyn,
Emma, Rufus

Chest Six:
Wini, Cnut, Ælfwyn,
Emma, Rufus

View of the chests on top of the stone screen
from the south transept

The stained glass windows on the west
front of the cathedral, from the inside

Coin of Cynetryth, queen of Mercia and wife of Offa

Image of Henry of Blois, twelfth-century Bishop of Winchester

Codex Aureus: the book ransomed from a Viking army by the ealdorman Alfred and his wife

Richard Fox, sixteenth-century Bishop of Winchester

Finger-ring bearing the name Æthelwulf, found in Wiltshire in 1780

Ninth-century 'two emperor' coin from the Herefordshire hoard,
showing Alfred and Ceolwulf side by side

isotope analysis of her tooth enamel to investigate where the woman had been born and, especially, whether she had grown up locally. The results clearly showed that she was not local, but that she had spent her childhood somewhere entirely different. To narrow the results down to possible locations and to get an in-depth understanding of her adolescent years, the team asked Dr Alistair Pike from the University of Bristol to use a method called laser ablation, which involved taking a sequence of minute laser samples of her teeth. Enamel forms incrementally during childhood, starting with the crown of the tooth when we are infants, then moving downwards, as the tooth is formed more fully, until it is complete. All the time this process locks in a series of isotope values, representing the food and drink consumed as the enamel is made. Normally when we analyse enamel for strontium and/or other isotopes, we use a long vertical slice of enamel that incorporates the entire time period, essentially giving us an average over the years it took the tooth to be created. But because of the way the enamel forms, our teeth lock in not just isotope values that represent the whole childhood on average, but potentially every month or even week of our lives too. All that is needed is to separate out each stage or period. It is precisely this that the laser ablation technology does: up to two thousand isotope values can be measured from a single tooth, giving a record from a person's birth up to around the age of fourteen.

In the case of the woman from Magdeburg, the results were spectacular. Overall, when looking at levels of both strontium and oxygen for Britain and Europe, southern England, with its chalky terrain, offered a very good match for where she might have lived as a child. This fitted well for a Wessex-born princess. But even more remarkable, looking at those gradual changes over time in her enamel, the scientists could show that during her early years she had lived in a number of different locations. This would fit a childhood travelling around her father's kingdom, as a member of his entourage. But from around the age of eight or nine, there was an abrupt change: from that point on, the values in her teeth remained constant, indicating a more stationary life. On the assumption that these remains were indeed those of Eadgyth, this could make sense: she was the daughter of Edward the Elder's second wife, Ælfflæd. We are not entirely sure what happened to her but by 920 Edward had remarried, and Eadgyth, and her mother, may well have been sent away to live in a monastery. She would have been around nine or ten and such a change in her circumstances would be a perfect explanation for the change in isotope values.

BRUNANBURH AND
THE LOST BATTLE-DEAD

For the year 937, the *Anglo-Saxon Chronicle* includes a seventy-three-line poem recounting what it describes as the greatest battle ever fought in England. The Battle of Brunanburh, which the poem describes, has become infamous because of this and its recounting of how King Athelstan successfully defeated an alliance of Scandinavians, Scots and Strathclyde Britons. The battle has been given a special place in the story of English nationalism and as recently as 2004, Brunanburh was called 'the Cradle of English Civilisation' by the *Independent* newspaper. At this battle, it is often claimed, 'Englishness' was forged. While this degree of nation-alism somewhat overstates its importance, the battle was certainly highly significant, if poorly understood. It is especially unusual that it was so widely reported in contemporary sources, as we have accounts of it in chronicles from Wales, Ireland and Scotland, in addition to the poem in the *Chronicle*.

Ultimately, the battle was the culmination of tensions that had built up due to Athelstan's aggressive policies in his ambition to become the most powerful ruler in Britain, with overlordship of the Welsh and Scottish, as well as the kingdoms he already ruled. The main rulers who engaged in battle against Athelstan were Olaf Guthfrithson, king of Dublin; Constantine II, king of Scotland; and Owain, king of Strathclyde.

According to the sources, the battle lasted all day and both sides suffered heavy losses, including the death of five 'young kings', seven of Olaf's earls and the son of Constantine. But the English victory was unambiguous.

The Battle of Brunanburh is infamous for another reason too: despite extensive description in the different sources, its location has never been found. In fact, there is not even agreement among historians on which side of England the battle was fought, with some favouring an eastern location, near the Humber, and others the western coast near the Irish Sea.

Brunanburh is not unusual; in fact, according to Historic England, apart from those sites with some prehistoric weaponry, 'secure and substantial archaeological evidence has yet to be retrieved from any English battlefield before the fifteenth century'. This leads to another intriguing question. With so many thousands of dead in battle, not just at Brunanburh, where are all the war dead from the past? Where are those battlefields filled with long-lost Vikings and Saxons?

A more recent battlefield may serve as a very relevant parallel and may even give us some answers. On 18 June 1815, one of the most famous battles of all time was fought at Waterloo in Belgium, between the French emperor Napoleon Bonaparte and a coalition led by the Duke of Wellington and the Prussian Marshal Blücher. The battle, in which Napoleon was defeated, led to the loss of approximately twenty thousand men, along with several thousand horses. According to documents written a few years after the encounter, the dead appear to have been buried in several mass graves. Their locations were not recorded, though, so although we know very well where the battle took place, none of these graves have ever been found. In fact, to date, out of those tens of thousands of dead only two near-complete skeletons have been recovered through archaeological excavations.

Sir Walter Scott, the Scottish novelist, visited Waterloo in August 1815, and wrote that by that time, 'All ghastly remains of the carnage had been either burned or buried.' Despite this, he noted that there was a lingering stench in several places across the battlefield, indicating that the burials must have been made 'hastily and imperfectly performed'. Another account reported bodies piled in mounds along with heaps of wood, to speed up the burning process. There are artists' depictions of naked bodies, with uniforms removed, tipped into shallow pits; another eyewitness reported the debris of soldiers' clothes, shoes and belts scattered all the way from the battlefield and along the way to places where the wounded had been taken. Within days, the detritus had been pillaged, weapons and uniforms stripped from bodies to be used or sold, other items ending up as souvenirs.

Digging graves is hard work and there are numerous descriptions of the dead being only shallowly buried. 'Here too,' said John Scott, another eyewitness, 'the heaps of the dead were scattered about – and numerous parties of the peasantry were employed in raking more earth over the bodies, their first thin covering of mould having been washed away by the rains.'

These observations must surely have paralleled what took place during an early medieval battle too, both the looting of battle debris and the need to dispose of the dead swiftly to avoid contamination from the rotting corpses. But although it might be easier to understand why thousand-year-old battlefields may have gone undetected,

why have we not found the Waterloo bones? Disturbingly, the reason
for this is not that we have been looking in the wrong place, but
rather because of what happened to the bones afterwards: it seems
many were deliberately dug up for profit. And this, of course, begs
the question of whether the same happened to other mass burials.
In the case of Waterloo, the bones appear to have been targeted for
the very lucrative fertiliser industry. Before so-called superphosphates –
chemically produced fertilisers – were discovered in the 1840s,
bonemeal was one of the main products used to fertilise soil in
Europe. In fact, an estimate published by the *London Observer* in
1822 suggested that more than a million bushels of 'human and
inhuman bones' had been imported into England from continental
Europe (a bushel is today equivalent to approximately 15–22 kilo-
grams). The bones were ground down and sold to farmers to spread
on fields. The same article states that human bones, in particular,
made the very best manure. In Scotland, another popular market
for ground-up bones, bonemeal proved especially good for growing
turnips. French newspaper articles from the 1830s record that permission had been given to excavate the battlefields of Waterloo in order
to access and use the bones. New research has also suggested that
the bones were used to filter brown sugar beet into refined white
sugar: the beets were cooked and pressed into juice before being
filtered through bone charcoal. There were at least two such sugar
factories within a few miles of the Waterloo battlefield, alongside
bone charcoal factories.

If the import of bones from overseas was so extensive and prof-
itable, and if there really were few concerns over *what* sort of bone
was used, it is very likely that ancient battlefields in Britain – if
chanced upon – would have suffered the same fate, either in the
nineteenth century or even earlier.

A KING REDISCOVERED?

Even if we *were* to be able to discover more of the ancient, lost dead, what would we really be able to learn from them? The identification in 2012 of Richard III, the fifteenth-century Plantagenet king, created a seismic shift in the public understanding of our ability to analyse and identify ancient remains, and has since been used as a benchmark for historical forensic investigations.

Interest in this case came partly from Richard's prominent position in English history. Although he was king for only two years, his reputation has been one filled with controversy, with many putting him down as a brutal tyrant, accused, among other things, of murdering his two nephews. Others have seen him as a noble king who was removed from his lawful position by Henry Tudor. The king's starring role in one of Shakespeare's plays, in which he is portrayed as a villainous hunchback plotting to take the throne, no doubt has added to the overwhelmingly negative image of him in many people's minds.

Richard died in 1485 at the Battle of Bosworth, where his army fought against that of Henry Tudor, a clash that signified the end of the Wars of the Roses. After the battle, he was buried at Greyfriars, a Franciscan friary in Leicester. However, when the friary was dissolved in 1538, what happened to the remains was uncertain, with one legendary story suggesting that his bones had been thrown in the River Soar. For decades, numerous historians had been interested in finding the location of his remains, but it was not until 2011 that action was taken. That year amateur historian Philippa Langley from the Richard III Society approached the archaeological department at Leicester University for help. The following year, excavations began in a now-famous Leicester car park that had previously been identified as the site of Greyfriars. Unusually, the team, led by archaeologist Richard Buckley, was in luck straight away, finding a skeleton in what was believed to be the choir of the church. In the hope that this might be the body of the lost king, experts carried out an extensive scheme of scientific analyses on it to attempt to verify the suggestion.

First of all, the osteological analysis showed that this was the body of a man aged between thirty and thirty-four at the time of death, which fitted well with Richard, who had died aged thirty-two. The skeleton showed eleven traumatic injuries sustained around the time of death, nine of them to the skull, suggesting the man had not worn a helmet. Three of his injuries could have been fatal and all of them could have been caused by weapons that were common in the medieval period. Further analysis of the skeleton revealed that the man had suffered from severe scoliosis, a condition that causes curvature of the spine. Radiocarbon dates, when correcting for a diet high in seafood (about 25 per cent), placed the year of death between 1456 and 1530. This same diet, as determined with the use of stable isotope analysis, led the researchers to conclude that he may have been of high status.

All of this evidence, then, seemed to support the preliminary identification. The osteologists even noted that the scoliosis observed on the skeleton would fit with the description from 1490 of Richard as someone who was small in stature and with a right shoulder that was higher than the left. But it was the DNA evidence that would put the final nail in the coffin, so to speak. Leicester geneticist Dr Turi King led the extensive ancient and modern DNA study. First, her team could confirm that the body was, as the osteology suggested, male. Second, they could predict his hair colour as having been blond and eye colour as blue, both of which matched one – but not all – of the early paintings of Richard.

Third, and most importantly, they looked for genetic links to modern individuals to attempt to secure an identification. Richard III had no children and therefore no direct descendants. Still, the lineages of noble families in England are very well recorded and studied, so the team was able to track down five living patrilineal relatives, that is, individuals from an all-male line going back to Richard's great-grandfather, Edward III. These five were genealogically related to Richard but very distantly so: between twenty-four and twenty-six generations apart. When the team determined the genetic haplogroup both of these men and of the Leicester skeleton, however, the result was disappointing: they were not a match. This was put down to one or more so-called false paternity events; in other words, that somebody had a different father to the one recorded. This, the team soberly noted, would not be unusual. Over the number of generations they were dealing with, they estimated the likelihood of false paternity events to be at least 16 per cent. Therefore, they concluded, we should not be too disheartened by the lack of a match between the Leicester skeleton and his proposed relatives on the male side.

But what about the female side? Again, the search began with the genealogies. It is often more difficult to track down female lineages because historically women's full names have not always been recorded. Luckily, the geneticists were able to identify an unbroken female line of descent from Richard's eldest sister, Anne of York. With the same mother, she would have shared Richard's mitochondrial genomes (mtDNA), along with all their other female-line descendants. A second unbroken line of female relatives was also found, leaving the researchers with two modern relations, who were nineteen and twenty-one generations removed from Richard respectively. The two were fourteenth cousins twice removed. With the mtDNA data, Turi's team had more luck: the three individual samples proved a match, showing that the distant cousins were indeed related, both to each other and to the skeleton. What was more, the mtDNA haplotype they shared seemed to be very rare, which made it less probable that the match had happened by chance.

Half the dataset, then, supported the identification of this body as that of Richard III. But how certain could they be? The rest of the process was based on statistics. As well as the DNA match, the team took the other factors that matched into account: for instance that the body was male, that the age of death was thirty to thirty-four, that there were perimortem injuries, and the evidence for scoliosis. Using a complex series of probability estimates, they combined all the evidence and found a very strong probability that the skeleton was that of Richard III. As they said in their *Nature* paper: 'Our sceptic would be driven to the conclusion that the probability that Skeleton 1 is not Richard III is less than 1 in 100,000.' In a less conservative estimate, taking into account even more of the circumstantial evidence, they concluded that the probability of it not being him would be one in a million.

Much of the identification, then, came down to statistics, and that's what's important to remember. Although the researchers used the term 'beyond reasonable doubt', the DNA analysis could not prove it beyond *any* doubt: the team could merely show how *likely* it was.

But is that really enough? To play devil's advocate, there certainly *are* doubts or, at least, a lot of uncertainties. The lack of a patrilineal match does not have to be because of a false paternity event but instead because this was someone else entirely. As for the mtDNA, just how rare the mtDNA haplotype is, is unclear. The team noted it as being rare because they found no matches in a European database with 26,127 samples, nor in a British database of 1,832 samples. They pointed out that across Europe, mtDNA haplotype frequencies don't vary too much. Because, they argued, female mobility among the European aristocracies was generally higher than among the general population, this makes the lack of a match even more uncommon. Another peculiar result came from the isotope analysis of the skeleton. As well as looking at markers for diet, a team of researchers studied oxygen isotopes in both teeth and bone, to look for evidence of mobility and geographical origins. By observing different parts of the body, they could investigate changes over time: teeth reflecting childhood, femur reflecting the past ten to fifteen years of life and rib reflecting the last two to five years. If this really was Richard, the data from the rib should reflect the time he became king – a period in his life we know a reasonable amount about from the historical records. The childhood and longer-term oxygen data proved pretty consistent with life in eastern England, as the records would suggest. The rib data, however, were surprising: the values became quite a lot higher, meaning that he had likely moved to an area that was either milder or with higher rainfall, such as much more westerly parts of England. But the historical records place Richard III quite firmly in eastern England in the last two years of his life, in locations that do not fit the oxygen data. Does this give us proof that the remains were not his? Possibly, but there could also be other reasons. Oxygen in human tissues comes largely through the water we have consumed, especially by drinking. But the isotope values in the water can be affected by how we treat it: if we boil water, for instance, the isotope ratios measured will change. The same is the case for processes like brewing – so if you got most of your water through drinking beer, the isotope ratios in your tissues would look different from if you drank pure water. In this particular case, however, the researchers proposed something more novel: that the king had drunk imported wine. Oxygen isotope values in wine reflect the area that the grapes grew in. Wine drunk in medieval England would likely have been imported from places like France. Testing the isotope values in modern French wines, the team concluded that if around 25 per cent of his fluid intake had come from such sources, it could result in the values they observed.

This explanation might also be supported by a change in nitrogen oxygen isotopes in the rib bone, suggesting a shift towards more high-protein food sources and, especially, luxury foods like fresh-water fish and wildfowl, something the researchers proposed would have been likely for a king. More recent research, however, has questioned such assumptions: a large-scale study of early medieval diets led by Dr Sam Leggett, comparing social classes in England up to the eleventh century, found little to no difference in isotope values between those at the higher and lower ends of the social scale. Of course, there may be differences between this dataset and the situation in the fifteenth century, but it does show that we need to be careful with our interpretations.

EDMUND I THE MAGNIFICENT

When Athelstan died, his eighteen-year-old half-brother Edmund succeeded to the throne, as the eldest of Edward's living male heirs. Edmund was the son of Edward's third wife Eadgifu, and it seems she now returned to court as *mater regis* – the king's mother – having disappeared from the royal retinue when her husband died. Alongside her young son, her role became important. Eadgifu was named on an unusually large number of witness lists, and her name often appears in charters alongside those of Edmund and his brother Eadred. Eadgifu happened to be incredibly wealthy, as she had inherited a vast amount of land from her father. She is said, in fact, to have been the wealthiest woman in England at the time. Edmund would marry twice, but neither of his wives appear to have had much influence or power at court – perhaps because of his mother's position and authority.

Although the kingdom Edmund inherited extended to the north, to include the regions that had previously been under Scandinavian control, this was not to last. The death of Athelstan was all the encouragement the Viking rulers of Dublin needed to take on the kingdom of York. Olaf Guthfrithson was swiftly recognised as king, keen to re-establish the Dublin–York network that had prospered since the ninth century.

Soon after he had taken the city, Olaf turned his eyes south, wanting to recapture the territories his predecessors had lost. After an unsuccessful attempt, in 940, to take Northampton, Olaf and his armies turned to Tamworth, with considerably more success but significant losses. Finally, when trying to retake Leicester, King Edmund was able to keep pace, besieging the town. However, the contest ended in a truce and Edmund was forced to concede a large amount of territory so hard won by his half-brother, at least temporarily: when Olaf died, Edmund recaptured this land – and more. There appears to have been a closer relationship between Olaf's successor, his cousin, another Olaf (Sihtricsson) and Edmund: this new ruler accepted baptism in 943 with the latter as his sponsor. Yet the relationship between the king and the Scandinavians was clearly complex, as both Olaf and the cousin he co-ruled with in some way, Ragnall, would be expelled by Edmund the following year.

On 26 May 946, Edmund was murdered. According to John of Worcester, he was stabbed by a robber when trying to save the life of his steward. He was buried at Glastonbury.

THE MISSING KING

*I*t is 2013 and osteologist Dr Katie Tucker stands in front of the so-called 'Unmarked Grave' in the grounds of St Bartholomew's Church in Winchester.

Katie is in charge of a team from the University of Winchester which has set out to investigate a brick vault containing a number of human remains, allegedly those of Alfred the Great and some of his closest relatives. This task is suddenly urgent, because the discovery of the remains identified as those of Richard III has led to a concern that these *remains, which are hardly protected at all, could be stolen.*

In reality, Alfred the Great's final resting place has never quite been confirmed. Initially, he was buried in Old Minster, in a tomb made of the finest porphyry marble. But according to some later historical sources, his remains were not at peace there: William of Malmesbury writes that Alfred's spirit wandered restlessly around the church and that for this reason, Edward moved him to New Minster in 903. New Minster lasted only until the early twelfth century, when new land was granted by Henry I to its monks to build a brand-new monastery. This land was located at the northern gate of the medieval city of Winchester. When finally complete in 1110, the entire minster was relocated along with, importantly, the monastery's relics, and renamed Hyde Abbey. Yet none of the records inform us what happened to the remains of the Wessex royal family, so it is only assumed that these remains were moved to the new monastery as well. The first written reference to it is from the sixteenth century, when antiquarian John Leland recorded that both Alfred's and his son Edward's remains had been moved from New Minster and placed in the tomb in front of the high altar at Hyde. Leland also reported that around the time of the dissolution of the monasteries, Alfred's and Edward's graves had been identified, as they were opened and lead inscriptions with their names were found in the tombs.

The monastery at Hyde was dissolved in 1538 and the fate of its relics at that point becomes unclear. One source, from 1901, suggests that when Richard Fox, the Bishop of Winchester, placed the Winchester royal burials in lead chests in the cathedral, he included those from Hyde – but no other accounts have corroborated this. The same source also suggests that after 1642 the bones were taken to Oxford and 'lodged in a repository building next the public library', but there are no other sources to back this up.

After the dissolution, the site that Hyde Abbey had occupied fell into disuse. In 1788, it was sold off for a new building, with disastrous results for the burials around it. According to a report made to the Society of Antiquaries of London in 1798, numerous burials had been found within the eastern end of the church, containing both lead coffins, bones and the remains of garments. The lead had been sold, the coffins broken into pieces and reburied, and the bones 'thrown about'. Apparently, numerous priceless remains of the ancient monastery were found, but were destroyed or reburied.

The first time someone deliberately searched the Hyde Abbey grounds for Alfred's remains would be in 1867, in a curious case set out in a series of letters written to the Hampshire Chronicle. First of all, an anonymous correspondent, naming himself only as Q, states that a 'so-called antiquarian' had callously dug up the remains of numerous ancient dead, without respect for the consecrated ground they were in, leaving corpses exposed and disrespectfully rearranged. The antiquarian in question, a man named John Mellor, responded that in no way had he acted disrespectfully: he had, in fact, been searching for the remains of King Alfred the Great and his family, in order to save them from 'further mutilation and violence'. Mellor claimed that he had been successful in identifying Alfred's bones, as well as the burial vault of Edward, along with a sceptre, gilt cloth and other precious items. Afterwards he had given the bones into the care of the churchwarden of Hyde parish church, where they were to be placed in wooden mortuary chests.

The anonymous Q refused to believe this version of events and claimed that Mellor had, in reality, offered human remains for sale to various households, one of which allowed a housekeeper to throw them into a dustbin in disgust. Mellor responded that none of this was true, and that the bones had been deposited in the exhibition rooms at a hospital. A few years later, Mellor published a pamphlet giving details of his work. Here he claims that not only did he find the bodies of Alfred and Edward, he had, astonishingly, also discovered those of Æthelweard, Ealhswith and Queen Ælfgifu, along with numerous precious artefacts, a plate of lead bearing the king's name, and even embers from a fire that had taken place in 1141. The bodies, he said, were still within the stone coffins. Even more incredibly, Mellor had accomplished the feat of discovering the skull of St Valentine, a relic said to have been housed in New Minster.

Clearly, Mellor's account is fantastical: for a start, there is no way he could have identified any remains he found as those of the lost royals, nor could he have so precisely dated embers from a fire. The lead plates he found, and used to prove his discoveries when questioned, were shown to be modern fakes. What is certain is that eventually the bones that were passed over to the churchwarden were reburied in the grounds of the parish church, St Bartholomew's, within a small brick vault. A photograph had shown that this included five fairly complete skulls.

More than 140 years later, Katie and her team began the task of clearing the unmarked tomb of soil, uncovering stone slabs within the vault of red bricks: between the slabs, they could make out a large number of long bones and a stack of five skulls, just as had been photographed in the 1870s. The bones were removed and five months later, permission was granted to analyse them. As Katie began her work, she realised the bones belonged to at least six different individuals, including a woman in her mid-twenties to mid-thirties who showed evidence of disease; two men in their thirties or forties with various signs of bone-related conditions like arthritis; and another man around the same age, with bones suggesting he had Paget's disease. The last two were much more fragmented.

In principle, the three male skeletons could be those of the three kings allegedly found by Mellor: Alfred, Edward and Æthelweard.

But Katie was suspicious: the remains seemed too well-preserved to have been exhumed and reburied so many times. Radiocarbon dating confirmed her suspicions, as the skeletons all dated from between the eleventh and twelfth century right up to the fifteenth. Katie wanted to investigate the site further and went to the local museum service that had been involved in an excavation there in the 1990s, when they had found human bone. These bones had been kept but never analysed, and an extensive trawl through the archives revealed that many of them were likely to be bones that had been disturbed and moved about in the eighteenth century. The bones were radiocarbon dated and all but one dated to later in the medieval period – the exception came from an adult male pelvis found within a pit dug by John Mellor, in a prominent location within the abbey. This sample was radiocarbon dated to between 895 and 1017, meaning that it could, in principle, have belonged to Alfred, Edward or Æthelweard. The only way, however, that this could ever be proven would be if it could be matched to the DNA of a known relative, and as yet no such person has been identified. But perhaps, one day, one of them can be matched to the remains in the bone chests?

CHEST III

PEACE

Eadred d. 955

Extract from *The Diary and Letters of Madame
D'Arblay* – Volume 2, by Fanny Burney

'We walked to the cathedral, and saw it completely. Part of it
remains from the original Saxon building, though neglected,
except by travellers, as the rest of the church is ample for all uses,
and alone kept in repair. The bones of eleven Saxon kings are
lodged in seven curious old chests, in which they were deposited
after being dug up and disturbed in the civil wars and ensuing
confusions. The small number of chests is owing to the small
proportion remaining of some of the skeletons, which occasioned
their being united with others. The Saxon characters are in many
inscriptions preserved, though in none entire. They were washing
a plaster from the walls, to discern some curious old painting,
very miserable, but very entertaining, of old legends, which some
antiquaries are now endeavouring to discover . . .

I could hardly quit this poor dear old building, so much I
was interested with its Saxon chiefs, its little queer niches, quaint
images, damp cells, mouldering walls, and mildewed pillars. One
chest contains the bones entire of Egbert, our first king. Edred,
also, I distinguished.'

Fanny rereads the entry in her diary as she puts the finishing touches
to her play, Edwy and Elgiva, *the story she started a year ago about
Eadred's nephew and his wife. She began writing while still in the*

job she loathed, the job she's just left; working as second keeper of the robes to Queen Charlotte. Now, in her new-found freedom, she is spending a few glorious months travelling the country and, hopefully, getting back to her writing career. Her novel Evelina *brought her roaring fame and she is itching to return to her literary circles. She found the inspiration for this new play in the British histories she has read, in books by authors like David Hume, the Scottish Enlightenment philosopher and historian. She is especially intrigued by the female characters, none more so than Elgiva – or Ælfgifu, as some call her, who, according to the sources, after marrying Edwy, who was actually her relative, was kidnapped and tortured by the abbot Dunstan. Fanny likes thinking of how these real characters of the past can be used to discuss issues important in the present; in this case, not just struggles for political power and the relationship between a ruler and his people, but also issues of feminism and control over the female body. This interest in the past is all the rage at the moment, as people are only now understanding the real origins of* England: *she saw that with her own eyes when she visited Winchester Cathedral and the antiquarians' work going on there. And to think, she stood only feet away from the remains of Edwy's uncle Eadred.*

THE KING OF YORK

On the murder of his older brother Edmund I in May 946, Eadred succeeded to the throne as king of England. The country he inherited was markedly different from that of his grandfather, Alfred. Under his eldest brother Athelstan, it had seen complete political unification for the first time in the wake of Brunanburh. Nevertheless, Eadred had to work hard to retain his territory. His authority over the kingdom of York, in particular, continued to be challenged: just as during Edmund's reign, the Scandinavian kings were keen to reassert their power. One of these would become a serious threat to Eadred: the Norwegian ruler identified as Eric Bloodaxe in later sources.

Eric first appeared on the scene in 947 when he was chosen as king of York by the Northumbrians. This may have come as a surprise to Eadred because only a matter of months before they had submitted to him, acknowledging him as 'father and lord'. Much of our knowledge about Eric comes from later Icelandic saga sources, not least because he was allegedly the son of Harald Fairhair, the Norwegian king credited with ruling Norway as a single country. Yet the sources we have are unreliable as historical evidence and the narrative in the English texts is also confused. The sequence of rulership between Eric, Olaf his predecessor, and an interlude in which Eadred appears to have been in control is unclear.

What the records state is that in response to Eric's rule and his support from the Northumbrians, Eadred launched a raid on their kingdom in 948, burning down the minster church of St Wilfrid at Ripon in the process. A battle further south at Castleford ensued with great losses on both sides. Eventually, facing the further threat of Eadred's wrath, the Northumbrians abandoned Eric and agreed to pay the West Saxon king compensation. The attack on Ripon's minster church may have coincided with the removal to Canterbury of the relics of St Wilfrid, who had built the church in the seventh century. This was a common strategy of the West Saxon kings: appropriating important saints' cults as a way of asserting their authority over captured regions. By this means, two aims could be achieved: the new ruler became associated with the established cult and the local region's control was weakened. Eadred's brother Athelstan had been particularly interested in relics and had clearly understood the power they could hold, both politically and religiously. In any case, the events that year sent Eric off into exile, allegedly, according to a later Norwegian history, setting sail for Spain to raid. Yet this was not the last the English would see of him: in 952, he returned, driving out Anlaf, the king who had acknowledged Eadred as overlord. Apparently, the Archbishop of York, Wulfstan, had supported Eric, so Eadred placed him under house arrest. Eric's rule came to an end in 954, although the circumstances are unclear: according to the *Anglo-Saxon Chronicle*, he was expelled by the Northumbrians, while another source records that he was betrayed and killed by his own people.

Eadred would eventually succumb to a mysterious, unknown stomach illness. Towards the end of his life, he was allegedly so ill that he could no longer eat properly: one account has it that he took to sucking the juices from his food and spitting out the rest, a sight that apparently repulsed all those who dined with him. He also appears to have had trouble with his legs, as his epithet named him *Debilis Pedibus* – 'the Weak in the Feet'. Finally, on 23 November 955, the illness took his life while he was at Frome in Somerset and afterwards his body was moved to Winchester.

Eadred would be remembered as the king who once and for all changed York's ruling dynasty from Viking to English. Nevertheless, his will makes it clear that he was nervous about the political stability of his kingdom. He left a total of £1,600 of silver to be divided between four leading churchmen in different regions: 'For the redemption of his soul and for the good of his people,' the will said, 'that they may be able to purchase for themselves relief from want and from the heathen army if they [have] need.'

A TEENAGE RULER

Eadred's mother Eadgifu still appears to have been attending court on a regular basis when he died, but with no other children she gave way to two new contenders for the throne: his nephews Eadwig and Edgar. As the elder of the two, Eadwig, also known as Edwy, was chosen to become king. Only around fifteen years old when he ascended to the throne, he found himself surrounded by a number of powerful figures at court, including his grandmother Ælfleda; the ealdorman of East Anglia, Athelstan Half-King; Oda, the Archbishop of Canterbury; and the abbot of Glastonbury, Dunstan. Dunstan, for instance, was entrusted by Eadred to keep safe the best of the royal treasures. But the young king seems to have had his own ideas on how to establish his independence. He clearly had little need for his paternal grandmother, as one of his first acts was to take away her land and wealth so that after more than two and a half decades, Eadgifu's place in royal society changed dramatically. But Eadwig also seems to have had issues with Oda and Dunstan. Most details of this come from the *Life of St Dunstan*, written around 1000, an account that has served to give Eadwig a reputation as a debaucher, a despoiler of the church and, not least, an incompetent king. A key part of the story concerns Eadwig's marriage in 956 to a woman called Ælfgifu, whose mother was named as Æthelgifu. In one of the manuscripts of the *Anglo-Saxon Chronicle*, the entry for the year 958 says the following: 'Here in this year Archbishop Oda divorced King Eadwig and Ælfgifu because they were related.' No further comment is given, but by tracing names and family relationships found in various charters, it seems possible that Ælfgifu was, in fact, a descendant of King Æthelred I, something that would have made her Eadwig's third cousin once removed.

The story told in the *Life of St Dunstan* discredits Eadwig for an entirely different reason, recounting an event that took place around his coronation. The day after the ceremony, during a grand banquet put on for him, Eadwig rushed out of the hall. Archbishop Oda ordered a search party to be sent out after him and eventually Abbot Dunstan found the newly crowned king, but he was not alone: he was having sex with two 'loose women'. These were a woman of noble birth and her daughter, the elder 'a woman of ripe age' who had frequently 'enticed him to intimacy' in the past. On this occasion, Dunstan was shocked to observe the king 'wallowing between the two of them in evil fashion, as if in a vile sty'. And not only that, he had thrown his beautiful royal crown, 'bound with wondrous metal, gold and silver and gems', to the floor. Eadwig had to be forcibly dragged from the women by Dunstan, who replaced the crown on his head and made him return to the party. We have no way of knowing if this is true, although it does sound very much like a scandalous story reported to discredit Eadwig. There were other accounts suggesting he was prone to liaisons with women thought unsuited to him, but it seems likely that the anonymous author of Dunstan's *Life* had a particular interest in disgracing Eadwig, who apparently was so enraged with Dunstan that he had him stripped of his status and possessions and driven into exile. The author also reproached Eadwig for his poor ability to govern his country, which he says led to him being completely deserted by the people of the north. What is certain is that in the summer of 957, the kingdom was divided, for reasons unknown, between Eadwig and his brother Edgar, with Edgar taking charge of the north while Eadwig kept the south – the Thames marked the line of division between them. Eadwig appears to have kept overall control, as seen by the evidence from coins: his were the only ones minted until his death.

Eadwig's reputation remained controversial, with some medieval writers describing him affectionately, while others, such as William of Malmesbury, stuck to the opposite view. Eadwig, said Malmesbury, was a 'wanton youth ... who misused his personal beauty in lascivious behaviour'. Little is known about Eadwig's death on 1 October 959, but it is said he was buried in New Minster.

EDGAR THE PEACEMAKER

We have surprisingly few details about Edgar's reign and life. After the division of Eadwig's kingdom in 957, he had become king of the Mercians, so when his brother died, there was little contest for his accession to the whole kingdom. Edgar was Edmund's younger son with his first wife, Ælfgifu, who died soon after he was born. While Edmund had married again, his new wife seems to have had little to do with her stepsons, who instead had been brought up by their uncle Eadred. Edgar was cared for by Ælfwynn, wife of one of the East Anglian ealdormen, and he was also influenced by his powerful grandmother, Eadgifu. Edgar would later become an important influence on church reforms and this likely came about from his education at a Benedictine house, possibly in Abingdon.

One important aspect of Edgar's rule can be gleaned from four surviving law codes attributed to him. The first relates to the administration of the hundreds, the administrative units that functioned as the subdivision of a shire. All landowners were legally obliged to attend the courts of the shire, and the hundred and the law code show the system to be well established by Edgar's time. Importantly, by the ninth century, all of the shires of Wessex have been recorded, but it is only after the kingdom's expansion in the tenth century that the shires of the Midlands are first recorded. Another law code attempted to standardise weights and measures throughout the kingdom, with a final command stating that only one coinage should be current throughout the land and that no man could refuse it – a key reform to ensure new standards for producing uniform coinage. A final important law code related to the parts of the country that were under Scandinavian, or Danish, legal rule. Although the code deals with a range of issues, one clause in particular is interesting: 'It is my will that they should be in force among the Danes such good laws as they best decide on, and I have ever allowed them this and will allow it as long as my life lasts, because of your loyalty, which you have always shown me.' The Danes Edgar refers to were the inhabitants of the former kingdom of York, now incorporated into Northumbria, which shows that during his rule Edgar respected and had a very positive relationship with the Scandinavians living in the north.

Strangely, although his brother died in 959, the *Anglo-Saxon Chronicle* says that Edgar was consecrated king as late as 11 May 973, in Bath. There is no good explanation for the delay and it is likely that it was actually a second coronation. Around the same time, he apparently took his entire naval force to have a meeting with six kings – thought to include Cumbrians and Scots – who pledged that they would be his allies. It is possible that he faced increasing pressure from the northern frontiers. Close to the Irish Sea, Chester may have been significant because it was an important centre of trade between England and Viking Dublin.

A vital aspect of Edgar's reign appears to have been his considerable power at sea: he was reported to have an exceptional navy. According to the *Chronicle*: 'Nor was the fleet so proud nor host so strong that it got itself praying England.' In other words, during his rule it looked as though foreign attacks from the sea were not likely. Later twelfth-century historians made a lot of this, John of Worcester crediting Edgar with a fleet of 3,600 ships that assembled every year after Easter, 1,200 from the east coast, 1,200 from the west and 1,200 from the north, meaning that the king could circumnavigate the entire island to demonstrate his strength and train his men. This would surely have repelled foreign invaders. However, one record suggests that Edgar did not man his fleet just with crew from England. Archbishop Wulfstan wrote that the king 'loved evil foreign customs and brought to family heathen manners within this land, and attracted foreigners and enticed harmful people to this country'. Later, William of Malmesbury was to specify that this meant the Saxons (Germans), Flemings and Danes who taught the innocent English ferocity, effeminacy and drunkenness respectively. It is possible therefore that Edgar, like other kings before him, had hired foreign crews and even ships, including those from Scandinavia.

Edgar died on 8 July 975 and was buried at Glastonbury Abbey: overall, his reign was thought of positively, as a golden age of peace and plenty, earning him the epitaph *Pacificus* – 'the Peacemaker'.

TRANSLATION

On Saturday 15 July 971, a large congregation was gathered outside the west door of Old Minster. The crowd included a large number of monks from both the Old and New Minster communities, led by their abbots and Bishop Æthelwold. According to a later legend, onlookers attempted to shelter from the pouring rain that fell on Winchester that day as they hustled and crowded in an attempt to get a glimpse of what was happening in front of them. Superstition now has it that if it rains on 15 July – St Swithun's Day – it will rain for the following forty days. Remarkably, we have two detailed accounts of what happened that day, when the bones of Swithun – former Winchester bishop and then its revered saint – were translated from their original burial place outside and into Old Minster. One of these is within a 3,400-line poem – the longest surviving pre-conquest Anglo-Latin poem – written down by a monk named Wulfstan, one of the clerics of Old Minster in the late tenth century.

Preparations for the translation had started the day before, through sermons, prayers and singing long into the night, when the people of Winchester brought out candles; in the twinkling light of gleaming lamps, they held vigil around the saint's tomb while the monks chanted. The following morning, the bishops, abbots and priests dressed in the finest vestments and began a procession, bearing candles and burning incense. Finally, they reached the tomb, around which tents had been erected to keep out the enthusiastic crowd, which had to be moved away. When they entered the sacred space, the work began, and Bishop Æthelwold was the first to put a spade in the ground. Afterwards he ordered attendants to continue digging until they reached the tomb. Finally, they struck the lid of the sarcophagus and used three poles to carefully prise it open. There, Wulfstan describes, they beheld a remarkable sight, matching precisely one that had been predicted in a vision by a smith three years earlier: the body of the saint was so beautiful that all the treasure of silver and gold seen in the entire world would look cheap in comparison. To add to that, a wonderful odour emerged from the body and filled the entire town with a sweetness that surpassed even that of cinnamon and balsam. The clerics set to work, apprehensively touching the precious body, washing it limb by limb and wrapping it in a clean shroud. When done, they placed it on a *feretory*, which was a sort of portable shrine that would allow them to move the relics. Two abbots carried the feretory on their shoulders to its new location, and the city of Winchester filled with the sound of crowds rejoicing and the church bells ringing. Finally, the bishop decorated the holy body and held mass, after which all the onlookers were sent home to refresh themselves with food and drinks. The saint himself immediately responded by carrying out new miracles, healing and consoling the ill and infirm. For the next five months, we hear, there was hardly a day on which the sick were not cured at his tomb. Soon after the translation had taken place, King Edgar commissioned a lavish gold and silver reliquary. According to Wulfstan, the king made available three hundred pounds of silver, ruby gems and gold for the purpose, and commanded goldsmiths to construct it. The reliquary was engraved with elaborate Christian scenes.

While this reliquary casket belonging to St Swithun does not survive, others do: there is the Gandersheim casket now in Brunswick, Germany, made of exquisitely carved walrus ivory or bone and brass. The casket is clearly of seventh- or eighth-century Anglo-Saxon manufacture, complete with deciphered runes, and it is thought that it ended up in Germany as a gift to members of the Saxon nobility; some have even linked it to the wedding of Otto the Great and Eadgyth in 930. Intriguingly, the fact that Eadgyth's half-brother Athelstan was an avid collector of relics could support this idea.

Caskets like this would also have been desirable targets for raiders: we know this because remarkably, in Norway, three complete reliquaries that originated in Britain or Ireland have been found, at least two of them from graves. One is the eighth-century so-called Ranvaik's casket, made from yew encased in decorative panels of bronze and enamel. A tenth-century runic inscription has been carved into its base, reading 'Ranvaik owns this casket'. Who Ranvaik was, or how the reliquary ended up in her possession, we will never know, but it seems unlikely it arrived in Norway through peaceful means.

While Swithun was certainly a real person, all we really know for certain is that between 852 and 863 he was the bishop of Winchester. We know that he was competent in Latin, far more so than his contemporary bishops, and he seems to have been key to formulating and executing the religious policies of Æthelwulf. The last we hear of him from a historical account comes in a poem, which states that he built a stone bridge at the east gate of Winchester. Apart from that, our remaining information comprises legends and tales of the miracles caused by his saintly body. Swithun passed away on 2 July, probably in 863, and was buried beside a stone cross in front of Old Minster. According to a later account, the humble saint wanted to be buried outside, so people could trample on his grave. It is hard to believe that we know so little about the person who, a century later, would become one of the best-known and most widely venerated Anglo-Saxon saints in England and elsewhere in Europe. But more than anywhere, Winchester was the place that had the strongest connection to St Swithun.

Around 250 years after his death, an anonymous author attempted to write an elaborate portrait of the bishop in the *Vita S. Swithuni* – the *Life of St Swithun* – with few sources and very few facts available to him. As a result, he used some educated guesswork to present a plausible story of the saint's life. He surmised that Swithun was born during the reign of King Egbert, who later appointed him as tutor for his son Æthelwulf. Æthelwulf, in turn, nominated him bishop and in his career the exceedingly humble Swithun restored a number of churches. It was the *Life*, too, which put forth the suggestion that Swithun wanted to be buried in an inconspicuous grave. Another, later tradition also credits the bishop with defending Winchester from Viking attacks. Later the number of miracles attributed to him became immense, especially the healing of the sick and disabled. Writing in the 990s, the monk Ælfric described Old Minster's internal walls as being completely covered in the stools and crutches of cripples who had been healed there.

On his death, Swithun was buried in a prominent position just outside the west door of Old Minster, in a house-shaped structure marked by a stone cross; hardly the humble and anonymous grave he had allegedly hoped for. However, it was not until Edgar the Peacemaker's reign that Swithun would really come into significance.

Not long after Swithun's reliquary casket was made, Old Minster had been extensively reconstructed by Æthelwold to incorporate his tomb.

The events of 971 are important because no translation on this scale had ever taken place in England before. Various other saints' relics had certainly been moved, but not in such a huge procession and ceremony. Why, then, did it happen now; why Swithun; and why Winchester? There are no simple answers, but it is crucial to understand the role of relics and remains in telling stories of the past.

The translation of saintly remains has a history that goes back to the early Roman period, at a time of the persecution of Christian martyrs. Many were executed in public places and their bodies left to rot, sometimes surreptitiously retrieved under cover of darkness either by family members or other devout Christians. It was only in 313 that it became formally permitted for those remains to be retrieved and moved – translated – to a more suitable place of burial. Often these places of interment then became centres for cults that grew up around the deceased. Throughout the Roman and post-Roman period, relics began to be moved around more extensively, especially in Italy and during periods of political upheaval. From the late eighth century onwards, churches in continental Europe, especially in France and Germany, started to acquire relics belonging to Roman saints and martyrs; to a smaller degree, this also happened in England and more extensively in Ireland. Elaborate translation ceremonies came to be included in the package. Eventually, trends shifted towards venerating and translating local saints too, in particular during the tenth century, and grand architectural embellishments of the local shrines became part of this as well. Bishop Æthelwold would no doubt have been aware that this was happening across the Channel and his discussions with continental monks, who we know were present in Winchester at the time, may well have given him the inspiration for creating the town's very own cult centre. There were, however, plenty of former bishops that he could have chosen for his cult and perhaps Swithun's prominent burial position – right outside that front door – informed his choice. While the description of St Swithun's translation is unique in early medieval England, the bishop would likely have followed the procedures specified in an *ordo*, the order of service. One such, for instance, explains how relics should first be placed on a *paten*, which is a metal plate or dish used during mass, then wrapped in cloth, before being taken to their new location, with a range of associated procedures to be carried out by the clerics.

A depiction of St Swithun's shrine may accidentally have been discovered in Winchester Cathedral in 1909, although it was only identified by John Crook in the 1990s. Concealed behind seventeenth-century fitted bookshelves in the Morley Library, which is located in a vaulted passage between the cathedral's south transept and the chapter house, was a wall painting covered over with whitewash. The painting, although fragmentary, is thought to date to the late twelfth century. On one side is a line drawing of a church, with an altar seen in an internal bay of the building. On this altar stand a chalice and a reliquary, and Crook believes the latter is the very one that was commissioned by Edgar.

While we cannot know Æthelwold's motivations for creating St Swithun's cult and for the improvements to the shrine, it is likely the reasons were not entirely religious, nor driven by genuine miracles. It may well have been down to money: cults, and the pilgrims they attracted, could be a significant source of income. If you travelled far and died at the end of your journey or pilgrimage, the likelihood was that you would make a donation to the saint, or rather to the institution that accommodated him or her.

The original reliquary survived until 1448, when it was melted down to create a new one after the death of Cardinal Henry Beaufort, Bishop of Winchester, who left money to the cathedral for new building projects.

After St Swithun's cult began to thrive in Winchester, it soon spread across England too. Ideally, other churches devoted to him would have liked to have a piece of the saint for themselves, but Swithun's remains were closely guarded. While saints' relics could often be legitimately dispersed, there was also an illegitimate trade in them – perhaps even a lucrative one. In Swithun's case, we know of at least one officially sanctioned dispersal. In 1006, Bishop Ælfheah, Æthelwold's successor at Winchester, was promoted to Archbishop of Canterbury and when he made the move from Winchester he decided to take with him nothing less than the head of St Swithun. The saint also became popular abroad, especially in Scandinavia. His cult is thought to have spread from Norway, possibly with some of the numerous missionaries that travelled across the North Sea from England. Stavanger Cathedral on the west coast, established sometime in the 1120s, is even said to have had one of his relics, as an arm bone is mentioned in a church inventory dating to 1517.

After being taken to Canterbury, the skull was apparently moved to Évreux Cathedral in Normandy sometime before the fourteenth century. How this happened is a bit of a mystery, but the skull survived the French Revolution and was recorded in 1919 as having since been enclosed in a reliquary made of gilded wood. This came to light in 1998 when a member of Winchester Cathedral's congregation came across a reference to Évreux, and a later inspection of the skull revealed a calvarium, the upper portion of a human skull, bound firmly to a red satin cushion adorned with gold braid. Whether this truly is the head of the Winchester bishop, we might never know.

It is unclear if any of the bones of St Swithun are still in Winchester Cathedral, and it would be extremely unusual if they were, as hardly any such early English saints' remains can be found in the place where the cult originated. Now though, there may be an exception, in Kent. In June 1885, a team of workmen employed to restore the north wall of the chancel in St Mary and St Eanswythe's Church in Folkestone, Kent, made a surprising discovery. While removing plaster work around a niche in the wall, they came across a cavity beneath a small slab and inside was an oddly shaped lead casket sixteen inches long. Prising the casket open, they found that it contained bones that appeared to be human, including parts of a skull and thigh bones. Canon Matthew Woodward wrote almost immediately to the newspapers and in an article soon after, it was stated that these were in fact the remains of Folkestone's and the church's revered female saint, Eanswythe. A member of the Kent Archaeological Society made an assessment of the bones and concluded they were likely from a young woman. The remains were subsequently placed in a glass case to allow visitors to view them.

Very little is known about Eanswythe but she is believed to have been a Kentish princess who founded a nunnery in Folkestone in the seventh century. After her death at a relatively young age, she is credited with numerous miracles, including the diversion of a spring upwards to provide water for builders.

We know from earlier records that relics said to be those of St Eanswythe were translated into this church in 1138, from one or more previous locations. There are records referring to the relics throughout the Middle Ages, including one dating to the 1530s. Like most other churches, St Mary and St Eanswythe was soon after to suffer the effects of the Reformation and the relics were thought to be lost. The 1885 discovery, however, suggests a different story: that the remains had been squirrelled away and hidden within the church wall.

In 2020, the claim would finally be investigated. A team of scientists was granted permission to remove and study the remains, concluding that they were likely those of a woman aged between seventeen and twenty-two at the time of death. There was evidence of minor trauma to the right foot and two of the fingers on the left hand, but other than that, there were no signs of poor health. Importantly, however, the radiocarbon dates gave the team exactly the result they were looking for: the bones dated to the second half of the seventh century. Isotope analysis was also carried out on the preserved teeth, but this was fairly inconclusive: the values were consistent with numerous parts of Britain, including the areas around Kent. In other words, nothing that could conclusively prove where the individual grew up. Nonetheless, the team and the local community were delighted, especially as, if right, this would make her the only pre-Norman saint with relics still in their original location.

EDWARD THE MARTYR

When Edgar died, the country was thrown into a serious succession dispute. In the *Anglo-Saxon Chronicle*, his death and the eventual succession of his son Edward are listed under the year 975, along with the sighting of a comet: one of many phenomena that were seen as portents of disaster, such as pestilence, famine, war and regime change.

Edgar left at least four children: Edward, the eldest surviving son from Edgar's first marriage; Edith, from a relationship with Wulfthryth of Wilton, who he may or may not have been married to; and finally Edmund Ætheling and Æthelred with his final wife Ælfthryth, the daughter of a powerful Devonshire thegn. Edmund had died before Edgar, in 971 – we don't know how old he was as his birth year is not recorded, but since Edgar and Ælfthryth had married in 964 or 965, and her previous husband Æthelwold, an ealdorman, had died in 962, Edmund was likely to have been aged nine at most. Some have suggested that he could have been born as early as 959, which would mean he was twelve when he died. There is no information about where Edmund was buried, but with Winchester being the centre of the royal court at the time, it would not seem an unlikely resting place for the intended heir to the kingdom.

When Edgar died, then, only two candidates remained as contestants for the kingship: Edward and Æthelred. Neither was a particularly obvious choice. Edward was aged around thirteen and Æthelred may have been as young as six or seven. While Æthelred's mother Ælfthryth naturally advanced her son's claim, Dunstan, by now Archbishop of Canterbury, eventually chose Edward as king on 17 July 975.

At such a young age, the boy would likely have been dependent on his ealdormen for help with politics and courtly affairs. The king appears to have had little influence over the north of the country and the Danelaw region. Tensions were brewing elsewhere, especially in areas where his brother Æthelred had been the preferred candidate for rulership. Coinage, much improved by his father, began to be debased and Winchester's monopoly on the cutting and issuing of coin dies was lost. Ultimately, Edward would not have the opportunity to make much of a mark on the country's history because on 18 March 978, aged no more than about sixteen, his life came to an early end.

The *Life of St Oswald*, an archbishop of York, is a work written by Byrhtferth, a monk at Ramsey Abbey between 995 and 1005, and in it we find the most detailed description of what happened to Edward. On that particular day, the king was travelling to visit his brother at the house of Ælfthryth, his stepmother, who had established herself on a large estate in Dorset at Corfe in the Purbeck Hills. According to the *Life*, when Edward arrived in the evening to meet his much-loved brother, his stepmother's retainers – nobles and chief men – came out to meet him. These men had plotted against him, because 'they possessed minds so accursed and such dark diabolical blindness that they did not fear to lay hands on the Lord's anointed'. Edward had few men with him for defence and was murdered while still on his horse. Servants picked up his body and took him to the house of 'a certain unimportant person', where he was unceremoniously given a shallow grave. There his body stayed until about a year later when Ealdorman Ælfhere rode to Corfe with a retinue to repatriate Edward's remains. On uncovering the body they found that it was still complete and looked unharmed; they took it for burial, first temporarily to Wareham, and then to the nunnery at Shaftesbury, where Edward would be venerated as a saint.

In this narrative, the blame for the murder is cast on Ælfthryth's retainers, but it is unclear if it was their own initiative. Æthelred was too young to be a likely culprit: another suspect was his mother; as later, post-conquest narratives argue, she would have had a lot to gain from Edward's death. Whether she had any part in it, we will never know, but a point often used to suggest her guilt is that little seems to have been done publicly to find the culprits and bring them to justice.

In the years to come, Æthelred appears to have been the biggest supporter of his half-brother's saintly cult and he may have been responsible for a second translation of his relics in 1001, something he did for his own, political motives.

THE FORGOTTEN PRINCES

A s the forensic team works its way through the Winchester bones, the archaeologists make an unexpected discovery. Not all the bones are those of adults, although the written records suggest they should be. Among the individuals they can piece together, they separate out two adolescent skeletons, including several bones that are not fully fused and a fairly complete skull. The remains show that when they died they were both between the ages of eleven and fifteen, or thereabouts.

Depending on the circumstances, age at death can be relatively well determined from a human skeleton. Over time our bones change and develop and the most extreme change – and therefore the most useful to the osteologist – happens during childhood. When a fetus develops in its mother's uterus, the shape that will eventually become the skeleton is first outlined in cartilage, as a template or blueprint for the baby it will shortly become. Soon that cartilage is replaced, gradually, with bone cells, in a process known as ossification. By the time the baby is born, the template has become a real-life model, but one that is still incomplete. In a long bone – like a leg or an arm – the ossification starts in the centre and at the ends – or epiphyses – with cartilage holding it all together in the right shape, until they eventually fuse together, in what's referred to as epiphyseal fusion, to form a single, solid bone. For this reason, a newborn has around 300 bones, compared to an adult's 206. Different bones fuse at different ages, and because this process is pretty well understood and reasonably regular, we can look at archaeological remains and work our way through the skeleton. That way we can see if the individual had reached adulthood at the time of death and if not, estimate the age. The femoral head, or hipbone, for example, fuses sometime between the ages of fifteen and twenty, while the epiphyses at the elbow fuse around the ages of thirteen to nineteen. The clavicle or collarbone can fuse as late as thirty. If a skull remains to be studied, we can look at the eruption of permanent teeth, as this follows predictable patterns: by the teenage years most children have their full set of adult teeth, except perhaps the wisdom teeth. For adults, it's more challenging. The enamel on our teeth – especially molars – may wear down over time, especially in times past when diets were rougher and toothcare less sophisticated. As we age, our skeletons continue to alter and change in other ways too, sometimes leaving subtle signs for the osteologist to discover: the bones that make up our skulls may start to fuse together and the shape of one of the pubic bones also changes subtly over time. Yet in the adult skeleton, these signs of ageing are far less precise and reliable than in a child's, so our estimates can only be very broad.

A preliminary ancient DNA analysis shows that the two skeletons were both male. But who were they? Winchester, and its minsters, was not only the burial place of kings and a queen – the city was also considered an appropriate resting place for a specific set of royal sons and senior aristocrats. The word 'prince' here is anachronistic. There was no such thing in the early medieval period: the word, with its *current meaning, did not come into use in England until the thirteenth century. Instead, boys and young men of noble, perhaps royal, birth were known as æthelings. Their presence in Winchester Cathedral shows that these two must have been of high status, likely of a royal bloodline, but if that is the case, did their premature deaths herald a crisis?*

CHEST IV

SUCCESSION

Edmund Ironside d. 1016

EDMVDVS·REX   OBIIT·AᵒDM·

QVE·THECA·HEC·RETINET·
EDMVNDV·SVSCPE·CHRISTE·
QVI·VIVENTE·PATRE·REGIA·
SCEPTRA·TVLIT·

WINCHESTER, 1539

*E*ngland is in the midst of a transformation. For two decades, trouble has been brewing across Europe and the Reformation is well underway; Western Christianity is splintering into Protestantism and what later becomes the Roman Catholic Church. In England the movement takes a different course from the rest of Europe, as the king, Henry VIII, has his own political incentives for bringing about change. With no prospect of a male heir, Henry demands an annulment of his marriage to Catherine of Aragon, but the church refuses. Henry decides to take matters into his own hands and removes the Church of England from the authority of Rome in 1534, allowing him to marry Anne Boleyn instead. As a consequence of that decision, major transformations take place throughout the country, not least the dissolution of the monasteries, a policy led by the king's chief adviser Thomas Cromwell. In this unprecedented act, more than nine hundred religious houses across the country will be disbanded; their substantial wealth and income expropriated by the crown.

This year a man by the name of Thomas Derby enters the town of Winchester through the city gates. Thomas, clerk to the Privy Council – the body of advisers to the sovereign – and newly appointed clerk to the Council of the West, has travelled to the West Country in the company of the president of the latter, Sir John Russell. Thomas is one of those who has observed the developments of the first few decades of the sixteenth century at close hand. Early in Henry VIII's reign, he was appointed to his role as a clerk by Cromwell and he is also a close acquaintance of Anne Boleyn's father, the Earl of Wiltshire.

Apart from his administrative skills, Thomas is well known to those in power for his talents as a writer and his thoughts on theology. A staunch Protestant, Derby has written a tract setting forth the reasons behind the dissolution of the monasteries. A year ago, Hyde, the monastery that took over from New Minster in the twelfth century, was disbanded, the fate of its wealth and relics unknown. What Derby does know is that around the country, the bones of saints have been specifically targeted and ecclesiastical treasures destroyed. He understands the cause, but is not sure he supports the means – vandalism is surely unnecessary? Even the remains of Winchester's most revered saint, St Swithun, have been attacked and he has heard the details of how it happened. Around six months ago, on the night of 21 September 1538, Thomas Wriothesley, a commissioner working on behalf of the king, entered Winchester Cathedral and demolished the shrine. In a letter to Thomas Cromwell, Wriothesley wrote: 'About three o'clock this Saturday morning we made an end of the shrine here at Winchester. There was no gold, nor ring, nor true stone in it, but all great counterfeits; but the silver alone will amount to 2,000 marks.' While dismantling the shrine, Wriothesley recorded that they made sure 'to sweep away al the rotten bones': the men were clearly not there just to appropriate the wealth and precious metals. Yet Thomas Derby knows that elsewhere there are those who have taken care to hide away the sacred bones of saints, either to protect them or to prevent them falling into the wrong hands. To preserve his thoughts and concerns, he writes: 'St. Swithan and other reliques whereabout abuse of ipocrasy was be layde save, and not, as it is untruely surmitted, brent, but according to reason collocate secretely, wher ther shal be no cause of superstition given by them; as some say that for the like cause, the body of Moyses was hyden lest the Jues should fall to idolatry.'

While he hasn't seen proof of it, Thomas has heard that the graves of those glorious kings, Alfred and his son Edward, who were both interred at Hyde, were opened and their remains moved to chests in the cathedral, but this may just have been a rumour.

Almost five hundred years later, Winchester Cathedral archaeologist John Crook will ponder those words, and ask himself whether the bones of St Swithun have been tucked away in the mortuary chests, hidden in plain sight?

THE SECOND VIKING AGE

'[Æthelred] is the only ruler of the male line of Ecberht whom we can unhesitatingly set down as a bad man and a bad King.'

E. A. Freeman (1870s)

Following the burial of his brother, Æthelred was consecrated king on 4 May 979. Reports say the English people were delighted, and Byrhtferth of Ramsey describes him as 'a young man in respect of years, elegant in his manners, with an attractive face and a handsome appearance'. These words stand in contrast to the reputation Æthelred would end up with for posterity – one that is almost entirely negative. Æthelred's name translates as 'noble counsel'. While he is now usually known by the nickname 'the unready', the name actually given to him, *Unræd*, essentially means 'ill-advised' – hence becoming something like 'good advice the ill-advised', a pun on his first name. The nickname also emphasises what is usually seen as the real problem with his rule: not that he was badly prepared, but that he was badly advised by those at his court.

Like his half-brother, Æthelred was very young when he inherited the kingdom and in his early years would have relied heavily on a group of councillors, one that may also have included his mother Ælfthryth. She may well have played a key part in his education too. As he reached his teenage years in the 980s, however, he would have become more independent, gradually needing less of the guidance and influence of those at his court. There is no clear age when the boy-king would have come to majority; the division between boyhood and manhood seems not to have been defined. Somewhere between twelve and fifteen seems likely; there were rules in some places, for instance, stating that at those ages thieves and sinners should be treated as adults.

Only a short time into Æthelred's reign, in 980, Viking raids on England began again, after a very long period marked by what seems to have been peaceful relationships and an almost complete lack of attacks. The *Anglo-Saxon Chronicle* records how Southampton was ravaged by a raiding ship-army that year, with most of the town-dwellers killed or taken prisoner; similar fates befell Thanet and Cheshire. While the initial attacks appear to have been sporadic, pretty soon the raids ramped up. The following year, 'great harm' was done all along the coast in Devon and Cornwall, but then the kingdom enjoyed some respite from attacks and around 985 Æthelred appears to have married for the first time. His wife was probably a woman named Ælfgifu, and although little is known for certain about her, she seems to have been the daughter of an earl of Northumbria. If so, the marriage would have given Æthelred an important alliance in the north. The two would have at least nine children together: six sons and three daughters – yet Ælfgifu herself left little imprint; it is possible she played a very low-key role politically. The six sons all bear the names of Æthelred's direct ancestors, even in order of succession with the exception of Ecgberht: Æthelstan, Ecgberht, Edmund, Eadred, Eadwig and Edgar. Naming his first heir after his great-uncle demonstrates how strong Æthelstan's legacy remained more than five decades after his death.

THE BATTLE OF MALDON

While Æthelred busied himself with internal affairs and establishing his own kingship, after just a few years of respite the Scandinavian threat returned. From 988, attacks began again and in 991 culminated in a battle that sent shockwaves through the kingdom. An Old English poem tells the story of this famous event: the Battle of Maldon. The poem, which may date to the end of the tenth century, survived in the Cotton Library in a single copy, but had already been transcribed with a copy taken elsewhere when the library burned down.

The anonymous poet describes how, in August, a large fleet of Vikings made their way to Essex up the Blackwater Estuary. Infuriatingly, the first page of the text is missing, throwing us straight into the action: on the sandy tidal shore, the East Saxon army led by Byrhtnoth, Æthelred's ealdorman, makes arrangement with a spokesman for the Vikings, shouting to him across the water. The raiders ask for tribute, payments of money, to stay away: if the English agree, they will turn away and not return. Byrhtnoth refuses – the only tribute they will receive are deadly weapons, he says, and prepares to fight. As the tide recedes, the two sides engage in battle. Initially, it goes well for Byrhtnoth, as he and his men have control over a bridge, or ford. But eventually, when the Vikings ask to be let across the causeway, he consents, and this turns out to be a fatal mistake. The poet observes that he offered them 'too much land' and in the close combat that follows, Byrhtnoth is killed, his finely decorated sword falling helplessly to the ground. Seeing their leader dead, several of the senior members of the Saxon retinue flee, with a big part of the army following them. Those who remain fight valiantly, and here the surviving text finishes and the climax of the battle is lost to us. Nonetheless, the English were clearly defeated.

While this poem is our main source of information about the Battle of Maldon, the event is mentioned in the *Anglo-Saxon Chronicle* and a few other sources. The earliest account comes in manuscript A of the *Chronicle*, where we read that the Scandinavians were led by a man named Olaf and that they came with ninety-three ships. Before reaching Maldon, they started out in Folkestone, Kent, plundering the countryside; from there they moved to Sandwich, then Ipswich, sacking both.

This Olaf is usually taken to be the Norwegian leader Olaf Tryggvason, and a later addition to manuscript A adds that he converted to Christianity and was sponsored by the king. The *Chronicle* also records that the English made peace with the Vikings after the battle.

Just as with the Battle of Brunanburh some six decades before, the exact location of this battle has never been found. Beyond naming the place as Maldon, we have a few clues. The poem tells us that the Vikings landed on the shore of the tidal river *Pantan stream* (the River Pant), now known as the Blackwater. A stretch of the river is still called Pant, near Braintree in Essex, and it is likely that this was once the name of the whole river and estuary. Beyond this, it is difficult to tell. There is an island at Mersea, just further north, on which the Vikings had set up a winter encampment in 895, and there is an ancient causeway there, connecting the island to the shore. Surviving wills also show that the West Mersea estate once belonged to Byrhtnoth. Yet Maldon is some distance away, so Mersea seems unlikely. Another possibility includes a stretch of land between the rivers Blackwater and Chelmer, closer to Maldon itself, but the most likely location is now thought to be Northey Island, just two miles to the south-east of Maldon town. Maldon, incidentally, was the location of a *burh* built in 916 by Edward, something that can still be seen in the modern town. Here detective work on the surrounding geography revealed that it fitted neatly with that described in the poem: there is an ancient causeway connecting the island to the land, mirroring the ford or bridge, and woodland on one side. The Saxon defenders would have kept to the land side and the Vikings in their ships, the island side.

The poem allows us insights into the culture and society of the warriors too. It shows, for instance, that the East Saxons turned up to battle on their horses, then dismounted to fight and sent most of their steeds away. We learn that the army had hawks. A young falconer, a kinsman to the second-in-command to Byrhtnoth, lets his favourite falcon escape into the woodland so the man can prove he is not a coward and join the fight. The poem describes how the army employs a shield-wall, with the commander riding along the ranks giving them instructions on how to stand, how to hold their shields and how to keep their courage and not be afraid. This could suggest the men were not seasoned, professional fighters but rather that many among them were farmers and others not used to being in battle.

A lot was at stake and its outcome had wide-ranging consequences for Æthelred's England. Some of those were reported in the written records a while later, with hindsight. The so-called 'Chronicle of the Reign of Æthelred', first appearing in manuscript C of the *Anglo-Saxon Chronicle*, for instance, explains that after the battle, 'it was advised that for the first time the tribute (*gafol*) should be paid to the Danish because of the great terror they were causing on the coast: at first this was ten thousand pounds. This advice was first advised by Archbishop Sigeric.' The entry is suggestive of things to come and this, it is emphasised, was the *first* of such payments. And worse definitely did come. Despite the tribute payments, the Viking force did not return home. Instead, they raided along the east coast in the following two years. Then, in 994, Olaf, now accompanied by Swein Forkbeard – a Dane who would later have a radical impact on the country's history – sailed up the Thames and launched an attack on London, ravaging the east and south afterwards. If the *Chronicle* is to be believed, the terror unleashed on the English was immense, with the Vikings seemingly unbeatable, both at sea and on land. At one point they 'wrought the greatest harm which any raiding-army could ever do, in burning and raiding and slaughter of men'. Finally, Æthelred decided he'd had enough, and sent messengers to the Vikings to tell them that he would pay them tribute and send provisions. The invaders moved to Southampton, where they took up winter quarters and were fed by the West Saxons. The tribute, or *gafol* payment, had risen to £16,000. Later the payments would increase even further. It is also notable that the entry about the first tribute payment states that the king was *advised* to make these decisions, one element of what would lead to Æthelred's infamous nickname: the ill-advised.

Around this time a peace treaty was struck between Æthelred and the Viking army led by three men named as Olav, Jostein and Guthmund; this was noted in the *Chronicle* and the treaty also survives as a text. It probably dates to 994, although this is unclear. A crucial clause in the agreement between the two parties stipulated that Olav was to be baptised (or possibly confirmed), with Æthelred standing as his sponsor. The bishop Ælfheah – of whom we will hear more later – was apparently key to the successful outcome of this agreement, something that may well have cost him dear when dealing with another group of Vikings nearly a decade later. Olav also had to promise that he would 'never come back to the English race in hostility', a promise he is said to have kept. Presumably, the wealth he amassed in England proved instrumental to his success in Norway, which he ruled from the end of the 990s. Interestingly, Swein Forkbeard is not mentioned in this particular text, even though he was clearly a member of the army. It has been suggested that this was a deliberate strategy on Æthelred's behalf, of manipulating England's enemies by dividing them and supporting those he found most helpful. Æthelred's support of Olav may well have been a provocation to Swein and the English interference could be seen as a strategic attempt to keep him occupied in Scandinavia.

Treaties such as this also give us an insight into the thinking behind what we might now see as military law. It outlines details like what sort of compensation was to be paid if one party slew someone from the other side: £25 for a freeman and £1 for a slave. The truce was considered breached if eight men were slain, regardless of whether this took place inside or outside a borough. There was also an amnesty on all killings and injuries committed before the treaty was signed: 'all of them are to be dismissed', the text records, 'and no one is to avenge it or ask for compensation'.

It has been suggested that at this point some of the Viking forces chose to join Æthelred's army as mercenaries. Relative peace returned for a few years, but by 997 the raiders were back, ravaging the southern counties over the next three years, although no tribute payments are recorded. In 1000, the Viking fleet crossed the Channel to take shelter in Normandy, where they were welcomed, presumably thanks to their heritage: Duke Richard II was descended from the Viking Rollo, who had founded Normandy sometime in the late ninth century.

As with the armies that were active in the ninth century, little evidence of these forces remains to us, as they left few permanent structures behind and the towns and settlements that they raided and in some cases torched would have been repaired and rebuilt. It is unlikely the damage was so extensive that it was not worth rescuing, while any that is still visible can be near impossible to date to a particular event.

In May 1001, the Vikings attacked Hampshire and Devon, so Æthelred decided to try another peace-keeping mission, which resulted in a payment of a staggering £24,000. This, too, would ultimately be in vain.

By November the following year, one event would make an indelible mark on Æthelred's reign: the so-called St Brice's Day massacre.

ST BRICE'S DAY

It's 13 November 1002. Today is the feast day of St Brice, a fifth-century bishop of Tours. The day would have been noted and observed, but not particularly celebrated, by the residents of Oxford for its original reasons; however the date would come to be commemorated more than a millennium later for another gruesome event that took place that day: a massacre specifically targeting the Danes, centred on St Friedeswide's Church. The *Anglo-Saxon Chronicle* describes it in the following way: 'Then in the middle of this ordered all the Danish men who were among the English race to be killed on Brice's Day, because it was made known to the king that they wanted to ensnare his life – afterwards all his councillors – and have his kingdom afterwards.'

Two years later, in a charter, King Æthelred justified what he had done. It was fully agreed, he said, that 'all the Danes who had sprung up in this island, sprouting like cockle amongst the wheat, were to be destroyed by a most just extermination, and this decree was to be put into effect even as far as death'. The charter went on to describe what had happened at St Friedeswide's. The Danes who resided in Oxford attempted to flee and decided to seek shelter in the church, breaking through its doors and smashing the bolts to hide from their pursuers. While in the church, they attempted to use it as a refuge and defence against 'the people of the town and the suburbs' – a description suggesting an extensive manhunt through the streets of Oxford. The Danes were clearly forced to barricade themselves against their attackers, who failed to break into the church. Consequently, the charter tells us, the locals had no choice but to set fire to the entire church, burning not only those in hiding within but also its 'ornaments and books' – the latter here meaning charters that were clearly valuable enough to be worth a mention alongside the casual description of the human lives lost.

Close to exactly a thousand years later, in 2008, a team of archaeologists in Oxford made a startling discovery. Before work could begin on a proposed extension to St John's College, at St Giles, near the centre of the city, the team excavated the site and found no fewer than thirty-seven human skeletons. They had been thrown carelessly into a prehistoric ditch, and were the remains of young men, mostly aged between sixteen and twenty-five, all robustly built and tall. As suggested by their irreverent burial, they had been brutally slaughtered: almost every skeleton showed extensive evidence of traumatic injuries. In fact, on eighteen of the skulls, a total of forty blade wounds were found, with individuals having up to nine such injuries each. There were no gravegoods buried with them: no weapons and no evidence of clothing. Radiocarbon dates placed the time of their death in the late tenth or early eleventh century – spot on for the events of 1002. Some of the bones even showed evidence of burning, evocative of that charter description of the church fire. Could this really have been the grave of some of Æthelred's victims? Chemical analysis suggested that might be the case, but the evidence was not conclusive. Strontium and oxygen isotope analyses of their teeth revealed that they *could* have grown up in parts of Britain, but equally in parts of Scandinavia. A crucial piece of evidence came from their diets, which showed traces of a higher proportion of marine food than was common in Oxfordshire at the time. The final piece of the puzzle would come almost a decade later, when a large-scale ancient DNA study was able to show that one of the bodies belonged to a man who was a cousin or half-brother of someone from a contemporary grave at Galgedil in Denmark. This, then, would seem conclusive proof that at least some of those who died there that day hailed from Scandinavia.

The St Brice's Day event has been described not just as a massacre, but also as a case of ethnic cleansing. But what were Æthelred's real motivations? According to the *Chronicle*, Æthelred had heard of a plot to kill him and seize power, presumably by those he refers to as the Danes. A critical question for debate has been whether those he targeted that day were locally resident Danes or members of a military raiding force. The political landscape by this time was complex. It seems likely now that the king's wrath was not aimed at everyone of Danish (or Scandinavian) descent, but a more select group. It could be that he was targeting recent arrivals or possibly even some of the mercenaries who had been recruited nearly a decade earlier in 994.

The 1004 charter is informative of Æthelred's thoughts at the time. The text uses the parable of the cockle and the wheat, a biblical reference from the New Testament. Here the kingdom of heaven is compared to a man's field of wheat in which cockles (also known as tares), a type of weed, have been planted by an enemy. To solve the problem, the farmer allows the cockles to grow, planning to burn them at harvest time, separating out the wheat for storage. In the parable the cockles represent sin and in the Middle Ages the parable was often used as a warning against false beliefs, as opposed to a call for toleration and for letting sinners be. The cockles, then, in Æthelred's version, represent the impure Danes among the pure English.

The charter's focus on Oxford means that there must have been people living there who fitted Æthelred's criteria. Although it was outside the area typically thought of as the Danelaw, there is archaeological evidence that Scandinavians had settled in Oxford. Other than that, it is difficult to know who he could have meant.

Ultimately, however, the outcome of the massacre would not be positive for Æthelred. Posterity, indeed, has it down as a blunder. One thing is pretty clear: this was a desperate act caused by an increase in tension at the king's court; rumours of plots and assassinations must have been severe for them to have resulted in a large-scale massacre. Æthelred must have been desperate after two decades of rather unsuccessful defence against an increasingly devious enemy. Nevertheless, the way the massacre is described in the charter shows that it was carefully thought through and agreed upon by both the king and his advisers.

Extraordinarily, the grave may also have a parallel some 120 miles away in Weymouth, where another was discovered in 2009 by archaeologists surveying land before scheduled construction of a relief road for the 2012 Summer Olympics. The chilling discovery, made in a landscape with plenty of prehistoric graves and monuments nearby but very little from the early medieval period, immediately signalled that this was an execution cemetery: a total of fifty-two individuals, all men, had been thrown into a large pit, with no gravegoods, weapons or fittings from clothing, and they had all been decapitated. Their skulls were stacked in a corner of the pit. But as in Oxford, there was nothing with them in the grave to suggest their origins or in any way identify them: the only evidence would come from the bones themselves.

Analysis revealed that they had all been adults, aged between about seventeen and forty-five. There was also a lot of evidence of lesions on the bones that could have come from repeated physical stress, suggesting that this was a group used to performing repetitive strenuous activities from early in life. Most of the men had been relatively healthy before death, although a surprising number showed signs of joint disease, metabolic disease, or inflammation caused by some kind of infectious disease. This included someone with a quite severe bone infection and another with a deformed right leg that would have meant he had impaired mobility.

Practically all of them, however, had evidence of sharp force trauma to the skulls, most obviously linked to the act of decapitation. The individuals had each sustained between one and seven blows to the head and cervical vertebrae; these blows had come from all directions but usually from behind. In addition, almost 70 per cent of the individuals showed sharp force trauma to other parts of their bodies, especially to their hands and shoulders.

So who were these men, and were they linked to the Viking attacks? Radiocarbon dates placed the grave to 970–1025. One possibility is that the men were victims of one of the raids on the south coast reported in the *Anglo-Saxon Chronicle*. In 980, for example, Southampton was raided and the town dwellers killed, and the 'great harm' reported thereafter must surely also have resulted in significant loss of life. But if they were locals, it seems far more likely that they would have been given more respectful burials. We know of other events too that led to losses on the Scandinavian side. In 988, for instance, the *Chronicle* reports that 'Goda, the Devonshire thane, was killed – and a great slaughter with him', but another account states that 'more of them [the Danes] were killed, and the English had possession of the place of slaughter'. Another theory is that the men in the mass grave were Scandinavian raiders caught up in Æthelred's massacre, just as those at St John's College are thought to have been. There is no direct record of the St Brice's Day massacre having spread to Weymouth, but it is certainly possible. Could the bones themselves tell us more? While the evidence for physical stress in many of the men could suggest they were members of a military force, surprisingly few of them had previous injuries or showed other evidence that they had engaged in combat. None had healed weapon injuries or defence injuries. So perhaps they weren't professional soldiers or, since many of them were quite young, perhaps they just had little experience before they met their end in Weymouth.

Occasionally it is possible to determine ancestry by looking at specific traits and measurements in a skull. Unfortunately, in the Weymouth material, only one individual's features were well enough preserved to do this: his skull most closely resembled similar material from Viking Age Denmark. The experts studying the skeletons also noted that the men were tall: not dissimilar from others in north-western Europe and Britain, but men of similar heights, they noted, were especially found in Denmark. A final feature that could suggest the dead were Scandinavians comes from a skull called SK3736: it has two horizontal grooves deliberately cut into each of the two front teeth. This form of dental modification was very unusual in early medieval Europe: three examples have been found at Galgedil in Denmark, but in Viking Age Sweden, a surprisingly high number have been found – a total of 132 individuals. Intriguingly, about 80 per cent of these have been found on the island of Gotland, located off the east coast, near Stockholm. The practice is exclusively associated with men, and some have suggested those with the filed teeth belonged to a particular social group. Some of those found in Sweden were associated with weapon graves or other high-status burials, but there is no clear trend.

Finally, strontium and oxygen isotope data may be able to help. The most intriguing result proved to be that the Weymouth group had a wide range of origins and most of them seem to have grown up outside Britain. Thirty-one of them had oxygen isotope ratios in the teeth that were consistent with childhoods spent in colder climates than the UK, or at higher altitudes. Five of them spent their childhoods in exceptionally cold locations, either in Scandinavia, north of the Arctic circle or perhaps in central Russia. Most of them had strontium isotope ratios that were very different from those prevalent in the south-west of England, although other places of origin in Britain could not be excluded. The group also showed quite differing diets, but overall they seem to have eaten a lot of protein, both from animals and marine sources. The researchers analysing their bones compared femurs and ribs to see if their diets had changed over time. Intriguingly, the data revealed that the men had altered their eating habits, consuming more protein and especially more marine food in the last few years before their deaths. This could be seen as evidence for a migrating raiding army.

If they were, then, caught by the English defenders in a raid, they may have been led up to Ridgeway Hill for a public execution. There is a parallel to the incident reported in the *Chronicle* for the year 896, when several ships were captured and some Vikings were taken to Winchester where Alfred ordered them to be hanged.

The mixed origins of the group found in Weymouth could fit well with what is known from other sources. We certainly know that you could be hired as a mercenary; even the English sometimes defected to the other side. Back home in Scandinavia, too, military groups seem to have been diverse. A cemetery at Trelleborg in Denmark, one of Harald Bluetooth's strongholds, contained the burials of people with local backgrounds as well as some who had travelled there from far away.

AFTERMATH

T hings certainly did not go well for Æthelred in the years following the St Brice's Day massacre, although whether this was a direct effect of those events is difficult to say.

In 1003–4, almost a decade after he had last raided England, Swein Forkbeard returned, ravaging the southern and eastern coast, including a brutal raid on Exeter, before moving inland. The *Anglo-Saxon Chronicle* claims the attack was aimed at murdering the reeve, a Frenchman called Hugh. The chronicler directly blames an ealdorman by the name of Ælfric for Swein's success. Ælfric, we hear, should have led the army but he 'pulled out his old tricks': as soon as the invading forces were close enough for hand-to-hand combat, he apparently pretended to vomit, faking illness and thereby betraying his people. As a result, Swein was encouraged to sack Wilton, then move up to Salisbury, before returning to his ships – something that would have put him within a very short distance of Winchester.

One medieval historian directly linked the return of Swein to the St Brice's Day massacre. William of Malmesbury reports in his history that Swein's sister Gunhild had been among the St Brice's Day victims. Gunhild had apparently married a powerful jarl named Palling, often thought to be the same leader who, in 1001, had deserted King Æthelred after previously pledging his loyalty and receiving plentiful gifts of land, gold and silver. We can't verify either of these suggestions: there is no other evidence that Swein had a sister, and certainly not one living in England, and equally we have no way of securely connecting the two mentions of a man named Palling. Yet many historians find the suggestion plausible, as Swein's previous raids on England may well have given him a link to the mercenary forces and raiding parties that were still present there at the beginning of the eleventh century. In fact, an ancient DNA study makes this even more likely, as one of the victims from Oxford was shown to have been a second-degree relative of a man buried at Galgedil in Denmark. The two could have been half-siblings, uncle and nephew, or grandparent and grandchild. For this reason, it would not be surprising if those who died at the St John's College site had been operating in the same sphere as Swein had back in Denmark.

The *Chronicle* describes the following years of Swein's sustained attacks as a devastating time, with the English powerless against the invading forces. After the south coast, Swein targeted East Anglia the following year, raiding and burning towns, and killing both 'chief men' and the local people.

In 1005, however, the Vikings were turned back by a force greater than anything Æthelred could drum up, namely a widespread famine that devastated not only Britain but also large parts of continental Europe. The respite was brief. Although the Vikings returned home, they were back almost immediately, with a fleet arriving the following year at Sandwich. Æthelred tried his best to repel them, ordering 'the whole nation from Wessex and from Mercia to be called out', campaigning against the Vikings throughout harvest time, yet with little success. Intriguingly, the *Chronicle* entry for 1006 gives an insight into the Vikings' tactics: not only do we hear that they had a secure base on the Isle of Wight, from which they could provision themselves with whatever they needed, but they are also described as having 'prepared depots' that they could dip into across Wessex. In the raids that followed, the attackers apparently gathered provisions and treasures far and wide, carrying them back to their ships. While in Wessex, the *Chronicle* tells us, 'the people of Winchester could see the raiding army, proud and not timid, when they went by their gates to the sea, and fetched themselves provisions and treasures from over 50 miles from the sea'. Presumably, the town itself remained safe from attack: as the jewel in the West Saxon king's crown, its walls and defences would have been particularly well built.

Æthelred's fraught political situation is also reflected in his coinage. In the first decade of the eleventh century, he issued coins now known as the 'helmet type', because instead of the more usual crown, the king is shown wearing full armour. It is tempting to imagine that some of this imagery might have been intended for his enemies, in the knowledge that large sums of money might have to be paid as tribute again in the future.

The Vikings didn't have to wait long, in fact, for in 1006, after every shire in Wessex had been severely burned and raided, the king consulted his councillors, deciding once again to attempt a truce. The following year, £30,000 worth of tribute was paid to the Vikings.

We can trace where some of this money went by looking at archaeological finds and coin hoards back in Scandinavia. Take Norway, for example, where a catalogue of all the Anglo-Saxon coins in museum collections has recently been published. In the first two decades of the Viking Age, the coins remain pretty few in number, but that picture changes dramatically from the 980s. Out of the 4,230 coins catalogued, a total of 80 per cent come either from Æthelred or from his successor. The Æthelred coins must represent part of the tribute and demonstrate that many of those who collected it came from Norway, which could perhaps be taken to be proof that the sagas' Olaf Tryggvason really was the Olav mentioned in the 994 treaty. These coins – often found in hoards – could have represented the hidden earnings of Norwegians who took part in one of these campaigns: a tantalising glimpse into the real people and individuals who made up those Viking armies.

By 1008, Æthelred seems to have really stepped up his defences. That year, the *Chronicle* tells us, he ordered warships to be built all around England, one from each of what is described as 310

hides, while from those of 8 hides, a helmet and a mail coat was
to be made. The ships were finished a year later and gave him a
fleet allegedly larger than any seen before in England. Yet bizarrely,
Æthelred's efforts seem to have been in vain, as a dispute between
his ealdormen led one of them, Wulfnoth, to take off with twenty
ships, and another, Beorhtric, to follow with eighty; the latter
getting into trouble in a severe wind that thrashed the ships to
pieces. Those that remained were swiftly burned by Beorhtric. The
incident led to confusion and panic: the king, with another part of
the fleet, went home and other commanders and noblemen abandoned their ships, leaving their crew to take them back to London.
With that, the *Chronicle* records, they had 'let the whole nation's
labour waste'. Soon after, the Vikings returned and Æthelred's efforts
had no impact.

DELIVER US FROM EVIL

In the years between the 980s and 1005, the constant threat of
the Viking invaders must have weighed heavily not just on the
king's mind but also on the English people. By this time, Æthelred
had replaced most of the advisers in his court, who had caused
him trouble in the early years of his reign. New clerics were now
advising the king. Remarkably, there was a flurry of activity relating
to the church and to ensuring that society was ordered according
to good, Christian ways: estates that had been taken from churches
were restored to them; new churches were built; others were
furnished with books and treasures; and people were recruited into
religious life. All of this may have been a direct response to the
attackers from the sea because in the same way as Alcuin had

reported the Lindisfarne raid some two hundred years earlier, the belief was widespread that the invasions were God's punishment for misdeeds and a lack of devotion to Christianity. By being a good Christian and encouraging those around you to do the same, you might be able to appease God and stop the punishment.

Winchester experienced a similar investment in good, Christian ways. At Old Minster, the preceding decades had seen building work on an immense scale by Bishop Æthelwold. The church had been extended, with huge apses built to enclose the site of St Swithun's grave, the length between them, from north to south, exactly one hundred Long Roman feet, precisely mirroring the rotunda surrounding the Tomb of Christ in Jerusalem, as well as the one Charlemagne had built at his palace in Aachen. The building was monumental and sophisticated, unparalleled by anything that had been built in England up to that time. St Swithun, and his miracles, were clearly to be honoured. Unfortunately, Æthelwold's ambition and religious devotion had not been matched by his knowledge of engineering. The new structure failed almost at once. It had been built partially on top of a Roman street, and the softer ground alongside its packed gravel surface failed to support the weight, causing cracks to form and pretty soon the entire structure needed rebuilding. Undeterred, the bishop created a huge square tower instead on better foundations, and on 20 October 980, the Winchester community took part in a two-day spectacular to dedicate the new structure. King Æthelred, nine bishops and the leading men of the kingdom all took part.

Æthelwold would continue his scheme of improvements until his death four years later, and his successor, Ælfheah, took up the work in the early 990s. We even have a contemporary depiction: an artist illustrating a manuscript at around the same time included an image of the three-storey tower above the altar of Old Minster, complete with ropes pulling bells and a high domed roof crowned by a glorious, golden weathercock. A description of the latter can be found in an exceptionally long poem written by Wulfstan, cantor of Old Minster in the late tenth century. Of the tower, he says: 'There is an added embellishment in that a weathercock stands on its summit, adorned in gold, awe-inspiring to behold. It gazes down the entire countryside, soares over all the fields, able to behold the bright constellations of the starry North. It holds the sceptre of rule in its proud talons and stands above the entire populace of Winchester.'

Poems and illuminations in manuscripts of this type reveal something we might otherwise forget. These internal spaces, and events like the dedication in 980, were filled with sound and colour: glinting golden arches and painted columns; robes of the finest silks and fabrics; and sparkling jewels adorning books, crowns and reliquaries. In fact, St Swithun's reliquary was made of gold and decorated with the finest jewels, in keeping with his status as a provider of miracles and defender against attacks. One of the burials in Old Minster excavated by Martin Biddle and his team, which may well have belonged to a member of the West Saxon royal family, was found with the remains of gold thread embroidery around his skull, including a braid 1.6 centimetres wide woven with the thread: he also had silver garter hooks at his knees.

Next door, New Minster seems to have been extensively improved too. The sight of the two churches side by side must have been phenomenal, and we can only imagine what the Viking raiders thought of the imposing towers, in 1006, when they passed the gates of the town on their way back to their base on the Isle of Wight.

Another key tool in the king's and clerics' toolbox was the utilisation of the potent power of saints' relics. Veneration of saints was well established in England by the tenth century. Relics appealed especially, as one historian put it, because they were 'where heaven and earth met, points of contact between the human and divine'. This was the ultimate way that the living could directly come into contact with the saintly powers. Here the bigger and more universal saints were venerated but so also were those of local importance.

Between 995 and 1002, a large number of relics were moved from one place to another, likely also to ensure their safety in the event of a raid. For example, in 997, Æthelred arranged for the remains of his half-sister Edith, around whom a cult had sprung up, to be translated, and on 20 June 1001, he instructed for the remains of his half-brother Edward the Martyr in Shaftesbury Abbey to be moved. With Wessex under such severe threat, the king clearly had the religious institutions' protection on his mind. By this time, a cult had also appeared focusing on Edward and it seems likely that Æthelred was still dealing with the consequences of the scandal surrounding his half-brother's murder. God's wrath, which brought on the Viking attacks, might in his and his contemporaries' minds have been linked in part to that fateful event. At the same time, the minster of Bradford-on-Avon in Wiltshire was granted to the nuns of Shaftesbury for use as a refuge 'against the inroads of the barbarians'; being further from the sea and in a relatively well-protected valley, it was presumably considered a safe haven. It is possible that the late Anglo-Saxon church at Bradford-on-Avon, built around that time, was meant to have housed Edward's remains: whether it ever did, we will never know.

A surprising consequence of this focus on religious institutions was that the fine arts also seemed to flourish. To appeal to more people and spread the good word, you would need more books and there were both resources and expertise available for their production. Some of the books produced also included explicit instructions both for prayers against attack and for more practical defence. A letter from around this time specified that every Wednesday the mass *contra paganos* ('against the pagans') should be sung in all the larger religious houses across the kingdom.

Simultaneously, other art forms like sculpture and metalwork also started to be prioritised. It is perhaps ironic that a time of prolonged threat of serious attacks across the nation could also be one of so much positive development, but the same had happened a century before when Alfred was battling the Great Army.

THE VIKINGS AT HOME

Why, then, after such a long period of relative peace, did the attacks from Scandinavia start up again at the end of the tenth century? And importantly, who were they, and what did they do? Were they distinct armies that returned home each year or did they overwinter and remain a constant threat to the English? To understand this, and what happens next in the history of England, we also need to understand some of the key developments back in the Scandinavian homelands.

Heading to the turn of the first millennium, Scandinavia was a very different place from what it had been when the first raiders set their eyes to English shores two centuries previously. Pretty soon, the countries of Norway, Denmark and Sweden would emerge as nation-states, under separate kings: the process was already well under way in Denmark, and to a lesser degree in Norway, in the last half of the tenth century. England was deeply entangled in these events.

The problem we have with understanding this period of Scandinavian history is that most of it needs to be teased out of the medieval saga literature, primarily written down in the twelfth and thirteenth centuries, as their historicity is difficult to verify. Archaeology and other sources can, in some instances, help. In Denmark, a substantial monument testifies to processes that were taking place at precisely this point in time. If you visit the small town of Jelling today, you will find a white-painted medieval church that serves as a surprising companion to the two vast burial mounds set just behind it. Around the burial mounds is an enormous setting of stones in the shape of a ship, 360 metres long from end to end. The church is a replica of one constructed in timber back in the tenth century; a church that was among Denmark's first. The Jelling burial mounds are associated with King Gorm and his wife Thyra, who were the first in a new dynastic line that would establish the kingdom of Denmark in something very similar to its modern form. Built between the 940s and 970s, the mounds are also linked to Gorm's more famous son, Harald Bluetooth (whose nickname has been made famous as a technology essential to our daily lives), who erected one of two runestones there. The stone is dated to around 965–70 and has the inscription 'King Harald commanded this monument to be made in memory of Gorm, his father, and in memory of Thorvi [Thyra] his mother – that Harald who won the whole of Denmark for himself and Norway and made the Danes Christian.' The stone is taken as evidence that Denmark, at this stage, was a defined kingdom and one where the process of Christianisation had been accepted on a formal, national level. Similarly, Harald also apparently moved his father Gorm's remains into a Christian monument; one of many examples of manipulating an ancestor's bones to express religious beliefs.

Around the same time, Harald also engaged in a number of large-scale projects at home, demonstrating his power, control, wealth and military prowess. A series of new fortifications known as Ringforts were constructed across Denmark between 975 and 980, military defences on a scale unheard of in Scandinavia. He also strengthened the Danevirke, a defensive structure marking the southern boundary of Denmark with the powerful German empire; all of this at a time when there was a lull in raiding activity in

England, when Edgar, Edward and Æthelred were able to deal with internal affairs rather than fend off foreign invaders. The Jelling runestone states that Harald also won Norway. Other sources suggest he won that kingdom at the Battle of Limfjord around 970, after the fall of a Norwegian ruler by the name of Harald Greycloak. Crucially, control over Norway gave access to lucrative resources, including troops and tribute, but also desirable products such as furs, falcons, iron, soapstone and whetstones. Luxuries such as these not only played a fundamental part in Viking society as objects in themselves – in a culture where gift exchange and social stratification were key to garnering support and followers – but were also significant because the wealth they could generate helped reward loyalty and arm forces.

Norway did not stay in Danish hands for long, however, and Harald's attempt at expanding his southern border led to defeat at the hands of the German emperor Otto II. Still, the Denmark he shaped proved a far more powerful and centralised entity than had ever been seen before.

Something else changed at around the same time that had a crucial impact on the Viking world, possibly providing an increased incentive for raids in the west. Since the very start of the Viking Age, trading routes to the east, down the riverine ways of Eastern Europe into what is now Ukraine, Belarus and Russia, had brought vast quantities of Islamic silver to Scandinavia. Goods such as furs, amber and, above all, enslaved people were exchanged as far south and east as Constantinople and Baghdad, within a well-developed network of trading sites that later turned into substantial towns. The silver, in the shape of dirham coins, was of superior quality, sourced from the large number of mines littering the central Asian territories under control of the caliphate. Europe, in contrast, had fewer known sources of silver to exploit. In Scandinavia, the metal was used as one of the main means of payment, in lieu of coinage, which would not be introduced on a large scale until the eleventh century. Eastern silver thereby represented an invaluable resource for those with ambitions to rule and expand their dominion.

Studies of silver hoards – hidden stashes of wealth deposited in the ground for safekeeping – provide us with a valuable insight into how this influx of coins ebbed and flowed over time. Across several time periods there seems to be a gap, with fewer coins travelling north, and sometimes this fits in with changes in the political and economic situation in the caliphate.

It is particularly intriguing that in the late 970s to 980s, production of Islamic dirhams went into a serious decline, owing to internal factors in the caliphate that resulted in a change in economic conditions. In earlier periods of the Viking Age, researchers have observed a possible correspondence between the lack of a silver supply and episodes of increased raiding in the west. We now know that these furthest reaches of the Viking world were deeply connected, through trade routes and mobility, right from the start. Perhaps this, too, then was a reason why the search for wealth in the west once more became necessary towards the end of the millennium?

While Harald consolidated a kingdom at home, it was his son – and later his grandson – who would have the most profound impact on England in the decades to come. In 987, Bluetooth died, an event that would have a cataclysmic effect not just on the future of Denmark, but also on England. His death apparently occurred during a rebellion led by his own son and heir, Swein Forkbeard, who inherited a kingdom both large and powerful, and so was able to lead raids himself, with the support of his own retainers and those working for other allied magnates.

While the Danish links to England would soon become obvious, the Norwegian involvement is a little harder to verify, because almost all the information we have comes from the saga sources that deliberately present a high medieval view of the time when the nation was allegedly formed. While Norway – or *Norðvegr*, the Northern Way – was known as an entity from at least the ninth century, it was certainly not a unified country until much later. A ruler by the name of Harald Harfagri (Fairhair) is given in the saga sources as Norway's first unifying king, but this is almost certainly fiction. The only sources that may be contemporary with Harald's life are two poems that describe a battle at Hafrsfjord, outside modern-day Stavanger, that took place in the 870s. Harald is said to have emerged victorious over local petty kings and chieftains. According to the Icelandic chronologies, he died in the 930s and left behind several sons with different women. Of these, Eric Bloodaxe is said to have co-ruled with his father during his final years, subsequently fleeing to England to rule York. While there is little historical basis in the saga narrative to confirm this biography, an Eric *is* known from the *Chronicle* as ruling York in 948; whether these two are actually the same or if they were later conflated is impossible to tell.

Finally, from Sweden, we have practically no written sources suggesting involvement on any large scale in English politics. Traditionally, it has been thought that the Swedes mainly travelled eastwards, down the riverine routes of Eastern Europe, interacting and trading with the Rus. We now know that the picture is a little more complex, and that there certainly was contact between Sweden and Britain. Most interesting, perhaps, are inscriptions on a number of runestones that can be found dotted around the Swedish landscape. These large standing stones, which carry inscriptions and sometimes a decorative pattern, are found across Scandinavia, but were particularly popular in Sweden, and from the late tenth and early eleventh centuries, we find many with useful inscriptions. The stones would be raised in someone's memory or to honour a particular deed; this could be something achieved at home, like building a bridge, but more commonly, fighting abroad. Here, then, we have the specific names of individuals, and often the names of their relatives who raised the stones for them. Around thirty stones specifically mention journeys to England. Several seem to mention the tribute payments: Runestone 241 from Lingsberg in Uppland, for instance, was raised in memory of a man called Ulfríkr by his grandsons. 'He had taken two payments in England,' the runic inscription states, presumably relating to such tribute. Another is even more helpful to us: translated into English, it says, 'And Ulfr has taken three payments in England. That was the first that Tosti paid. Then Þorketill paid. Then Knútr paid.' We can assume that Þorketill is Thorkel the Tall, and the Knútr is Cnut the Great.

Several others refer to men who died in England and among these one is intriguing. The inscription reads, 'Gunnkell placed this stone in memory of Gunnarr, his father, Hróði's son. Helgi, his brother, laid him in a stone coffin in Bath in England.' Apart from a rough date in the eleventh century, we have no more details of this Gunnarr but the inscription must presumably date to a time when south-west England was under Scandinavian control, if a Swede were to have been granted such a permanent and apparently high-status burial as a stone coffin. Bath has very little evidence of Viking activity, one of very few objects found there being a sword that was discovered in a ditch outside what was one of the city's Saxon walls. The sword is known as an 'Ulfberht' type because it bears the inscription 'Ulfberht made me' in runes. Or at least that is what it is meant to say; the spelling is not quite right. This means that the maker of the Bath sword may well have been imitating swords thought to have been made in a workshop somewhere along the River Rhine in what is now Germany. With the sword discovered just outside the city gates, could it have been lost by someone taking part in a failed attack? Or was the sword's owner, like Gunnarr, someone resident in Bath when it was in Scandinavian hands?

THE COMING OF THE NORMANS

In 911, an event took place that would have an impact not only on the Frankish kingdom but eventually on the future of England. That year the Frankish king Charles the Simple granted Rouen, a town on the Seine, along with the surrounding region, to a Viking leader by the name of Rollo. The territory was given 'to the Norsemen of the Seine, that is, to Rollo and his companions, for the protection of the kingdom', according to a charter granted in the king's name a few years later. The intention of Charles, in other words, was to use Rollo and his compatriots to help protect them against other bands of Vikings. The territory would soon be named after these Northmen: Normandy. Scandinavians had plundered far and wide in Francia at least since the first recorded attack in 820. A crucial fact that is often overlooked is that the Vikings who were active in Francia were often the very same Vikings that harried the English shores: the documentary evidence makes this clear. In 879, for instance, the *Anglo-Saxon Chronicle* states that the raiding army that had settled at Fulham went across the sea to Ghent in the land of the Franks, settling for a year. In the following years, this army continued further inland, raiding, fighting and setting up camp each year.

How much territory was given to Rollo initially, however, nobody knows. The boundaries were never spelled out and the archaeology is practically non-existent: there are no Viking burials, no runic inscriptions and only a handful of Scandinavian-style metal objects to be found in this part of Normandy.

It is likely that when the territory was granted to Rollo, significant numbers of Scandinavians were already living there and by then it may have been under their control. The territory was extended westwards in 924, into an area where more Scandinavians had apparently recently settled.

Because of the lack of archaeological material, the number of Scandinavians who settled in Normandy is unknown. It's tempting to draw parallels with England, where our knowledge has changed drastically, thanks to things like metal-detected artefacts. In France, metal-detecting is illegal, and it has also been pointed out that the objects found in England – such as jewellery and brooches – display very specific Scandinavian characteristics that signal an identity: even if we're not necessarily conscious about it, we often wear and use clothes and things that convey messages about who we are and our place in society. A cross worn as a necklace, a turban or a hijab are obvious examples of religious symbols, but other signs, such as an expensive watch or handbag, or a car, can also be used to express our place in society. In the first half of the tenth century, competition between the West Saxons and the Scandinavians over territory may well have fuelled subtle or not-so-subtle ways of displaying which side you were on. Perhaps in Normandy there was no such need. The lack of burials with gravegoods might be explained by the control of the church, as it may have been forbidden, or the possibility that the settlers quickly converted to Christianity. The only real clue we have lies in the continued use of the Norse language, especially in place names, where we can find a significant number of Scandinavian elements, such as Caudebec (*Caldebec*, from Old Norse *kaldr*, 'cold', and *bekkr*, 'stream' – a name that can also be found in north-west England). Other names include Old Norse elements like *toft*, *dalr* and *hólmr* that survive as the French *tot*, *dal* and *houmet*. There are even surviving family names that stem from Scandinavian laws and rights: the names Dodeman and Floteman come from the Old Norse *dauðamaðr* ('man condemned to death') and *flóttamaðr* ('fugitive') respectively. Nevertheless, comparatively speaking, the impact of Old Norse on the French language has been minute and certainly nothing like the impact of Norse on English. Intriguingly, many of the settlers may well have come from the Danelaw, not directly from Scandinavia.

The Scandinavians successfully and swiftly mixed and integrated with the Franks, which means that the new identity, that of the Normans, appeared quickly. In the early years, however, it is difficult to know the true nature of Rollo's rule, but clearly he had an arrangement with Charles, perhaps something similar to the agreement that was made between Alfred and Guthrum in England only a couple of decades earlier.

Rollo's background is obscure. There has been a longstanding debate on whether he came from Norway or Denmark, with both countries claiming this Rolfr, as he is known in Norse sources, as theirs. Most of the information we have comes from Dudo of St Quentin, whose accounts are questionable at best. In its later manuscripts, the *Anglo-Saxon Chronicle* records that Rollo invaded Normandy in 876 and ruled for fifty-three years.

Rollo and his settlers were not the only Scandinavians to be interested in Normandy and over the decades that followed, several other Scandinavian-led takeover attempts are recorded, likely from men of wildly different backgrounds, since Scandinavian Normandy was a real mismatch of identities. Nonetheless, Rollo successfully established his dynasty and at his death around 928, his son William Longsword acceded to the territory, followed in 943 by Rollo's grandson Richard I, after William was assassinated.

Richard I, also known as Richard the Fearless, would have what would prove to be an important relationship with England and with Æthelred, forging a treaty with his English counterpart in 991 that included the provision that Richard was not to receive 'any of the king's men or his enemies'. Although the identities of those enemies are not specified, it seems possible that this clause was designed to end the support Scandinavian raiders may have received from Normans allowing them to shelter on their shores in between attacks on England.

It appears, however, that almost a decade later, in 1000, this treaty may have been forgotten, as now the Viking fleet is recorded to have travelled to Normandy, presumably able to use it as a safe port, thanks perhaps to the different views of Duke Richard II, who had by then succeeded Richard I. There was also an English attack on Normandy recorded around 1002, which further suggests animosity between them.

Yet that same year a new change was in the making as negotiations were initiated between Æthelred and Richard II, culminating in another event that would be instrumental to England's future: the marriage of Æthelred and Richard's younger sister, Emma.

The daughter of Richard I – one of his nine children – and the Danish-descended Gunnor, Emma was the great-granddaughter of Rollo, giving her Scandinavian ancestry on both sides of the family. She would also be the great-aunt of William the Conqueror, something that William would actively use to help justify his own right to England some decades later.

In 1002, probably aged in her late teens or early twenties, Emma was sent to England to marry Æthelred as his second wife. The marriage was clearly a strategic one, aiming to strengthen an alliance between England and Normandy in light of the harrowing attacks on both English and Norman shores by Scandinavian raiders. Æthelred had apparently accused Emma's brother, Duke Richard II, of harbouring the Vikings and enabling their raids, and the marriage was designed to ensure the duke's allegiance. The alliance proved unusual, as although in the past several English princesses had been married off to French and German rulers, no English king had married a foreign wife for almost 150 years.

Emma was given the English name Ælfgifu, one with royal connotations in her new homeland: it was the name of several women in the royal family and probably also the same name as Æthelred's first wife. Such renaming was not uncommon at the time and was likely a deliberate strategy by Æthelred to make her fit better into his dynasty. Although other queens were more resistant to using their new names, Emma seems to have embraced them both, likely understanding well that it gave her a foot in each camp. In any case, she had grown up multilingual at the court in Normandy.

The marriage resulted in three children: sons Edward (later known as the Confessor) and Alfred, and daughter Godgifu. Few sources say much about Emma's political activity in these years and it seems her role was mainly one of being a wife and a mother, the most common description of her being *conlaterana regis*: 'she who is at the King's side'. In this first decade of her career she was the least powerful, and one source, William of Malmesbury, suggests that she and her husband were never on good terms with each other. These first two decades of the eleventh century were marked by ongoing trouble and threats of Scandinavian attacks and the peacemaking marriage appears to have done little to prevent Norman aid to Viking attackers.

With her own Danish ancestry, it is difficult to know what Emma might have felt about the situation she found herself in, especially in the aftermath of the St Brice's Day massacre. But pretty soon things would change severely for the worse, not least with the return of Swein Forkbeard.

DUKES' GRAVES

M uch ink has been spilled over the question of whether Rollo was Danish or Norwegian because the question has inevitably been bound up with both countries' national pride, not least in the nineteenth and twentieth centuries when new national identities were being formed and reaffirmed in Scandinavia. A few years ago, researchers tried once and for all to get an answer using modern DNA analysis. After much negotiation, a Norwegian team was given access to burials in the floor of the monastery in Fécamp, Normandy, the coffins of which were said to have contained the bones of Richard I and Richard II, grandson and great-grandson of Rollo. Rollo himself has a tomb in Rouen, but it had been opened previously and shown to be empty. In Fécamp, however, the researchers were in luck. Not only did the lead coffins in the floor contain bones, but they also appeared to contain enough material for DNA extraction. With the press looking on, the team took samples and rushed them back to the lab in Copenhagen. Sadly, this was where their luck ended. Before any DNA could be successfully extracted, the radiocarbon dates delivered the blow: one of the skeletons dated to the early eighth century, while the other was even older, apparently dating as far back as the third century BC. There was no way these bones could have belonged to men born in the tenth century and therefore nothing that could link them to the Normans. Nobody knows why such very early bones had found their way into the lead coffins, or when they were placed there, and Rollo's geographical origins remain hidden.

SWEIN FORKBEARD

In the English story, the first time we come across Swein is during the raids on England in 991, when he was a member of the group that defeated the English at the Battle of Maldon with Olaf Tryggvason. By this point, Swein already held the kingdom of Denmark. Soon after Maldon, he returned to Scandinavia and turned his attention eastwards, extending his domain in Sweden by subordinating a group known as the Svear. However, in 992 or 993, Erik, king of the Svear, attacked Denmark with the support of his brother-in-law, the Christian Polish ruler Boleslav. Although the medieval historian Adam of Bremen claims that Swein was forced into exile until Erik died fourteen years later, this is unlikely to be true. Instead, Erik died during the campaign or soon after, and Swein married his Polish widow. Forkbeard was then acknowledged as overlord of Sweden by Erik's son Olof Skötkonung (the 'Tribute-king').

A couple of points are important here. First, it is crucial to understand that the people who became some of the most significant protagonists in the English story in the late tenth and eleventh century were part of a much wider, European scene. The interaction with Poland, through Swein's marriage, shows alliances were formed in easterly directions as well. Swein's wife, whose name is unconfirmed but who is referred to as Gunhild in the medieval Icelandic sagas, was apparently the daughter of Mieszko I of Poland. Second, Swein's actions show that the significant income that could be generated through raiding or tribute in England fuelled the ambitions of Scandinavians back home, allowing them to pay for the logistics and loyalty needed to extend their reach. We have numerous sources to inform us of Swein's life, but much of the information is known to be false, for instance the particularly hostile comments made about him by Adam of Bremen in his *Gesta Hammaburgensis ecclesiae Pontificum* – the *History of the Archbishops of Hamburg-Bremen*. This source reminds us that such writers were far from objective. In Adam's case, his problem was that he was dissatisfied with Swein because the latter did not acknowledge the authority of the Archbishop of Hamburg-Bremen.

In any case, after his activity in Sweden, Swein led another raid on England in 994, again with Olaf Tryggvason. Olaf subsequently returned to Norway, where he was accepted as king in the Trøndelag region, with the help of money obtained in England through his deal with King Æthelred.

Incidentally, it seems all the money obtained in England also had an impact on the development of coinage in Scandinavia. The economy in the homelands was largely based on silver, usually through bullion or silver ingots. The coins received as tax and tribute would normally have been melted down and turned into weighable and often *wearable* currency, like arm-rings. There were no national currencies resembling those that Æthelred and his ancestors created. Some coins were minted at Hedeby in southern Denmark (now Germany) from at least the ninth century, but coinage bearing legends only appears in the 990s. A few coins were struck in Swein's name during the reign of Olav as king of Norway, modelled directly on English coins struck between 991 and 997. Some coins may also have been associated with Harald Bluetooth, but what is certain is that by the first decade of the eleventh century, well-made, English-looking coinage flourished in Denmark. The rulers who travelled west had clearly taken lessons from the successes of their English counterparts.

THORKELL THE TALL AND
THE BEGINNING OF THE END

'Yet in the end, he stands as an example of a failed hero; one who, having no one to tell a story, faded into the mists of time, leaving only his name behind.'

Ann Williams (2016)

There is one person who is key not just to the downfall of Æthelred but also to what was to follow, but who is often forgotten: Thorkell the Tall. It has even been said that without him the future Danish conquest could not have taken place. Thorkell appears on the scene in full force in 1009. According to saga tradition, he was the son of a Danish earl and had become successful back home in Scandinavia. That year he arrived off the coast of Sandwich with a large fleet and was immediately joined by other Viking forces from far and wide, who took to raiding and plundering across the country for the next three years. The devastation that followed was immense and the chronicler of the Peterborough manuscript of the *Anglo-Saxon Chronicle* makes it clear he thinks poor tactics were to blame: the misfortunes, he says, were due to a delay in making decisions and especially a delay in offering tribute.

Eventually, aided by internal treachery, a band of Vikings managed to enter the city of Canterbury, where they captured several abbots, bishops and, most importantly, Archbishop Ælfheah. Apparently free to stay in the cathedral city for as long as they pleased, the marauders finally moved on to London. Here the chronicler and later sources describe what happened in graphic detail: a week after a *gafol* payment of a staggering £48,000 was made to the Vikings in London, another demand of £3,000 was made for the archbishop's release. Ælfheah apparently refused to allow anyone to pay this, enraging his captors. The Vikings had set up camp at Greenwich on the Thames and on 19 April they held an assembly, or perhaps some kind of trial. The meeting turned raucous, as the Scandinavians had had wine brought to them from 'the South' (presumably Normandy), and they were soon outrageously drunk. The archbishop became their target: the *Chronicle* describes how he was cruelly and humiliatingly tortured as they threw the remains of their feast at him; the most sacred and holy servant of Christianity in England pelted with bones and the half-eaten heads of oxen. Finally, a member of the army struck the archbishop at the back of the head with an axe in a blow that killed him. Ælfheah had previously helped bring peace to another Viking band led by Olav, back in 994; perhaps this had made him overconfident in his ability to negotiate with his captors. The following day the Vikings allowed the body to be taken away and buried in the minster church that would later be known as St Paul's Cathedral, and very soon after a cult emerged.

After the money was finally paid in 1012, the Viking force dispersed, presumably returning home to Scandinavia, but in a remarkable turn of events forty-five of the ships remained and instead offered their services to King Æthelred as mercenaries. This fleet was led by none other than Thorkell the Tall. In return for helping to protect Æthelred's kingdom, his men received food and clothes. It seems that for Thorkell, with an army to manage and maintain, and probably no territory of his own to return to, there was more profit and success to be had in England than in Scandinavia. With his kingdom's defences severely weakened by the continual raids, a presumably exasperated Æthelred took on the mercenaries – it would have been nothing new to him and keeping his enemy close may have seemed like a good approach. That very year Æthelred introduced a new type of tax called *heregeld* – 'army-tax', a form of regular taxation that would allow him to pay the mercenaries. This term later morphed into the concept of *Danegeld*, although this word is more commonly (though incorrectly) used for all sorts of payments made to the Vikings.

Thorkell's worth would soon be tested when Swein Forkbeard returned to England in the summer of 1013, establishing a base at Gainsborough on the eastern bank of the River Trent and receiving submission of the so-called Danelaw area north of Watling Street. Afterwards, Swein moved south, conquering Oxford, Wallingford and even Winchester: there, in the heart of Wessex, the city submitted without a fight, offering Swein hostages. The Viking also unsuccessfully attempted an attack on London, where King Æthelred was based. He next went to Bath and received the submission of the south-west, at which point Æthelred admitted defeat to avoid further destruction. England now lay in Danish hands, with Swein Forkbeard its ruler. After initially staying with Thorkell's force, Æthelred decided to flee the country and travel across the Channel to Normandy, to where he had already sent his wife Emma and the two Æthelings Edward and Alfred to safety, as well presumably as their sister Godgifu, whose whereabouts are not mentioned. Notably, Æthelred's sons from his first marriage remained in England, as they were older and more likely to be either militarily active or at least capable of defending themselves. Tensions within this generation of sons would later come to breaking point: it has been suggested that this division may have been the start of that.

The reasons behind Forkbeard's invasion have often been discussed. Medieval legends have it that the alleged death of his sister in the St Brice's Day massacre provided the trigger. But as many have pointed out, that happened more than a decade before and wouldn't justify a full conquest. An intriguing suggestion is that Thorkell may have represented a challenge to Swein, and to the stability of the Danish kingdom he ruled over: with the increased wealth Thorkell must have obtained by working directly for Æthelred, he could well have been a threat to Swein. Thorkell also had family connections and powerful allies in what was then eastern Denmark, now Sweden. With Thorkell's money, connections and reputation as a powerful warlord, Swein may have seen the necessity of stopping him in his tracks.

Sometime between Swein Forkbeard's arrival on English soil in 1013, and his death early the following year, a wedding took place somewhere in England. The groom was Swein's son, Cnut, and the bride, a woman by the name of Ælfgifu, the daughter of Ælfhelm, a Northumbrian ealdorman, a member of an influential Mercian aristocratic family with close ties to King Æthelred. Back in the 980s, Ælfgifu's wealthy uncle Wulfric Spot had entered the king's entourage and a decade later her father appears in royal charters. Her two brothers Wulfheah and Wulfgeat followed their father into politics. Ælfhelm's role as an ealdorman gave him authority over much of the region and his wider family belonged to a circle of influential figures in the north of England; members of a faction of northern nobles. We still don't know the details of how this region of England was administered in the late tenth and early eleventh centuries, but it seems likely that aristocrats such as these acted as an important link between King Æthelred's royal court and the north. But in the first few years of the new millennium, something happened to cause this particular family to fall from grace: Wulfric died in around 1002 and for reasons unknown, in 1006, Ælfhelm was executed by the king and his sons blinded. While Ælfgifu survived the palace intrigue unscathed, what happened to her in the following years is a mystery, until she emerges as the new wife of England's future king. Why her? The choice may well have been a strategic move for Swein, allowing him to create ties with the northern English aristocracy through his son; a way to help his position in the future.

To understand the circumstances around the union, we need to backtrack to the years around Swein's invasion and early rule. The north of England seems to have been particularly important to him, which can be seen from his choice of Gainsborough (in Lincolnshire) as a command base, and from the suggestion that he may have been planning a coronation in York just before his early death. To marry his son to the daughter of a family so deeply entangled in the networks of northern power would therefore have ensured him vital support. Soon after their wedding, Ælfgifu bore Cnut two sons: Swein and Harold (later known by the nickname Harefoot), born sometime between 1013 and Cnut's second marriage in 1017.

Swein's rule over England was to be very short-lived, as the Danish king died on 3 February 1014, apparently from illness. According to William of Malmesbury, however, local legend had it that it was St Edmund who led to Swein's demise: the saint appeared to him in a vision and complained about the misery the Dane was causing his people. When Swein replied insolently, St Edmund struck him on the head with a blow so hard that it killed him. We don't know what happened to Ælfgifu after Swein's death, though Cnut returned to Denmark and she would likely have followed him. However, around this time, a curious story appeared about an English *matrona* – a woman – and the body of Swein Forkbeard. On his death, Swein was apparently buried in York, but according to the eleventh-century chronicler Thietmar of Merseburg, an unknown English woman took it upon herself to exhume the body and repatriate it to Denmark, concerned that it would be destroyed by Æthelred in revenge when the king returned to England. It has been suggested that this woman was none other than Ælfgifu, anxious to keep her father-in-law safe, because the account makes it clear that this was a woman with important political allies and connections at court. The body was moved to Roskilde to be buried alongside Cnut's grandfather, Harald.

With Swein dead, his men and followers were determined that his son Cnut, who had come across to raid with his father, should be elected king. The recently conquered English disagreed, however, sending for Æthelred to be their ruler once more. Æthelred dispatched his son Edward across the Channel with messengers to speak on his behalf, declaring that if they accepted him once again he would be gracious and improve on everything they disliked about his former rule, as long as they swore loyalty. It was clearly enough, as Æthelred was reinstated and all Danish kings were outlawed from England 'forever'. Æthelred returned to the throne, with Thorkell apparently still by his side, but Cnut, despite being outlawed, did not return to Denmark. Instead, he remained in England and gained the loyalty of people in Lincolnshire: Æthelred fought against him but the Dane escaped by ship, stopping off only briefly to mutilate hostages that had previously been granted to his father, sadistically cutting off their hands and noses.

After the death of his father, and even though he had been chased out of England back to Denmark at last, it is clear that Cnut's appetite for the west had been whetted. With his brother in charge of Denmark, and no political home for him there, Cnut appears to have forged his own networks to assemble an army, including allies from Norway. When conflict raged between Æthelred and Edmund Ironside in 1015, Cnut clearly saw an opportunity. Raiders and invaders often took advantage of political turmoil to make a move, and now Cnut had contacts of his own, not least a large number of English collaborators and defectors, no doubt helped by the bonds he had forged through his marriage to Ælfgifu of Northampton.

In 1015, Cnut launched renewed attacks on England, initially with success in the south-west, where by Christmas the kingdom of Wessex recognised him as overlord. Several reasons lay behind his success, not least the devastation that his father had wreaked upon the kingdom. Cnut had also taken advantage of the fact that Æthelred was sick while the internal conflict with Edmund Ironside raged. By now the eldest of Æthelred's surviving sons, Edmund had defied his father to marry the widow of a Danelaw thegn murdered by one of Mercia's ealdormen, Eadric Streona, who had been one of the king's dominant advisers. The union was a strategic move on Edmund's behalf, earning him the submission of much of the Midlands, which would come in handy later, and it may have been the reason behind Cnut's move straight to the south-west – avoiding Edmund and the strife in the heart of England.

However, around the same time, Eadric, who had gathered an army on Æthelred's behalf, defected from the English side and joined Cnut's force, taking forty ships with him. Edmund tried to hold on to the north-east by seeking an alliance with the Northumbrian Earl Uthred, but this was not to last: when Cnut and Eadric headed north, Uthred abandoned Edmund and submitted to the Dane instead. Taking no chances, Cnut had Uthred executed and replaced him with his own brother-in-law, the Norwegian Erik of Lade. In the meantime, on St George's Day, 23 April 1016, Æthelred died in London. Edmund arranged for his father to be buried in St Paul's, which may have been the only possible alternative to him, seeing as Wessex – and Winchester – had submitted to Cnut. Yet London had always been close to Æthelred's heart, and this may have made it a favoured location.

Edmund Ironside was elected king, and he put up an admirable fight against Cnut. Eventually, a series of clashes culminated on 18 October 1016 in the Battle of Assandun, a location thought to be in Essex. At some point previously, Eadric Streona had changed sides again, returning to the English, but perhaps fearing the upcoming battle, he deserted to Cnut a final time. Edmund Ironside was defeated and the English suffered heavy losses. There are obituary lists from Ely that include numerous of the landed aristocracy of the region who fought and died on Edmund's side. Curiously, in another record from the same place, we hear that in the course of the encounter, the relics of a saint by the name of Wendreda of March were carried into battle by the monks of Ely. We know little about Wendreda, except that she was a female saint who was important locally and had once founded a nunnery at March in Cambridgeshire. The *Liber Eliensis* notes that after his victory Cnut seized the relics and had them moved to Canterbury, keeping the reliquary – a gold shrine set with costly jewels – safe, so either he understood and respected the saint's religious importance or he did it for pragmatic reasons. It has been speculated that Cnut made this move strategically so that he could continue to display the relics on his campaign, something that would have been common throughout Europe at the time. Although St Wendreda may not have been widely known, she was, it has been pointed out, English: the fact that she did not make a saintly intervention to stop her bones from being taken may have implied divine support for the Scandinavian invaders.

Later that year, Cnut and Edmund met at Deerhurst in Gloucestershire, on the River Severn, agreeing to divide the country between them, with Edmund receiving Wessex and Cnut Mercia. Yet the arrangement would prove short-lived.

IRONSIDE

As Æthelred turned out to be a prolific producer of offspring – he fathered many children both with his first wife Ælfgifu of York and his second wife Emma of Normandy – Edmund Ironside's path to kingship had not been obvious from the start. Understandably, in time tensions between the sons had become rife; not least later, when those Æthelred fathered with Emma faced competition from the sons of Cnut. Æthelred's eldest son Æthelstan had initially been set to be the heir but died in 1014 before he had the chance to get to power. It is unclear what happened to three of Æthelred's other sons: Ecgberht, Edgar and Eadred all disappeared from the records between 1005 and 1012, so they most likely died. This left only Edmund and Eadwig. Being the eldest, Edmund clearly had ambitions to rule. However, after Æthelred's death, as the child of his father's first wife, not of his latest, Edmund's position was uncertain. To make matters worse, according to the life of Edward the Confessor written some fifty years later, when Emma was pregnant with Edward – Edmund's half-brother – all the Englishmen swore that they would accept the boy child she carried as king. Perhaps this, and the fact that when Swein had conquered England only Emma's children – and not Ælfgifu's – were sent to Normandy for protection, was among the causes behind Edmund's later rebellion against his father. The manner of Edmund's death is not recorded in any contemporary sources but from the eleventh century onwards various tales, each wilder than the last, report that not only was it a case of foul play, but it was also both painful and humiliating. Adam of Bremen, in the 1070s, states simply that he was poisoned, but in the twelfth century Henry of Huntingdon puts the blame on the son of Eadric, the ealdorman. Edmund died, says Henry, when one evening he had to retire to his house to relieve a call of nature. Eadric's son had hidden himself in the latrine and when the king sat down, he stabbed Ironside twice from beneath, leaving the short dagger still in his bowels. A similar theme is reported by Geffrei Gaimar in his *Estoire des Engleis*, but with the offensive weapon apparently being a crossbow.

At some point, Edmund Ironside's remains appear to have ended up in Winchester Cathedral and his name is painted on one of the mortuary chests. In addition, a marble slab, located on one of the screens of the presbytery, bears the inscription 'Here lies King Edmund son of King Æthelred'. The letter forms suggest the inscriptions were made in the later twelfth century, but the slab itself was moved there only in the early nineteenth century from elsewhere in the cathedral. It is possible that the slab once marked the location of a tomb.

But there is a problem: the written accounts state that Edmund Ironside was interred in Glastonbury and there is no record anywhere of his remains having been moved to Winchester. Edmund's burial took place in 1016 and the choice of Glastonbury may have been made because its monastery already housed his grandfather and great-grandfather. The decision could also have been strategic on Cnut's behalf: it was away from Winchester and London, both of which held crucial political importance. Winchester was still the seat of power in Wessex, and the home of the ancestral burials, while London was rapidly becoming a new political battle-ground. London had been Æthelred's favoured city and his choice of burial location, and Cnut was still working hard to maintain the Londoners' allegiance. By removing the body of the king to a less convenient location, Cnut lessened the chance that it might become a rallying point for those who did not support him. It has also been pointed out that the funeral itself may have been of strategic use to Cnut: the hundred-mile journey Edmund's body had to make could have helped the transition to the new reign, especially if Cnut took part in the funeral himself. This strategic investment in Edmund's burial would continue. On 30 November 1032, on the sixteenth anniversary of his death, Cnut would travel to Glastonbury to pay his respects at Edmund's tomb in the abbey, laying down a cloak decorated with peacock feathers; perhaps a garment made of precious, Byzantine silk. It has been suggested that this was a deliberate act by Cnut to reinforce his position of power, reminding anyone in attendance that his right to the throne was a result of the treaty he had made with Edmund to divide the country, until the former's untimely death.

Glastonbury Abbey claims to have kept Edmund's tomb for several hundred years and there is no record of his translation throughout the Middle Ages. But if the inscription in Winchester really was made in the late twelfth century, one of the sites must be fabricating evidence. An alternative explanation is that Cnut's visit and gift of a royal cloak could have been the result of all, or some, of Edmund's remains being moved to Winchester, which was among Cnut's efforts to make Old Minster into his family mausoleum. The record states that he paid homage 'as a brother'; William of Malmesbury recorded a century later that Cnut was accustomed to describing Edmund this way.

DATES

Scientifically dating the bones is one key task, in order to find out if they really could have belonged to the names listed on the chests. So often, so-called relics found in churches turn out to be of the wrong date entirely. The only reliable method of dating bones is radiocarbon dating, but even that is not without its problems. First, most radiocarbon dates will provide you with a relatively wide range, sometimes as much as a hundred years or more. Second, radiocarbon dates can be problematic because they can be affected by diet: if you eat a lot of seafood, the dates can be skewed because the carbon we date in bones comes from the carbon that was consumed during a person's life. If you eat mainly a terrestrial diet, that's not a problem, but carbon that comes from fish or other marine sources is different. In terrestrial food sources, such as plants and animals, the carbon we date comes straight from the atmosphere and the radiocarbon clock – which allows us to date archaeological materials – starts ticking straight away.

The Watlington hoard

The Alfred jewel: a gold, enamel and rock crystal *aestel*
bearing the inscription 'Alfred ordered me to be made'

Sarcophagus of Queen Eadgyth from Magdeburg Cathedral

Tenth-century St Peter's coin, with a sword and Thor's hammer

Frances Burney, an author

replen . ut cum of caelestis spon
si thalamum ualeaus ingre
di · quod ipse ·

Illumination of
Old Minster drawn
c. 994, from *The
Benedictional of
St Æthelwold*

Eleventh-century 'helmet type' coin of Æthelred

Human remains from Ridgeway Hill, Weymouth, associated with the 1002 St Brice's Day massacre

Runestone 241 from Uppland, Sweden, raised in memory of Ulfríkr by his grandsons. Ulfríkr had taken two 'payments' in England

Grave marker bearing the inscription 'Here lies Gunni, the Earl's companion'

Tomb below a niche in the south screen of the presbytery, with the inscription 'Here lies Richard son of King William the Elder, and Duke Beorn'

Emma receiving the *Encomium* with Edward and Harthacnut watching, from *Encomium Emmae Reginae*

Emma and Cnut by the altar in New Minster, from the New Minster *Liber Vitae*

Runestone from Jelling, Denmark, raised by Harald Bluetooth

Section of the Bayeaux Tapestry

Drawing of the tomb of Earl Beorn and
Richard, son of William the Conqueror,
by F.J. Baigent, which was opened in 1887

Carbon that gets into the ocean and in turn into fish, however, stays there for a very long time, up to around four hundred years on average. This means that the carbon we date in anyone who has consumed a lot of fish could also be up to four hundred years too old. Fortunately, there are ways to assess how much marine protein someone has had in their diet so that we can make a pretty good estimate of how much of the older carbon to account for.

When the dates from the bone chests come through and are corrected, where needed, for seafood consumption, the results are as hoped: although the findings are broad, the bones that have been tested date to the early medieval or early Norman period. This is especially intriguing for the two juveniles, because it makes a Viking Age or Norman date for their death very likely.

CHEST V

CONQUEST

Wini d. 670

Cnut d. 1035

Ælfwyn d. 1042

Emma d. 1052

Rufus d. 1100

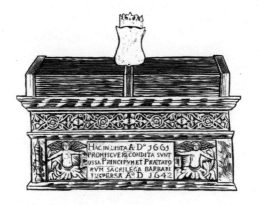

DORSET, 1646

*B*runo Ryves *unwraps the leatherbound book he has just received from the printing press in Oxford and holds it in his hands, gingerly turning the precious pages. It's the culmination of three years of hard work, finally compiled into a single volume:* The Mercurius Rusticus, OR The Countries Complaint of the barbarous Outrages committed by the sectaries of this late flourishing kingdom together with a brief chronology of the battels, sieges, conflicts, and other most remarkable passages, from the beginning of this unnatural war, to the 25th of March, 1646. *To play a part in the Civil War that raged across the country, Ryves, a Royalist, turned his efforts to journalism. Here he could employ what he had learned as a vicar and royal chaplain: he was regularly complimented for his notable, florid style as a preacher. The catalyst had been the night that he, his wife and his four children were torn from their beds, having all their possessions seized and being chased outside, finally having to hide under a hedge in the rain before being rescued and supported by Lord Arundel. A few months later, Ryves began to publish regular issues of a newsbook, in which he detailed the murders, robberies and plundering carried out by the Parliamentarians, with a specific emphasis on the atrocious sacrilege directed towards the country's cathedrals.*

Taking in the craftmanship of the engraved frontispiece in his collected volume, he turns to one of the events that really stayed with him: the attack on Winchester Cathedral in December 1642. At the time Ryves was a member of the Royalist army and served on the

Council of War, so he had access to informants throughout the country. Based on reports he received, he wrote a description of the event in his newsletter of 24 February 1643, merely ten weeks after it took place, and has included it in his new compilation. Ryves knows Winchester well and wanted his readers to know of its importance, setting out the city's former significance as a royal seat and the magnificence of its cathedral. Rereading his account, he is pleased with his detailed and stirring words, right down to his description of the beating drums and colours flying, and the order in which the Parliamentarians desecrated the building. He reminds himself of the way they targeted the ancient dead, beginning with Bishop Fox, defacing his chapel and breaking its painted glass windows. After directing their malice towards the numerous other bishops around the church, the soldiers set their sights on those chests that Fox had so piously placed on top of the choir screens: 'We could not have imagined', Ryves now reads out loud, 'that any thing but the like Piety that here inshrined them, or a Resurrection should ever have disturbed the repose of these venerable, yet not Popish Reliques.'

He is pleased he could report that the destruction of the chests was stopped before it was complete, that only the chests inscribed with the names of the bishops, of Emma and of some of the kings had been targeted. He often wonders how much remained of those bones. How much could be salvaged, collected and reinterred afterwards? He knows that now, four years later, the cathedral is still in disrepair; its stained-glass western window still shattered.

What Ryves doesn't know is that it will take another fifteen years for the bones to be recovered and placed in new chests matching those that were made by Bishop Fox, the fragmented remains of the four destroyed chests having been divided between two new ones. A Dutch artist, William Schelling, will visit on 8 September 1662 and describe the new chests as plain and without inscriptions. Eventually these two chests will be painted as well, and on one side will be a permanent reminder of the fate that befell the others: 'In this chest AD 1661 were promiscuously laid together the bones of the princes and prelates which had been scattered about by sacrilegious barbarism in the year AD 1642.' On the other side, the list of names of the five thought to be distributed between them: Wini, Cnut, Ælfwyn, Emma and Rufus.

A SCANDINAVIAN EMPIRE

Cnut's conquest of 1016 has been called England's *neglected* conquest, especially in comparison to that of 1066. But even though it was not as long-lasting, historians argue, it was no less important. Reigning for almost two decades, Cnut should certainly be considered an immensely successful king, not least because this was the only time a king ruled England, Norway and Denmark at the same time. Granted, his father Swein had – if briefly – almost done the same, as he had been the king of England and Denmark and overlord of both Norway and Sweden. It is also puzzling to compare the memory of Cnut with that of Alfred, the two of them the only monarchs of England ever to have been given the epithet 'the Great': yet it is mainly the latter whose impact most people seem to really appreciate. Alfred gained much of his fame for his fight against the Vikings, so much so that he is usually credited with having 'defeated' them. It is somewhat ironic that the only other king with a comparative label was a Viking.

In the saga dealing with Cnut's life, he is described as extremely tall and strong, and outstandingly handsome, with a fair complexion, thick blond hair and beautiful, piercing eyes: handsome, that is, if one ignored his nose, which was slightly crooked, too thin and too high set. While the saga writer is keen to assert Cnut's strength and positive qualities, there was one area he did not excel in. Like his father, grandfather and great-grandfather before him, Cnut was not very reflective. 'None of them,' the author says, 'were great thinkers.' Yet this description seems at odds with a king who so successfully ruled a North Sea empire for several decades.

Back in that summer of 1013, Swein had prepared for his invasion of England with a specific target in mind: conquest, not merely raids. Ships, supplies, weapons, strategy, everything was meticulously planned ahead of the mission. Swein's previous experience and in-depth knowledge of the conditions in England no doubt helped enormously. His kingdom of Denmark was in the safe hands of his eldest son Harald, who was well aware that he needed an iron grip to quell any lingering resentment relating to Swein's rebellion against his own father Bluetooth. But this was the first time a Scandinavian ruler could leave his home country and feel safe in the knowledge that it was well protected. One day Swein summoned his younger son Cnut, eager to hear his views ahead of the invasion. Cnut had been offered the chance to take part, and there can be little question that he understood the opportunity this gave him. With Harald as the heir, Cnut was the spare. By helping his father gain new land, this might also pave the way for him, in time, to gain territory of his own. This, then, may have been the precise moment at which Cnut's future was determined and with it, England's.

Cnut's early success as a ruler owed much to the way he gained the throne in the first place. Edmund had only had lukewarm support in some quarters and Cnut's use of English collaborators helped him along. Ultimately, the English were weary of decades of war, and the potential for political stability must have been an attractive one, especially from a ruler who might – finally – be able to stave off further Viking attacks. With such a large territory to control, Cnut had to appease both the English and the settled Scandinavian population, as well as those who were somewhere in between: English nobles who had swapped sides in previous regimes.

Ruling what essentially amounted to an empire, across three different countries, required a well-functioning system of administration. Throughout the early medieval period, monarchs surrounded themselves with a series of advisers and nobles, and during Cnut's rule in particular, none more so than the earls. When he took complete power over England in 1017, he divided the country into four: Wessex, the country's control centre, with Winchester as its nucleus, he kept for himself; East Anglia went to Thorkell; Mercia to Eadric; and Northumbria to Erik.

The word *eorl*, in earlier English literature, used to mean nobleman or warrior. However, in prose from the ninth century onwards, the word changed meaning to describe a high-ranking Scandinavian leader, thanks to the very similar word that was in use in Old Norse, *jarl*. When Cnut came to power in 1016, he gave the word *eorl* more of an official status, assigning the title to all the new provincial governors he appointed, though any *ealdormen* still in power could keep that title.

In addition to the myriad of historical accounts, we also have information about these particular people from contemporary charters, which typically record events such as the grant and exchange of land. Such charters usually include a list of witnesses and from those lists we can begin to reconstruct the names of the earls in both Cnut's inner and outer circles. It is clear that the lists incorporate a combination of Scandinavians and English men, at least judging from their names, without there necessarily having been a hierarchy between them. In fact, the numbers show that there were more with English names: of around 110 thegns (that is, including other nobles and not just earls) attesting charters, forty have Scandinavian names while seventy have English names.

One of the best known of these earls was Godwin, Earl of Wessex, whose daughter Edith would marry Edward the Confessor and become queen of England, and whose son, Harold Godwinson, would briefly become king after Edward's death. Cnut appointed Godwin earl in 1018 and over the coming decade he apparently took part in all of the king's expeditions abroad. Godwin married Gytha, the sister of Earl Ulf, who was Cnut's brother-in-law.

Another who was significant was Beorn Estrithson, the son of Estrith, Cnut's sister, with her Danish husband Ulf: this also made him Godwin's nephew. In 1045, Beorn would receive an earldom in the East Midlands from Edward.

Intriguingly, there are also links to the east at Cnut's court: someone by the name of Wrytsleof (an Anglicised version of Vratislav) attests two charters in Old Minster. This is perhaps not surprising: Cnut's mother was Polish, daughter of Mieszko I of Poland, and one of his sisters apparently married Wyrtgeorn, described as 'King of the Wends', the Wends being Slavic peoples settled along the southern fringe of the Baltic and further inland. Another of Cnut's sisters, Astrithr, was married to 'the son of the king of Russia'. As would later become apparent, Cnut's kingdom was deeply connected with the rest of Europe.

In the first few years of his rule, Cnut seems to have been especially concerned with removing rivals to the throne. Edmund Ironside's sons, for instance, had to be swiftly dealt with. When he died, Edmund had left behind two infant sons, Edward Ætheling (later known as Edward the Exile) and Edmund, their mother presumably Ealdgyth, the widow he had married against his father's will. Both were sent out of the country when Cnut took over. What happened to those boys is a mystery because the sources vary tremendously. One states that Cnut sent them to Sweden, hoping they would be murdered, and that they were then sent on to Hungary, something other sources agree with. There, Edward apparently thrived and married a woman named Agatha. He only returned to England just before his death in 1057, with his son Edgar, who would go on to become a contender for the throne, and his two daughters Margaret and Christina: Margaret would later become the queen of Scotland.

When Cnut married Ælfgifu of Northampton, the union between them had strong political incentives, as it had given his father – and later Cnut himself, too – important allies and networks. With the country now formally his, the king had different priorities: he needed a new way of obtaining alliances, while at the same time countering the threat of Æthelred's sons by reinstating Emma.

In 1017, Cnut asked for Emma to be 'sent for', so that he could marry her. Taking the widow of his predecessor as his own wife was a shrewd move by Cnut. As someone who was already a significant political character in her own right, she had key contacts and networks of her own, not to mention an in-depth knowledge of the English political system. Emma provided Cnut with a bridge to the past rulership, alongside a renewed alliance with Normandy and Duke Richard. The two married in a full, Christian ceremony. It is unclear what Emma herself thought about the marriage at first but later on, in her *Encomium Emmae Reginae*, 'In Praise of Queen Emma', a text she herself commissioned, she stressed that not only did the marriage bring peace, but it also formed an equal union and one she entered into by her own consent. Her own ancestry may well have affected her feelings about her marriage. After all, her mother was the daughter of recent Danish settlers in Normandy, while northern origins made up a key element of Norman self-identity. Thanks to her family and her childhood growing up at court, Emma already likely spoke Danish.

Following Cnut's union with Emma, Ælfgifu's status becomes unclear. She may have remained in Denmark, although there is an intriguing document that has an Ælfgifu witnessing a lease of land in the Midlands dating to around this time. Could it be that Ælfgifu stayed in the Midlands too, perhaps with some land of her own, perhaps in Northampton as her name would suggest? Support for the alternative explanation, that she stayed in Denmark, comes from the thirteenth-century Icelandic text known as

Heimskringla, which claims that in the 1020s Ælfgifu and her son Swein had been in charge of territories in the east of Denmark.

A particular problem with our knowledge of Ælfgifu is the way she was described by near contemporary writers and later discussed by scholars. Very little is known about her from written sources and many of those sources that do – sparsely – detail her life are heavily biased towards Cnut's second wife, Emma. One aspect that has been especially problematic is that of Ælfgifu's status when Cnut married Emma in 1017. Did he simply repudiate her as his spouse, so he could take up the more politically advantageous union with someone who was not only the wife of the former king but also provided him with an alliance with Normandy? We know little about procedures for divorce in the eleventh century, nor are the details of what happened with this particular union spelled out in any of the sources. And was Ælfgifu actually Cnut's full wife, or, as many later accounts would have it, merely his concubine? One of the major sources for what we know about Ælfgifu is the *Encomium Emmae Reginae*. In it Ælfgifu is referred to as a concubine rather than a wife but it is important to remember that the aim of the book was to further Emma's own political career and the position of her sons. Similarly, Adam of Bremen uses the same term, but he was writing in the second half of the eleventh century, when Emma's son Harthacnut had already risen to power in Denmark. He, too, may well have been biased towards Emma.

In reality, there is no reason to think that Ælfgifu was anything other than a full wife. But while the term 'concubine' is usually used in a derogatory way, especially in order to highlight lower status, some scholars have pointed out that in Scandinavia, and in the cultural sphere that Cnut belonged to, the term may have had quite different connotations.

During the Viking Age, customs around marriage seem to have

been different in Scandinavia from England. Evidence from law codes and sagas shows that in Scandinavia, divorce was not only common, but also easy to obtain: a woman could leave her marriage for reasons ranging from spousal violence to her husband's failure, through 'negligence', to consummate their union. In Scandinavia, women retained economic independence in their marriage and, crucially, afterwards too: she would take with her what she had brought into the marriage after a divorce. This also says something about societal attitudes to divorced women. While the loss of association with a particular man (and whatever status he held in society) could affect her social standing, the act of the divorce in itself would not. At the same time, although marriage would include just one single spouse, having multiple partners was not unusual or unheard of in Scandinavia, especially in the higher echelons of society. Among the Norwegian and Danish royal families in the eleventh and twelfth centuries, extra-marital sexual relationships involving large numbers of aristocratic women were apparently very common. This is because the systems of inheritance and royal succession did not depend on legitimacy, that is, on a child being the offspring of a formal wife to the king. Those women described as *concubines* in Denmark and Iceland commonly formed important alliances between high-status or influential families. So regardless of whether Ælfgifu was originally Cnut's formal wife, if we consider their marriage in Scandinavian terms, her status may not have been significantly reduced even after his marriage to Emma.

Her family connections apart, Emma was clearly important to Cnut, not least because of her knowledge of English politics. It seems likely that the partnership between the two developed over time, helped by the fact that their age difference was considerably smaller than that between her and her first husband. In a document from New Minster in Winchester, the two are depicted either side of an altar, as an illustration of the monastery's loyal benefactors.

What is important about this, and similar depictions, is how the couple are shown as a double act, which emphasises Emma's political importance. In any case, Emma and Cnut's marriage would last until his death in 1035 and they had two children together: Harthacnut and Gunnhild.

By 1018, Cnut had managed to create a pretty stable situation in England. But not all of his decisions had been popular: that year he collected tribute, or *gafol*, according to the *Anglo-Saxon Chronicle*, amounting to £72,000, with Londoners forced to pay an extra £10,500. It is possible that such arrangements had been in place since the agreement with Edmund in 1016. Crucially, similar tax demands would continue throughout Cnut's reign, allowing him to finance a substantial military force, likely providing the funding for exploits abroad and for hiring and maintaining mercenary troops. The early payments may well have been necessary to settle his expenses relating to the invasion. What would have undoubtedly been popular was the fact that he sent a substantial number of his forces back to Denmark that year, proving that he – unlike any other king before him – could trust that Scandinavian raiding parties would be kept away from English shores.

With plans in place for England, Cnut also had to focus on Scandinavia after his father died in 1014. Swein had left behind three children with the Polish ruler Mieszko's daughter: Harald II, Cnut and Estrid, as well as at least two other daughters whose identities are obscure. It was Harald who became king of Denmark, having already been in charge while his father invaded England.

We know little about Harald's rule of Denmark, but it seems he died of an unknown cause in 1019, when only in his twenties or possibly thirties. That same year Cnut travelled to Denmark, presumably to formally succeed his brother and take control.

From his time away, a remarkable letter is preserved, written by Cnut to reassure the English people as to the reasons for his absence: his trip to Denmark, he says, was to ensure peace, remove a potential threat and to make sure a possible enemy was instead turned into an ally, as long as the English kept their faith and support in him. Along with these promises, he emphasised his devotion to God and reminded them that he had, in fact, used his own money to help protect them in the past.

Cnut returned to England in 1020. Back in his new home, his attention appears to have been focused strongly on the south; from his Wessex heartland, he ruled as an 'absent overlord' who showed little to no interest in Scotland, Wales or even Ireland. Yet the relationship with those he chose to help him rule was clearly complex. Eadric Streona was initially able to hold his position of power in Mercia, but by 1017 he had outgrown his use. While his actual fate is tricky to untangle from a garbled set of sources, that year his apparent disloyalty saw him beheaded: this was, according to Emma's *Encomium*, 'so that soldiers may learn from this example to be faithful, not faithless, to their kings'.

Cnut's relationship with Thorkell also proved complex. In November 1021, the two obviously had a disagreement because the king outlawed Thorkell, banishing him. The reasons behind the conflict are unknown: some suggest Thorkell may have made a bid for the throne. He returned to Denmark, but within a couple of years whatever had happened between them was clearly forgiven: the two met and not only reconciled, but Cnut decided to entrust Denmark and his son Harthacnut, who was no more than about five years old at the time, to Thorkell's care. It is unclear if this son really was Harthacnut, however, as none of the records spell it out. In return, Thorkell's son apparently came to England with Cnut. All of this may have been a way for Cnut to ensure the fidelity of Thorkell, a warlord who had previously shown himself more than capable of amassing his own armies; there may have been a lingering threat underneath it all. However, Thorkell disappears from the historical records after 1023 and may have died around then. Harthacnut subsequently ruled Denmark for several years, and in that time struck coins with the title 'Rex'.

During the 1020s, tensions spilled over in the contest for ruler-ship in Scandinavia. The Norwegian ruler Olav Haraldsson, in power since 1015, launched a joint attack on Denmark with the Swedish king Anund Jakob in 1025 or 1026, forcing Cnut to bring a fleet over from England in defence. Around the same time, Cnut fought against the Swedes at the Battle of Holy River (Helgeå). In 1028, Cnut sent a force to Norway, allegedly of fifty ships. It appears that Olav fled without much resistance and Cnut officially took charge of Norway, which he placed under the sub-rulership of Earl Hakon, the son of Earl Erik of Northumbria. However, Hakon died soon after.

As a result, Cnut needed someone he could fully trust to take control of Norway and the choice fell on his son. Swein, however, was only around fifteen years old at the time and too young to rule on his own; even more so in a foreign country. He had likely grown up in Denmark and would have had little knowledge of the intricacies of Norwegian politics. For this reason, he was sent there in the company of his mother, Ælfgifu, whose status would change once again. By ruling alongside Swein, she had effectively been made the queen of Norway. The fact that Cnut entrusted Ælfgifu with this task says a lot about her status and the power available to her as the mother of the king's son, regardless of his new marriage to Emma.

Details of Swein and Ælfgifu's rule in Norway are obscure and mostly come from later sources, many of which seem intent on emphasising the negative aspects of their regime. Their time in Norway is typically described as being one when heavy taxation caused intolerable hardship for the population: so much, in fact, that one of the poets, in a skaldic verse, reported that to avoid starvation the people were forced to eat foods normally only given to cattle and goats. Some of this taxation and other initiatives apparently came directly from Cnut. But in the sagas, they are described as Ælfgifu's laws: it is *she* who is portrayed as a wicked and harsh ruler and not her son, following on from a common pattern when describing ruling queens. Importantly, there was every reason for the local elites to resent the incoming Danish powers. Swein and Ælfgifu had, after all, replaced a local, Norwegian candidate, Cnut's intended satellite ruler Hakon Eriksson, heir to the northern dynasty of the Earls of Lade and the son of Earl Erik of Northumbria, who had drowned at sea in 1030, apparently after returning to England to fetch his wife. Nonetheless, the mother and son stayed in power for almost five years, which would not have been possible without the support of at least *some* of the local nobles.

However, by 1034 opposition to the two had grown too strong. In 1031, an alleged illegitimate son of Olaf Tryggvason had arrived in Norway and been defeated, and afterwards a group of Norwegian nobles led a major revolt. In 1034, two of Trøndelag's most powerful men, Einar Tambarskjelve and Kalv Arnesson, who had formerly led the coalition against Olav Haraldsson, travelled to Russia to bring back Olav's young son Magnus (later known as 'the Good') from exile. Ælfgifu and Swein fled back to Denmark without a fight and Magnus – aged eleven – was crowned king. Swein would never rule again; he died in Denmark soon after, and his father Cnut died in 1035.

However, this was not to be Ælfgifu's last experience of political power. She had another son – Harold Harefoot – and now she was intent on advancing *his* claim to the English throne.

While much is often made of the impact the Scandinavians had on England in the early eleventh century, it is clear that this contact across the North Sea had a significant effect back home too, beyond just the wealth arriving from raids, tribute and taxation in Britain.

While the vast quantities of silver Cnut was able to procure through taxation of the English would undoubtedly have increased his wealth, his reign also had an influence on the church. At this point, many parts of Scandinavia were still in the early phase of Christianisation, and it seems the connections between religious institutions there and in England grew closer towards the end of the tenth century. Adam of Bremen mentions an English bishop arriving in Denmark to teach, and stone churches – previously unheard of in Scandinavia – appear by the early eleventh century, many with clear, direct parallels in their architecture to examples in England. Moneyers appear to have come across from England to Denmark too: some of their artefacts bear legends with distinctly English moneyer names. In Lund in Sweden, a wooden pencase lid dating to around this time was carved with Winchester-style decoration, bearing the inscription 'LEOFWINE': an English name and coincidentally also the name of a known moneyer. Even more telling is the appearance of wheel-thrown pottery at elite sites: these wares were of types very similar to English wares, but made from local clays, which means that English potters must have taken up residence in Scandinavia.

By the end of the 1020s, Cnut had truly established himself as the head of an empire. But his connections and interests showed a wider, international perspective: he took a great interest in Rome and attended the imperial coronation of Conrad II in 1027. Perhaps Cnut took inspiration from this event; certainly the crown he is depicted with in the Winchester *Liber Vitae*, or *Book of Life* – a crown placed on his head by an angel – most closely resembles that used by Conrad. Winchester, at this point, could essentially be described as the capital of the empire. While he was away, Cnut wrote another letter to the English people, much like the one he sent when he travelled to Denmark in 1019, again assuring them he was acting in their interests. But this time he also emphasised his links to Rome and – importantly – acclaimed himself the king of all England, Denmark, Norway and parts of Sweden.

His links further east continued too, thanks to his family connections to the Polish Piast dynasty. Back in England, his court showed considerable cultural diversity: not just Anglo-Scandinavians but travellers and ambassadors from Slavic and imperial courts must have been present. The longer-distance connections between the Rus and the Scandinavians were well developed by this stage and these, too, must surely have had an impact on England.

THE KING'S CITY

The king must have had a royal palace in Winchester but none of the archaeological investigations have ever found trace of it. Early medieval kings did not live in a single place, instead they moved around the country between the different estates. The earliest reference to the royal residence in Winchester comes in the late tenth century, when Bishop Æthelwold is said to have resided there. Later, in 1053, records state that Earl Godwin fell ill at the 'King's Table' on Easter Monday, which presumably must have been in the palace.

Originally, the minsters in Winchester had been integral to the town and the gridded streets, with its residential buildings, once laid out by Alfred. This had all changed in the 960s. Alongside other bishops and on the orders of Edgar, Bishop Æthelwold undertook a substantial scheme of reformation of the monasteries, many of the changes dramatic. In doing so, he also enclosed the minsters in Winchester to ensure they were secluded, away from the bustling urban life surrounding them.

The minster we know the least about is Nunnaminster, founded by Queen Ealhswith, King Alfred's wife, after his death in 899. Retirement to a religious community was common for royal women and archaeological excavations have uncovered structures to the east of New Minster, on land known to have been granted to Ealhswith by Alfred.

The town's plots and tenements, many along the original streets, had by the late tenth century turned Winchester into a centre of manufacture and trade, with crafts being practised everywhere. In one plot, for example, in a property that had reused the surviving walls of a Roman building, more than two thousand pieces of scrap glass were found, ready to be melted down and turned into new products. There are records of specialised trades: in the 990s there is a street of tanners and in 996 reference to streets of shield makers and butchers. There is evidence of pottery production, metalworking, spindle whorls and loom weights testifying to textile manufacture, and remains of the working of bone, antler and horn: the discovery of discarded horn cores shows that everyday objects like spoons, knife handles and drinking vessels were produced to furnish the tables of the residents of the town. Other things came from further afield: honestones used for blade sharpening had found their way to the town from the Telemark region in southern Norway, while the most sought-after quern stones had travelled from Niedermendig in the Eiffel Mountains of Germany. Sherds of a particular type of amphora (a large ceramic vessel) have been found in excavations at the cathedral car park right by the minsters: these would have been used to import wine from the Rhineland, no doubt to fuel the feasts at the royal palace or among other well-to-do residents.

Among the discoveries made during the excavations of Old Minster, one set of artefacts may well reveal something about the beliefs, stories and legends that were shared between the kings and people of Wessex and Denmark in the early eleventh century. During their work, the excavators came across more than ninety fragments of sculpture and among these one exceptional block of stone, found where the church's eastern apse had once been. The stone, measuring roughly 70 x 50 centimetres, has a carved image in relief that shows parts of two distinct scenes. On the left, you can see a man wearing mail, with a sword hanging from his hip, walking out of the picture, while directly behind him, on the right, there is the head and shoulders of another man, who is lying on his back. We can't see his facial expression, but the man has his hands raised either side of his head and a rope around his neck, which appears to be tied to a stake in the ground. A canine is standing on top of him with its teeth bared and large, clawed paws bearing down on the supine man's neck and chin; the animal's tongue reaches down into the man's mouth. This is presumably a wolf or a dog in the midst of an attack on the helpless character who is holding his hands up to protect himself. The carved stone has been nicknamed the 'Sigmund' stone because it seems to relate to an episode from one of the Icelandic sagas, the Saga of the Volsungs. In this story a man named Sigmund and his nine brothers were taken prisoner after King Volsung, their father, died in a battle at the hands of the rival King Siggeir. Before Siggeir could kill the sons, his wife Signy, who happened to be Volsung's daughter, intervened and convinced him to put her brothers into stocks in the woods, in the hope that she could at least save one. Each night a she-wolf entered the woods and killed and ate one of the brothers, until only Sigmund remained. Desperate to help him, Signy instructed a servant to smear honey on Sigmund's face and to put some of it in his mouth. That night when the she-wolf appeared again, instead of killing Sigmund, she started licking his face and eventually reaching her tongue into his mouth. At this point, Sigmund bit down so hard that the wolf jerked her body back in pain and in the process split the tree trunk he was tied to, allowing Sigmund to escape through the woods to safety.

Although much is missing from the Winchester stone, the parallel to Sigmund's story is extraordinary: it seems to show the precise moment the wolf extends her tongue into Sigmund's mouth.

Martin Biddle believes the scene was once part of an immense frieze that adorned the inside of Old Minster, positioned around the interior of the apse. A panel like this would have acted much like the Bayeux Tapestry, showing a series of events and telling an important story. If he is right, the frieze would have communicated a shared knowledge of stories and legends, told through images to an audience with their feet in both the English and the Scandinavian world.

Fittingly, both archaeological and other forms of evidence have suggested that during Cnut's reign Winchester was the place in Wessex with the highest concentration of Danes. Even afterwards, it continued to be a key location for Anglo-Danish interests.

GUNNI, THE EARL'S COMPANION

While the presence of identifiable Scandinavians can be read in the written records and, obliquely, in place names with Scandinavian elements, we rarely come across individuals any more directly. One unique exception is found in Winchester. During the Old Minster excavations, the archaeologists discovered numerous graves around the old church. Most of the time, ancient graves are anonymous and unremarkable, marked out only by a vaguely defined grave cut, a different colour from the surrounding soil, perhaps marking a coffin of wood that has long since rotted away. In an important location like this, however, graves are occasionally better defined and to the east of Old Minster, several were covered with stone grave slabs or other markers. Among these, one stood out from the rest, not least because of its unusual shape, and also because – exceptionally rare for the period – it gave us the name of the grave's occupant: a man called Gunni.

The stone that covered the grave in question is rectangular with a curved or coped top, and it resembles a stylised version of a very particular kind of grave monument: a so-called Hogback tombstone, a type of carved stone found largely in northern Britain in Anglo-Scandinavian contexts. While other versions are decorated and finely carved, sometimes to resemble the curved roof of a Viking hall or the back of a hog – hence the name – the Winchester grave cover has no decoration apart from the text inscribed along its top. The inscription, in Old English, reads 'HER LIÐ G[VN]N[I] : EORLES FEOLAGA' – 'Here lies Gunni, Eorl's [or the Earl's] fellow'. The inscription is peculiar, because it incorporates Old Norse elements: *Feolaga* is an anglicisation of the Old Norse word *félagi*, which means something like fellow, partner or companion. The word is very rare in England. One of the few occasions it has been found is in the pact made between Edmund Ironside and Cnut at Deerhurst in 1016, when they agreed to divide the country between them. The term therefore seems to say something very specific about the relationship between Gunni and Eorl/the Earl, perhaps even in legal terms. Elsewhere in the Norse-speaking world, this particular word seems to have meant something relating to either raiding or trading – or both – perhaps even some kind of joint enterprise or business partnership. Gunni's grave also had a footstone, a freestanding grave marker with the so-called 'hand of God', a relief of a right hand holding a cross, indicating the deceased's Christian association. Similar symbolism has been found on the hilt of a sword from Langeid in Norway, dating to about the same time.

The name Gunni is Scandinavian and has the same root as more common names like Gunnar, and it is rare in England: in Domesday

Book, only three men named Gunni are mentioned as landholders in 1066. On Danish and Swedish Viking Age runestones, it occurs around thirty times. We don't know who the earl in question is, or whether Eorl is actually a personal name. One possibility is that the earl could be Eorl Beorn, Cnut's nephew who died in 1049 and whose tomb can be found in the cathedral. There, according to an inscription, he lies with Richard, son of William the Conqueror. Earl Godwin of Wessex is another possibility. The elaborate style and prominent location of Gunni's grave means that it is clearly that of someone significant: the close fellow or companion of a royal relative would certainly fit the bill. Intriguingly, some of the runestones in Sweden that mention a Gunni may well also have links to England. One states that a man called Tosti raised it in memory of his in-law Gunni who 'was westwards' (a phrase usually referring to England), while another stone, located in Sävsjö in southern Sweden, has the following inscription: 'Vrái placed this stone in memory of Gunni, his brother. He died in England'. Could any of these Gunnis be the man buried in Winchester? Perhaps that would be too much of a coincidence. However, a nearby runestone commemorates Vrái, Gunni's brother, after his death, and this second stone states that Vrái was Earl Hakon's marshal: this is believed to be Hakon Eriksson, a Norwegian earl thought to have ruled Norway as a vassal of Cnut both in the 1010s and the 1020s. Hakon was the son of Erik Hakonsson, who had campaigned with Cnut and who was given the kingdom of Northumbria after Uthred was killed in 1016. Based on its location, Gunni's grave in Winchester is thought to date to the 1020s to 1030s. The connections may be tenuous, but with the close links between the elites in Scandinavia and England at the time it is, at least, a possibility.

A final chance to find out more about Gunni's identity comes from his remains. Underneath the stone grave marker, the skeleton was relatively well preserved. The bones were analysed by forensic pathologist Bob Stoddart, who determined that the body was that of an adult man, aged between thirty-five and sixty at the time of death. Apart from this, there was little to be teased from his bones: the skeleton showed he was healthy in life, with few or no signs of disease. There were no obvious marks of trauma or injury to his remains either, nor a clear cause of death. Radiocarbon dating, when corrected for marine foods in his diet, placed his death between 852 and 1023, but from what we know about the development of Old Minster, the cemeteries around it, and the later development of New Minster right next to it, only the later part of this range fits: the archaeological evidence suggested he was buried in the 1020s or 1030s.

Oxygen and strontium isotope analyses of his teeth were, unfortunately, inconclusive in terms of his geographical origins: the values obtained could fit either the local area or parts of southern Scandinavia, especially Denmark. Yet his diet was more informative. The dentine in his teeth – a partially organic tissue that preserves isotopic signals of childhood diet – showed that as a child he had been raised on terrestrial foods, with very similar carbon and nitrogen isotope values to those of others buried in southern England. However, this had changed later in life. A sample taken from his femur, indicative of the last ten to fifteen years before his death, proved very different: he was consuming significantly more seafood. This marine diet in adulthood would have been very different from those in southern England, and much more similar to that of individuals from places like Scotland and parts of Sweden. While none of this provides a clear-cut identification, taken with all the other evidence it seems very likely that the man in this grave had strong connections both to England and to Scandinavia; a member of Winchester's Anglo-Scandinavian elite.

CNUT AND THE CHURCH

Throughout his reign, Cnut deliberately fostered a close relationship with the church. This may seem surprising to those
familiar with the stereotype of the pagan warrior: even some
twentieth-century scholars have assumed that this devotion to
Christianity would have been something very new to him, something the Dane must have picked up from those advising him at
court. Some even credit Emma as his guide towards religious devotion. It is important to remember, though, that by the time Cnut
came to power in England, the Danish kings had been Christian
for three generations. His grandfather Harald Bluetooth was the
king credited with Christianising Denmark, and his grandfather
on the Polish side, Mieszko, was baptised in 966. Coupled with
the time Cnut spent in England during his father's invasion and
brief rule, this must mean that he had a pretty good understanding
not just of the religion itself, but also of how beneficial it could be
for a king. In fact, another accusation sometimes levelled at Cnut
is that his investment in the church was purely for strategic reasons,
to gain the support of the people he had conquered. Whether or not
this is true, we'll never know, but he also took an interest in local
English saints, many of them with direct connections either to victims
of Viking attacks or to his predecessors, such as the cult of Edward
the Martyr, which by the time Cnut came to power had grown
massively and which he continued to support. Perhaps by doing
so, he hoped to show continuity with the West Saxon royal line.

In 1023, Cnut was involved in removing the relics of St Ælfheah –
the archbishop cruelly murdered by raiders in 1012 – from St Paul's
to Christ Church, Canterbury. By this point Ælfheah had become
one of London's most popular saints and in these early years of his
reign the city still harboured uneasy feelings towards Cnut. The
citizens had to pay exceptionally high taxes and to put up with the

king's special military garrison, his *huscarls*. Losing their favourite saint, and the income that came with it, clearly did not prove popular. Besides, Ælfheah had been murdered by the Viking invaders, so his relics acted as a reminder of the injustices that had been visited upon the English by the Danes. One source records the translation in dramatic terms: a troop of Cnut's *huscarls* faked an attack on the city gates while the king, the archbishop and a small number of men snuck into St Paul's and used an iron candelabrum to smash open the saint's tomb and retrieve the body – which was as complete as it had been when interred ten years previously. They carried the saintly remains out on a plank, covered with the altar cloth (for which they had left a pound of gold as payment), all the way to the bank of the Thames, where an armed longship lay in wait. Having loaded the martyr himself, Cnut steered the ship to the opposite bank. Eventually, the body of Ælfheah was taken to Canterbury, to the delight of the residents. Another account is far more positive: one of the *Anglo-Saxon Chronicle*'s manuscripts describes the event as a joyous occasion, rather than a heist, in which the return of the martyr was welcomed by everyone involved.

Another saintly cult to receive attention from Cnut was that of St Edmund, martyred by the Great Army more than two centuries before, and already popular among Scandinavians; East Anglia was a key constituent of the Danelaw. If we are to believe William of Malmesbury's account, Cnut retained a further link to St Edmund, since it was the saint who had struck the king's father Swein down in a vision. It's unclear if this legend dated back as far as Cnut's time, but William certainly thought so. He writes that not only did Cnut do all he could to appease the saint, he also built an abbey, fully staffed with an abbot and monks, at the site of St Edmund's body. Cnut certainly supported the Abbey of St Edmund, but the link to Swein may have been something William invented as a way of explaining the king's interest in the saint.

Cnut also moved the relics of St Wystan in Repton; again, a site that had been targeted by the Great Army. The fact that they were even there is a little puzzling; we don't hear about them until Cnut moves them to Evesham, an aside that is rarely commented on but is informative of two things: first, that the relics had remained unharmed during the Great Army's attack on the church, either because they were deliberately spared or, as seems more likely, because they had already been removed for safekeeping. Second, new archaeological and bioarchaeological evidence from Repton suggests that a community with Scandinavian links remained there for about three generations after the Great Army's conquest of Mercia; this could have lasted into the late tenth century. Perhaps there, like in Bury St Edmunds, a local saint had been adapted by the Scandinavian community?

How much did Cnut and others in the eleventh century really know about these events that had taken place well over a century before? *Knutsdrapa*, the praise poem written in Cnut's honour, includes references to Ælla, the king of York who was killed by Ivar in the alleged blood-eagling. The poem makes Cnut's link to those former warriors clear, reminding the audience of his role as an invader. Could this connection make it more likely that Cnut's support of both Repton's and Bury's saints was somehow meant to appease the local communities?

As an aside, Cnut is often known as Canute in English. When and why this change was made has been debated. The reasons for it range from Pope Paschal II's inability to pronounce the name in the twelfth century to the disappearance of the *Cn-* sound after the English *kn-* sound was simplified to *n-* during the seventeenth and eighteenth centuries, to a simple desire to avoid confusing the king's name with the word *cunt*. The issue may seem inconsequential but when a tenth-century hoard discovered in Silverdale in 2011 was found to contain a coin with the inscription 'AIRDECONUT', the discussion took on a new significance. Several experts believe this to be the rendering of the name Harthacnut by an English moneyer who was struggling to spell an unfamiliar name; but it could also provide proof of a previously unknown Scandinavian king in the north of England around this time (Cnut's son Harthacnut's rule, of course, dates to almost a century later).

The change in spelling of Cnut's name, however, could tell us something else. The spelling 'Canut' is found in two charters dating to the reign of Cnut, making it earlier than both the Pope with pronunciation problems and the later shift in the English language. It also pre-dates the first known use of the word *cunt*, which is found as a word describing female genitalia on its own for the first time in 1325 and a little earlier in place names. Instead, by looking at the earliest records of Cnut's name, researchers have shown that it was exclusively written with the *Cn* spelling by French and Norman authors writing in Latin. Eventually, these sources were translated into English, complete with the name in the form Canute. Could this imply that the Silverdale coin also came from a Norman source? There was, in fact, a king of Denmark by the name of Harthacnut in the early tenth century who, according to Adam of Bremen, travelled to Denmark from Normandy. The Silverdale hoard also contained numerous other objects and coins of Frankish, Islamic and Scandinavian origin, so a Norman coin would certainly have been possible too.

In English history, one story about Cnut has taken on huge significance in the public perception of this king and his legacy, in a similar way to the story of Alfred and the cakes. The tale, popularly known as Cnut and the Waves, involves Cnut attempting to hold back the tide. It is typically used as a parable to describe someone fighting against a raft of challenges and opposition, and Cnut is often portrayed as foolish, attempting to stop the inevitable: with this interpretation, being like Cnut means being someone unable to accept their own limitations. The story was first recounted by Henry of Huntingdon in his twelfth-century *Historia Anglorum*, which placed the event in the year 1035. What Henry described was something of a miracle and a clear demonstration of Cnut's immense power and success as a king. The king, the chronicler says, when at the height of his reign – the powerful king of four countries (Henry includes Scotland) – ordered for a chair to be placed at the seashore, just as the tide was coming in. As the waves slowly but surely made their way towards him, the king uttered the following words, in a direct order to the sea: 'You are subject to me, as the land on which I am sitting is mine, and no one has resisted my overlordship with impunity. I command you, therefore, not to rise onto my land, nor to presume to wet the clothing and limbs of your master.' The sea, however, took no notice and continued apace inland, drenching both the king's feet and his clothes. In response, Cnut jumped up and cried: 'Let all the world know that the power of kings is empty and worthless, and there is no king worthy of the name save Him by whose will heaven, earth and sea obey eternal laws.' As a way of demonstrating his understanding of God's greater power, Cnut thereafter never again wore his golden crown but put it instead on a crucified figure of Jesus. Instead, then, of being the story of a king not realising the limits of his strength, it is the opposite, that of a king very aware of them. Cnut's tale found its way into children's lessons after it was incorporated into school textbooks in 1896 (along with Alfred's cakes), when the author James Baldwin stated that in Cnut's time, 'the Danes . . . were not so fierce and cruel then as they had been when they were at war with King Alfred'. We don't know if a version of the story existed in Cnut's own lifetime or where Henry got it from. It may well have been a legend he had heard of. Henry also says that never before had there been, in England, a king of such great authority as Cnut and so his limitation in the face of nature speaks even more powerfully about God.

Cnut's success no doubt rested in part on his ability to take advantage of internal turmoil, from the first conflict in 1015 between Æthelred and Edmund to the lukewarm support that Edmund had in some parts of the country, to the changing loyalties of significant players like Eadric Streona, especially in light of Æthelred's death. Decades of defeat and repeated attacks by the Scandinavians had left the English exhausted and the aristocracy weary. Ultimately, it has been claimed, it was the promise of *stability* and an end to Viking raids that paved the way for a Scandinavian to take the throne.

Cnut's repeated and lengthy trips abroad, leaving England in the capable hands of his earls, give us a clear sign of just how stable his reign was. Few rulers before him had been able to do the same.

There are few sources to inform us of Cnut's activities in the early 1030s, and it has been suggested that he suffered a long period of illness, before he died in Shaftesbury on Wednesday, 12 November 1035. It has been speculated that early death was inherited in Cnut's family, perhaps caused by strokes or aneurysms.

According to the *Anglo-Saxon Chronicle*, after his death Cnut's body was moved to Winchester, where he was buried. There is a legend that his heart remained in Shaftesbury; in fact, a glass bowl was excavated from beneath a heart-shaped marble slab on the floor in front of the high altar at Shaftesbury Abbey in 1904 – a bowl said, for highly dubious reasons, to have held Cnut's heart. The general consensus among the medieval writers is that Cnut was buried in Old Minster, with one even specifying that he was given pride of place in front of the high altar.

SUCCESSION

When Cnut died, the North Sea empire he had built and successfully maintained for almost two decades was not to last. The dispute over the succession proved fierce, one in which his sons by his two wives were to compete for the throne alongside Cnut's stepsons: a contest intensified by the actions of their mothers. Harthacnut, whose name means 'tough knot', was Cnut's only son by Emma. With the complications surrounding the status of Ælfgifu and her sons – not to mention the sons already mothered by Emma with Æthelred – it is not surprising to see her encomiast claiming that Emma had refused marriage until Cnut promised that her male offspring with him would be first in line to the throne.

After his father's death, Harthacnut initially stayed in Denmark, where he had been for some time, as its ruler. By this point, he had already struck coins in his name, along with the title 'Rex', which shows that he certainly had some power to rule. Yet although he was the prime pretender to the English throne (at least according to the *Encomium*), Harthacnut found himself unable to travel to England because he was facing threats to his kingdom from the Norwegian king, Magnus the Good. England, instead, fell to Harold Harefoot, Cnut's son with Ælfgifu. According to some of the chroniclers, this had been Cnut's arrangement all along. However it came about, in late 1035, the agreement was finalised, and Harold was elected regent with the support both of troops in London and those to the north of the Thames. It seems likely that his mother's family origins in the Midlands helped him gain support there. Emma, meanwhile, was sent to Winchester to hold Wessex for Harthacnut, where she also took charge of the royal treasury. There is some archaeological evidence for this joint arrangement to be found in the coins that were minted at the time: south of the Thames we find silver pennies struck in the name of Harthacnut while on the north side they are almost exclusively pennies minted for Harold.

Competition between the royal sons also led to some serious slander directed at Ælfgifu and Harold. In the *Anglo-Saxon Chronicle*'s entry for 1035, it explicitly says that Harold was 'claimed' to be the son of Ælfgifu and Cnut but that this was not true. The *Encomium* went into more detail: Harold was, it claimed, nothing more than a lowly servant's son, stolen by Ælfgifu and smuggled into her bedchamber, so she could present him as her own and provide Cnut with a rightful heir. Emma, of course, had other sons who were keen to stake their claim to the kingdom. Alfred and Edward had been in exile in Normandy, and Edward (who would later become known by the nickname 'the Confessor') made the first unsuccessful attempt on England by attacking the south coast. Soon after, Alfred the Ætheling returned to England too, but with disastrous results. Both the *Chronicle* and the *Encomium* recount what happened, in slightly different versions. According to the *Encomium*, he was intercepted by Earl Godwin, who until this point had been at Emma's side; the earl, apparently, duped him into travelling to England by sending him a forged letter in her name. On arriving, Alfred and his men were captured; some of the men were murdered at once and others sold as slaves. Alfred's fate was worse: he was blinded and either died straight away from his injuries or was kept alive for some time. Eventually, he would be buried by the monks at Ely.

The competition for the throne ended with Harold Harefoot becoming king in 1037. At this point, Emma was exiled to Flanders, where she stayed with a distant relative, Count Baldwin and his wife Adela. Nonetheless, Emma's ambitions for herself and her sons would remain.

Ælfgifu vanished towards the end of her life; after her career as the mother of queens was over, the writers showed little interest in her. Yet a brief mention in the records of an early twelfth-century monastery in Aquitaine in southern France suggests she may well have retired there: it records that an Englishman by the name of *Alboynus* (Ælfwine), the son of a king by the name of Harald and a woman named Ælfgifu, came there on pilgrimage and convinced the local authorities to make him the prior of the church. This Harald was likely the son of Harold Harefoot and historians have argued that the Ælfgifu in question was not his mother, but his grandmother, escorting her young grandson. Whether or not this is true, it would seem a fitting place for Ælfgifu to end her long life.

HARTHACNUT

'He did nothing worthy of a king as long as he ruled'
Anglo-Saxon Chronicle manuscript C, 1040

Later Scandinavian sources record that in 1038 an agreement was made between Harthacnut and Harold that whichever of them lived the longest should inherit the other's kingdom. If true, it is possible that this provided the stability needed for Harthacnut to leave Denmark and stake his claim to England. After gathering an invasion force and meeting his mother Emma in Bruges, Harthacnut crossed to England after Harold Harefoot died in March 1040. Landing with an invasion force of sixty-two ships at Sandwich on 17 June, he successfully became ruler of both England and Denmark that year. Harold had been the first ruler to be buried in Westminster, but apparently Harthacnut ordered his body to be exhumed and thrown into a marsh.

We know little about how Harthacnut governed England during his brief rule, but his reign is heavily criticised in two versions of the *Anglo-Saxon Chronicle*. The report of his exhumation of Harold clearly angered his critics, as did the heavy taxes he levied to pay for his extensive fleet. One of these taxes, amounting to £21,099, was so unpopular it caused severe trouble in Worcestershire, when the *huscarls* responsible for collecting the tax were killed by the locals. In response, Harthacnut sent an army with orders to burn Worcester, slaughter the men there and devastate as much as they could of the whole shire.

A short time into his rule, Harthacnut sent for his half-brother Edward to return from Normandy and according to manuscript C of the *Anglo-Saxon Chronicle*, the latter was sworn in as king that year, alongside his brother. It seems likely that Harthacnut, who had no wife or children, had selected him as his heir. The two are depicted in a contemporary manuscript, Emma's *Encomium*, alongside their mother, demonstrating the collaboration between the three.

Harthacnut's early death, aged perhaps only about twenty-five, may have come about due to illness. The circumstances of his demise are described as follows in the C-version of the *Anglo-Saxon Chronicle*, in the entry for 1042: 'Here Harthacnut died as he stood at his drink, and he suddenly fell to the earth with an awful convulsion; and those who were close by took hold of him, and he spoke no word afterwards, and he passed away on 8 June. And all the people then received Edward as king, as was his natural right.'

The fuller version of this story explains that Harthacnut, on that day, was attending a marriage feast at Lambeth, on the south bank of the Thames. Another reference says he had been 'merry, in good health, and in great heart' but that he fell while drinking. There is little more that we can tease out of the sources, but it really does seem like early death ran in the family, with both his father and uncle dying relatively young of unexpected illness.

Although brief, Harthacnut's rule was significant, and many have mused that if he had lived longer, the Norman conquest may never have happened. Another view on his significance comes from Henry of Huntingdon's twelfth-century account, in which he stated that with Harthacnut's death, 'the English nobles are joyful now to be freed from Danish rule'. This, in other words, he saw as the end of the Vikings' stranglehold on England.

EDWARD AND EDITH

Harthacnut was formally succeeded by his half-brother that same year: Edward was crowned at Winchester on Easter Sunday. By this point, he was aged at least thirty-eight, unusually old by the standard of recent English kings. While he would be remembered as a stable and successful king, ruling for almost twenty-four years, his success was not a given as he took over from two short-lived rulers, who were the sons of a foreign invader – albeit an effective one. Many of the challenges that Edward faced related to internal issues, such as maintaining his control over the church and the aristocracy. While some suggest he had a positive relationship with Emma before his rule, before long Edward turned very demonstrably against his mother, arriving in Winchester a few months after his coronation to take away her treasures of silver and gold, as well as most of the land she owned. She was allowed to stay in the city and eventually regained her position at court, but the precise reasons are unclear: Emma was later accused of having been too harsh on Edward; of offering aid to Magnus of

Norway for an invasion of England; and even of having had an affair with Ælfwine, the bishop of Winchester. It seems none of these were true. Edward most likely wanted to reduce her political involvement and give her a simpler status as the widow of two former kings, leaving him to rule independently. At the same time, Edward's rule was marked by his marriage to Edith, daughter of Earl Godwin and Gytha. The Godwins were among the most prominent Anglo-Danish families in the country and the marriage gave both sides a distinct advantage. Edith also provided Edward with a tie to Cnut's family: her mother Gytha was the sister of Ulf, who married Cnut's sister Estrid. This meant she was cousin to Swein Estridsson, who ruled as king of Denmark between the 1040s and 1070s, and who would later become a threat to England as he attempted to assert his claim to the country.

Much of what we know about Edward's reign has come to us through the *Vita Ædwardi Regis*, an account commissioned by Edith and written by an anonymous author in 1065–7. The book begins as a history of Edith's family and later turns to her husband's life, something that might explain its depiction of her: Edith is not only physically beautiful, but she is also very accomplished in numerous skills, from literature to embroidery, as well as in her dealings with her household and care for her husband. However, for unknown reasons, the couple would remain childless.

During 1051 and 1052, a crisis erupted between Edward and the Godwin family, causing him temporarily to outlaw most of them and attempt to divorce Edith, sending her to a nunnery and depriving her of all her possessions. After Earl Godwin and his sons gathered a large force against the king, Edward reinstated both them and Edith. During this time, a later chronicler claims that William of Normandy made a visit to Edward's court and that the latter promised William the succession to the English kingdom: whether there is any truth to this, we will never know.

The remainder of Edward's rule was one of relative peace and few serious conflicts. The death of several family members who could have caused problems for him may have helped, including Emma, his brother-in-law Swein and his father-in-law Earl Godwin. Nonetheless, Edward's other brother-in-law Harold Godwinson became a powerful figure at court during this time, something that would have significant ramifications later.

Early in his reign, Edward had established a royal palace in London, on a low-lying island by the Thames known as Thorney Island. Nearby lay a Benedictine monastery established during King Edgar's reign in the 960s, which he also chose to support with the building of a brand-new stone church in the decades to follow. Although dedicated to St Peter the Apostle, this church became known as *West Minster* to separate it from *East Minster* – now known as St Paul's Cathedral – in the City of London. At the time, Edward's church was remarkable and of grand proportions. Little remains of that actual structure today in what is now Westminster Abbey except one remarkable part: a door thought to be Britain's oldest. The door, which is now in a vestibule leading to the chapter house, has been dated using dendrochronology (tree-ring dating), which showed that its timbers were felled after 1032 and that it was made sometime in the 1050s. This fits well with the time we know the church was built.

Edward's new church was due to be consecrated on Holy Innocents' Day, 28 December 1065, but by that point he was too ill to attend. When he died only days later he was buried there, in a tomb in front of the altar, following the example of Harold Harefoot. There his remains would stay until they were translated into a new tomb in 1161, when he was canonised. In the twelfth and thirteenth centuries a cult sprang up around St Edward the Confessor, one that would later gain significant support from the English church and monarchy. Edward's significance continues to this day: at the coronation of Charles III in May 2023, the new monarch wore the so-called St Edward's Crown, a seventeenth-century crown allegedly modelled on that worn by Edward in the eleventh century. An original was in use throughout the Middle Ages until, during the Civil War in the 1640s, it was either sold or melted down.

ORDEAL

The clergy at the Winchester court formed an important part not just of the religious administration, but also of the wider political world. This, of course, did not make them immune to scandal. There is one particular story that threw dishonourable light not only on Emma but also on one of Winchester's bishops. Formerly a member of Cnut's royal clergy, Ælfwine became infamous in the twelfth century when, in a record written down by a chronicler by the name of Richard of Devizes, the *Winchester Annals*, he was accused of having an affair with Cnut's widow Emma.

The story takes place some years after Cnut's death, when Emma had returned to England with Harthacnut. According to Richard, her other sons Alfred and Edward were of no interest to her; not even when Godwin brutally murdered Alfred. Emma, he says, was perfectly content living in Winchester and ruling alongside Harthacnut. At the same time, most of her attention was taken up by an illicit romantic affair with Bishop Ælfwine.

To prove their innocence, Emma convinced King Edward, her son, to let her go through a trial by ordeal: walking over nine white-hot ploughshares lined up in the nave of Winchester's Old Minster. She escaped unscathed, and Ælfwine's reputation was restored and his career reached a new peak in the aftermath. According to the inscriptions on the bone chests, the two now lie together, an ironic fact considering that this is precisely what Emma had to prove she had avoided during her lifetime.

A WOMAN OF POWER

She had kings as sons and kings as husbands
She shone forth in the glory of her progeny of kings
She excelled in virtue even the ranks of her glorious ancestors

Godfrey of Winchester, eleventh century

The information available to us about Emma's life is sparse, and much of what we know comes from the *Encomium Emmae Reginae*. Written down in 1041–2 by a monk from St Bertin, in what is now France, and commissioned by Emma herself, the *Encomium* is not a straightforward biography but an account – modified in several later versions – of the role she played in English politics during the reign of Cnut and his successors. A famous illustration shows her seated on a throne, a kneeling character handing the book to her, with her two sons Harthacnut and Edward watching from the wings. The *Encomium* conjures the position she was in at the height of her power, aimed at her sons and written to influence the future.

We know that Emma owned a property herself in Winchester because a grant exists that was made in 1012 by Æthelred. In it, he gives his queen a property on Winchester High Street known as Godbegot. Conveniently, the estate also benefited from a special legal status, exempting its owner from taxes and the so-called 'three burdens' of having to contribute to the repair of bridges and defences, and towards military service. There is also a church there, and although some of the property would later be given to Old Minster, Emma kept the remainder as her own Winchester residence.

Emma's career in England can be divided into three parts: the first two relate to her marriages and the third to this period after Cnut's death. In the fierce competition for the English throne that ensued, Emma worked to manoeuvre her sons into kingship, taking an active part in the political sphere as the queen mother. When Harold Harefoot died in 1040, she returned from Flanders and Harthacnut, her son with Cnut, took to the throne.

The role of queen mother was clearly an important one, and she was recognised as an authority: she is listed as *mater regis* in witness lists during these years. Emma may have learned about queenship from her mother, Gunnor, who was later hailed as the matriarch of the Norman aristocracy and dubbed the 'mother of the dynasty' in the twelfth century.

Despite her remarkable political career, Emma's best-known legacy is no doubt the link her Norman background gave her to William the Conqueror, enabling the events of 1066 to run their course. In the words of Henry of Huntingdon, describing her marriage to Æthelred: 'from this union . . . the Normans were justified according to the law of peoples, in both claiming and gaining possession of England'. Two portraits survive of Emma, one with and one without Cnut, something that is very rare as we have virtually no other portraits of early medieval queens. Before her, we have generalised portraits of Cynethryth, Offa's wife, on her coins, and the single other example is of a seventh-century Northumbrian queen, Æthelthryth, but only in a manuscript that depicts her as a virgin abbess rather than a queen.

On 6 March 1052, Emma died of an unknown cause, and she was buried next to Cnut and Harthacnut in Winchester Cathedral.

QUEEN?

*W*ithout DNA analysis, determining the sex of a skeleton is only possible through distinctive differences in certain bones. In children and young adolescents, it is impossible, because the morphological differences that separate men from women only begin during puberty: this is when boys' jaws broaden and become more square and girls' pelvises widen to allow for childbirth later in life. These two parts of the skeleton, the skull and the pelvis, are in fact the most useful for us in determining sex, as they are the most distinctive and most likely to give accurate results. Differences in height and stature do, of course, also vary between men and women, and there are often subtle differences between the sexes in things like muscle attachments. Yet we have to be careful to make conclusions on this basis. A very tall, broad-shouldered skeleton may well have belonged to a man, but not necessarily: nor must a smaller, more gracile frame have belonged to a woman. For this reason, arm and leg bones don't reveal much about sex, nor do the smaller bones from fingers and toes.

The use of ancient DNA has completely changed the game. If the bones are well enough preserved, it can be possible to extract DNA from even small fragments that we would otherwise get very little information from. If successful, the DNA can make it possible to estimate biological sex from such fragmented bones and even from juveniles: this is done by looking for the X and Y chromosomes that all humans store in their genetic data. Although there are variations, put simply, most of us have either two X chromosomes, making us female, or an X and a Y chromosome, making us male. Unfortunately, archaeological material is often disappointingly poorly preserved.

The team makes a breakthrough: among the bones distributed between several chests, they put together a set that they confidently determine to be from one person. There is a relatively intact skull belonging to an adult: described as 'mature', typically meaning over *fifty. There are two matching shoulder blades (scapulae); four bones from the arms (two humerii, a radius and an ulna); five ribs; the right thigh bone (femur); the left lower leg (tibia and fibula); some ankle bones; and, importantly, a large part of the left-side pelvic bone. With these bones, the team is in luck. The measurements and morphological features of the remains agree: this is a female skeleton. The radiocarbon date from this individual places her in the Anglo-Saxon period. Could it be the body of Emma?*

CHEST VI

IDENTITY

Wini d. 670
Cnut d. 1035
Ælfwyn d. 1042
Emma d. 1052
Rufus d. 1100

*E*dmund Cartwright Jr, an officer in the West Yorkshire Regiment
of Militia, senses the excitement of the people gathered around
him. For a while now he has been stationed in Winchester. During
this time, fuelled by a nationwide interest in the past and not least
the flourishing work of fellow antiquarians, he has taken a keen
interest in the area's ancient artefacts. A few months ago, he opened
three prehistoric barrows nearby to investigate their contents, but with
little luck, as he found neither bones nor relics inside any of them.
Then he approached his good friend Newton Ogle, the dean of
Winchester, who he has spent much time with during his posting in
the city. Might he, Cartwright wondered, have Ogle's permission to
investigate some of the many tombs and monuments in the cathedral?
Thankfully, Ogle agreed, as long as it was done with privacy and
decency, and under the direction of the master mason of the chapter.
Today, alongside the mason, he has brought with him two other
gentlemen: Henry Howard Esq. and Mr John Hasting, surgeon of the
North Gloucester militia. Others have gathered to watch the proceedings too, and local hired hands are helping with the heavy work.
Cartwright has already searched out the tomb he was told belonged
to the venerable saint Swithun. Within he has found an oak coffin
with an almost perfectly preserved skeleton inside, complete with leather
boots on its feet – the elegantly shaped, pointed soles of which he traced
with a pencil before keeping one of them. Cartwright knew others did
not agree the body was that of the saint but personally he was inclined
to believe. They opened what was allegedly the tomb of Bishop Fox

too, but disappointingly it was empty. Now it is the turn of the six wooden chests that sit on top of the stone screens around the presbytery. As far as he knows, nobody has investigated the contents of these chests before: they may not even have been opened since they were desecrated during the Civil War. Do they even contain bones anymore? And if so, how many? And could those bones really be the remains of the kings, queens and bishops whose names are listed on the outside?

Once all the chests are safely lifted down from their lofty positions, Cartwright and his colleagues start working their way through them methodically. To his delight, they really do contain bones, and a lot too. Two of the chests even have inner chests within, painted chests that are presumably the predecessors to those created by Fox. The skulls and long bones are carefully counted, and Hasting uses his medical expertise to reveal as much as he can about them, from their appearance, shape and size.

By the end of the day, the inventory is complete:

Box one, with the names 'KINIGILS' and 'ADULPHUS', contains two skulls and two sets of thigh and leg bones, so he assumes these must belong to the kings listed. Hasting measures the skulls to see if their size differs from what you would expect from someone living today, and finds they are nothing out of the ordinary.

Box two, with the names 'EGBERT' and 'KENWOLPH' painted on the outside, contains three skulls, one of which is very small. There are also two pairs of thigh and leg bones that match, including a hip bone that appears to have belonged to someone who was either lame or deformed.

Box three, with the inscription 'EADRED', contains two skulls and many thigh bones.

Box four, bearing only the name 'EDMUND', contains five skulls and many other bones. One of the skulls appears to have belonged to a man of extremely old age, judging from the way the sutures have fused together. Ælfwyn or Wini, perhaps?

Box five, claimed to be a 'promiscuous collection', contains no skulls, but numerous other bones. Some of them, his colleague notes, appear to be those of a woman because they are smaller and weaker. Presumably, they are those of Emma.

Box six, labelled the same as the previous, has no skulls either.

In the report he is drafting on the chests, Cartwright notes that the number of skulls – twelve – corresponds exactly to the number of names on the outside, while the large quantity of thigh bones presumably belonged to those same people.

He is pleased with his discovery. As he watches the bones being placed back in the chests and the lids secured once again, he ponders their history and longevity, especially here in this cathedral that was built soon after the Norman conquest, by the Conqueror himself. But why, he wonders, would a foreign, invader king take such care to preserve these bones from the distant past?

THE SECOND CONQUEST

There is a very neat division in the history of England, a 'before' and 'after', where one stage ends and another begins: the Norman conquest of 1066 – the most famous date in the country's past – separates 'Anglo-Saxon' from 'English' history, and starts it again from scratch. Even the Edwards of the thirteenth and fourteenth centuries represent a new beginning, numbered, as they are, from I instead of IV, despite being named after their forebears Edward the Elder, Edward the Martyr and Edward the Confessor. Often this is the very place that history begins, but for Winchester – and those whose remains ended up in the mortuary chests – this was the beginning of the end. And yet the conquest itself could only take place thanks to a chain of events stretching back many decades.

The year 1066 began with the very brief reign of Harold Godwinson, who was crowned on 6 January 1066, the day after Edward the Confessor died. Edward had suffered a period of illness and the succession question had been at the top of the royal agenda for some time, as it was apparent that he would die without a legitimate heir. Harold, the son of Earl Godwin, made his claim for the throne immediately but his coronation provoked trouble. One of those who was dissatisfied was Tostig, Harold's brother, who returned to England from exile that summer. After ravaging parts of the country, he fled to the Scots, where he found an ally: the Norwegian king Harald Hardrada, who had seen an opportunity in the English succession dispute and wanted to capitalise on it. Together, Hardrada and Tostig sailed up the River Ouse with a joint fleet and defeated a force led by two of the earls at Fulford in September. Five days later, on 25 September, Harold arrived in the north and fought against them at the Battle of Stamford Bridge, leaving both Tostig and Hardrada dead on the battlefield. Yet this was not the only threat to Harold's reign, for an even more serious sequence of events had been set in motion many months earlier. Over in Normandy, Harold's coronation had provoked William into preparing for an invasion. He may have sought support from the Pope and had gathered a huge fleet, as many as 700 ships according to a later document, and somewhere between 7,000 and 14,000 men. William's wife, Matilda, even commissioned a ship, the *Mora*, for her husband to sail. While he was away, Matilda would rule Normandy, and later also England, in his absence.

At the same time as Harold was occupied in the north, William landed at Pevensey in East Sussex – only a short overnight passage across the Channel – in late September. He moved east to Hastings, where he set up camp, constructing earthworks on top of a pre-existing Iron Age hill fort and proceeding to ravage the countryside for rations and resources, but also as a ploy to lure Harold back south. It worked. News quickly reached the English king and in the immediate aftermath of his victory at Stamford Bridge, he marched south with his troops and reinforcements gathered in London. On 14 October, William and Harold met in battle at Hastings. On the morning of the battle, after hearing mass William picked up a reliquary containing holy bones, just as so many others had done before him – to carry with him for divine support.

The exact events of the battle, despite having been told and retold in numerous narratives, are actually not very well known, but a few facts are clear: the two sides were well matched, and William had a slight advantage in his mounted army with effective archers. Harold's advantage lay mainly in his use of higher ground, situating his army on a hill. By the afternoon, the English army was depleted and exhausted, and William's archers advanced until, at some point, King Harold lay dead on the battlefield. Most schoolchildren will have learned that he died from an arrow shot into his eye: a tale first recorded in around 1080, as well as, seemingly, in a panel on the Bayeux Tapestry. Whatever the truth of this, the death of the king meant the defeat was a reality. Two of Harold's brothers died too, as well as significant numbers of the aristocracy.

William's victory didn't hand him the throne at once, however, as in London, two earls, Edwin and Morcar, were putting forward Edgar the Ætheling as king, supported by the archbishops Stigand and Ealdred. Yet doubt was rumbling and there were divisions among the English so that by the time William came closer, after further ravaging the south and then marching on London, most of the English submitted to him. Later records are also at great pains to state that sometime in 1051 or 1052, William had visited England and Edward the Confessor offered him the succession. By this reasoning, 1066 merely saw him making good his claim, having been usurped by Harold.

Ultimately, 1066 was one of many succession disputes, and an exceptionally complicated one at that. The candidates for the throne were many, and the military threats to England – not just from Normandy but also from Norway, in the actions of Hardrada, and Denmark, in the figure of Swein II, cousin of Harthacnut and nephew of Cnut – continued to be very real.

A visual record of the conquest and the events that led up to it – or at least, one version of those events – survives in the form of the Bayeux Tapestry, from Bayeux Cathedral in Normandy. A 68-metre-long strip of linen, it is actually not a tapestry at all, but a stitched embroidery of woollen threads that was once even longer. The story the tapestry tells begins around 1064, with Harold travelling to Normandy, and ends with William's coronation on Christmas

Day 1066, and can best be described as a Norman propaganda piece, with some curious pro-English elements thrown in. It was made within a few decades of the Battle of Hastings, perhaps even within a couple of years. Historians broadly agree on this because the style matches that of manuscripts produced at the time and also because of the way it relates the events: the storytelling seems to be very specific to a certain moment in time, when the conquerors and the conquered were actively attempting to reconcile. There is even a poem by a churchman named Baudri of Bourgueil dating to 1100, describing a tapestry that tells the story of the conquest – although the details don't entirely match, some suggest Baudri must have seen the tapestry that survived in Bayeux. Nevertheless, the first record we have of the tapestry dates to 1476, in one of the cathedral's inventories.

While we have no records to tell us for certain, it is likely that Odo, Bishop of Bayeux, who was William the Conqueror's half-brother, was the person to commission the tapestry: wealthy and powerful, Odo was a loyal ally to William and was present at Hastings. He is pictured on the tapestry in a very favourable and instrumental manner, urging William to build his fleet and advising him on tactics, as well as rallying troops at crucial moments, something that we don't see in any other description of the conquest. Did Odo enhance his role by manipulating the narrative shown on the tapestry? Odo and William fell out in 1082: another clue to the early manufacturing date of the panel.

We are pretty certain that the tapestry was made in England and most likely in Canterbury, where Odo was also the Earl of Kent. Another theory is that it was not commissioned by Odo but *for* him, by none other than Archbishop Stigand of Canterbury, who would stay in post until 1070, and who is shown on the tapestry. In any case, the tapestry probably ended up in Normandy soon after it was made and recent work on the eleventh-century cathedral in Bayeux has shown that its original dimensions fitted perfectly with the length of the nave behind the choir screen.

A NEW CATHEDRAL

A stranger walking through central Winchester in 1093, over two decades after the conquest, would be met with a remarkable and bewildering sight. A complex of spectacular buildings would have vied for her attention: Old Minster, now almost half a millennium old, with the hundred-year-old New Minster squeezed tightly up against it – both of considerable size and grandeur. The two lay so close together, according to William of Malmesbury, that the walls actually touched and the voices of one choir would disturb the other; one of many issues that caused significant offence between the two communities. Not far away lay St Mary's Abbey, and Nunnaminster, built by Alfred's queen Ealhswith, as well as the ancient royal palace and the palace of the bishop. But for the past decade or so, a brand-new building had been starting to take shape: the Norman cathedral that stands in the city today, a powerful symbol of the new regime's hold on not just Winchester but the country as a whole.

In November 1066, Edith, Edward the Confessor's widow, surrendered the city of Winchester to Duke William, handing it over without a fight; Edith was left to live in peace in her house on the north side of the high street, although others were not so lucky, as many landowners had their property forcefully taken over. With its historic significance as capital, Winchester's importance was clearly not lost on William, and the palace remained the location of the royal treasury. Its wealth ranked in the top four in the country and the strategic location near roads and the port of Southampton made it even more important to protect. The incoming Normans wasted no time in creating new city defences, starting the construction of a new castle in the south-west corner of the walled city within weeks. The site, the highest point within the walls, later became Winchester's Great Hall – which, incidentally, was imaginatively identified as Camelot, King Arthur's castle, in the fifteenth century.

Every year from 1068 onwards, William chose Old Minster as the place to celebrate Easter, in a so-called crown-wearing ceremony. His initial coronation took place on Christmas Day 1066 in Westminster Abbey, only months after his victory. This was where his predecessor Edward the Confessor was buried, so his choice helped to form a link and thereby legitimise his rule: it would also be where every coronation in England has taken place since. Yet four years later, William held a second coronation in Winchester. This time he chose Old Minster, which was home to the grave of his relative Emma – his great-aunt, sister of his grandfather Duke Richard II of Normandy – as well as so many illustrious former monarchs. The ceremony saw him re-crowned by two cardinal priests, John and Peter, who had been sent from Rome by the Pope, in part to dispose of Stigand.

That same year, 1070, William turned his attention to the city in earnest. In order to accommodate his Easter crown-wearings, he needed new residences: although there was already a royal palace to the west of the minster, he required more space, including a new hall and palace. A few years earlier, in 1065, a fire had destroyed most of the domestic buildings belonging to New Minster and the head of the minster, Abbot Ælfwig, had fought against William at Hastings and died, alongside many of his monks. The New Minster community found itself in no position to object and ended up giving the king a large portion of the precinct in exchange for much less valuable land elsewhere. Pretty soon, the new palace occupied at least a third of the minster's former precinct, and an area of about two hectares. Alongside this, Winchester's urban landscape was vastly impacted by new developments both in the sacred and secular spheres.

But it was the new cathedral that would have the most enduring impact on the city.

The building project started in 1079 and because the cathedral would be located slightly to the south-east of Old Minster, the latter could remain in use for a little while longer. This was important, because there were crucial clerical functions that could not be interrupted. The transepts and east arm of the new church were built first so that for a short while the three churches – all of spectacular proportions – existed side by side. Bishop Walkelin, the Norman bishop, was in charge of the new build. What would the monks of Old Minster have thought, when Walkelin oversaw the digging of huge foundation trenches to the south of the minster church, right through what had been their cemetery for more than four centuries? Around nine hundred years later, in 1969, the archaeologists investigating the site found out what they did with them: the bones of over a thousand individuals had been placed together in a huge charnel pit. To the west, skull upon skull was lined up neatly and next to them, the long bones had been thrown together to a depth of over a metre.

When the eastern sections were complete, they were dedicated in a grand ceremony, on 8 April 1093, the Friday before Palm Sunday: all the bishops and abbots of England attended and watched as the monks from Old Minster made their way across to the new cathedral. But although Easter could now be celebrated in the new, Norman church, one more event needed to take place: a final translation of St Swithun. Exactly 122 years after the first translation, on 15 July 1093, the relics would be moved once again, into a new cathedral, where they were placed behind the high altar by a new regime.

Now, with Winchester's most sacred saint safe, Walkelin ordered the demolition of Old Minster to begin. According to Richard of Devizes, it took no more than a year, leaving only the high altar and one porticus behind. Some of the stone was reused for the new cathedral but it would take another thirty years or so for the cathedral to be complete.

The new building project was part of a wider, nationwide scheme, described as an 'ecclesiastical building explosion', one component of the larger programme that William had initiated to transform the church. Around England, every cathedral was rebuilt. Many of them were moved from their former, more isolated locations to more populous towns. Winchester proved a key element of the scheme, although here there was no reason to move the former religious centre: the town was already a hive of activity and an active pilgrimage site for the cult of St Swithun. These points served the new conqueror well. Rather than wanting to be seen as a suppressor of old traditions, he wanted to demonstrate his legitimacy and continuity with previous kings. What better way to do so than to associate himself with those kings' mortal remains?

ARCHBISHOP STIGAND

The Bayeux Tapestry shows that at Harold's coronation on 6 January 1066, it was Stigand, by then the archbishop, who crowned him king. He had risen to power as a wealthy and influential cleric.

Stigand began his ecclesiastical career as a royal clerk for Cnut, a role befitting his Anglo-Scandinavian background. His wealthy family appears to have come from East Anglia and he has a Scandinavian name, Stigand meaning 'the swift footed one', while his brother's name was English.

The first time we come across Stigand is in 1020, when he is named as the clerk to whom Cnut gives the church he had built at Assandun, commemorating his victory in 1016. After this Stigand fades into obscurity, reappearing only occasionally as a charter witness, but making little or no impression otherwise.

His story starts in earnest in the 1040s. At that point he re-emerges briefly as the bishop of an East Anglian see in 1043, early in Edward the Confessor's reign at a time when conflict was brewing between Edward and his mother Emma. Stigand had become closely involved with Emma's court and for this reason, when Emma had all her possessions taken away by Edward, Stigand was quickly deposed and had all his belongings confiscated too. As the *Anglo-Saxon Chronicle* states, this was 'because he was his [Edward's] mother's closest adviser and because she did just as he advised her – so men supposed'. Yet for unknown reasons, a year later, Stigand was restored as bishop and in 1047 moved to Winchester when his predecessor Ælfwine died. From now on, he was clearly a key member of Edward the Confessor's court, regularly witnessing charters, his star on the rise, as can be seen by his increasingly prominent position on the witness lists.

Stigand's long-lasting clerical duties saw him embroiled in the political crisis of Edward the Confessor's reign in the early 1050s, and he became critical to hostage negotiations between Edward and Earl Godwin after the latter was banished from the kingdom. Later Stigand succeeded to the see of Canterbury, holding down the post at the same time as being the bishop of Winchester, something that would later prove a deeply problematic issue. Technically, holding two sees at the same time – and England's two richest ones at that – was something that Rome objected to. Perhaps for this reason, Stigand made the decision not to travel to Rome to receive his sign of office, the *pallium* – a stole of white wool – from the Pope, as he should have done.

Collecting your pallium was an essential duty and we have a record of this from the late tenth century, when Archbishop Sigeric of Canterbury travelled to fetch his in 990. Sigeric kept a diary on the way, giving a unique insight into his travels, including all the overnight stops he made and the churches he visited en route; at least eighty stops are mentioned. The journey was long and at times perilous, but the effort and risk showed dedication fitting the importance of a personal interaction with the Pope. Stigand, however, appropriated the pallium that had belonged to his predecessor, who had been forced to escape the country after being outlawed by the king. This turned out to be a decision that would come back to haunt him.

Pretty soon, Stigand began to amass significant wealth. We can track some of his money through Domesday Book records: he had a total of £2,940 in 1066, of which £755 was his own, personal wealth, not related to his sees – a vast sum for the time. If you search out his name in the records, the amount of property in his name is staggering. It seems that some of it came into his hands by dubious means, as there are various allegations that he misappropriated funds and neglected the administration of property that belonged to the church. Worse, he was also accused of taking advantage of his position of power and driving too hard a bargain with the monks he was meant to support. In addition to his monetary wealth, he also had the important resource of personal loyalty, with over a thousand thegns and freemen in some way indebted to him.

Yet at the end of 1066, it wasn't Stigand who crowned William the Conqueror in Westminster on Christmas Day, but Archbishop

Ealdred of York. At least that is what most sources suggest, although Stigand was certainly present and may have had a bigger role than later described. In any case, soon Stigand's power and wealth – and the fact that this may have been gained dishonestly – did not go unnoticed by the new king, who clearly distrusted him. After Hastings, Stigand initially backed Edgar the Ætheling, and only submitted to William when it became clear that Edgar's metaphorical ship was sinking. But William recognised that Stigand's power made him a tricky adversary and even took him on a tour of Normandy after the conquest, presumably in an attempt to keep his enemy close. A few years later, it was clear that the Pope was severely hostile towards Stigand too, describing him in a letter as a 'source of evil'. William may also quite deliberately have used Stigand's problematic appointment as a way to gain support from the church and legitimise his English land grab. With Stigand so closely associated with Harold, William, by replacing him, would also bring order to the church. In 1070, legates were sent from Rome to depose him, both for the sin of holding two sees at the same time and for accepting another's pallium, apparently in defiance of the Pope's order. With the prelate's considerable wealth in mind, William would no doubt have seen several benefits of this outcome – much of the archbishop's wealth would now go to the king.

It appears, however, that Stigand was not happy to go quietly: he is said to have fled, eventually reaching Ely, 'with the whole contents of his treasury . . . until the outcome of his trial was known'. But in Ely, his luck ran out and he was captured, then imprisoned in Winchester. The former archbishop was allowed only a meagre pension. Queen Edith apparently went to visit him, pleading with him to eat more and dress less austerely. On either 21 or 22 February 1072, Stigand died. Despite having been removed from his post, his career of over fifty years afforded him a burial in Old Minster. There is a story that on his death a key was discovered around his neck: the key led to the discovery of hidden treasures he had squirrelled away before his arrest.

At some point Stigand's bones must have been translated to the cathedral along with so many others; his name is mentioned a few times in records relating to the cathedral's burials over the years, first as the occupant of a lead coffer near the high altar and later as being in one of the chests intermingled with the remains of Bishop Wini.

THE RED KING

A tomb, or more strictly speaking a stone coffin with a coped top, which for some centuries past has been described as the tomb of King William Rufus, in Winchester Cathedral, was opened, and its contents ascertained, by direction of the Vice-Dean (the Ven. Archdeacon Jacob) on August 27th 1868. Subsequently to the examination it then under-went, its position within the building was changed on the 15th September following. No previous notice of the transaction having been given, except to a few persons residing in the town of Winchester, I have to regret that it was not in my power to be present either at the opening or the removal. As an interest of no ordinary kind attaches to this monument, I have considered the matter to be of sufficient consequence to collect together a summary of the particulars. The tomb has long been reputed to be the resting-place of the first of the great line of English sovereigns of the present dynasty buried in England; but besides this, the fatality which caused his death, the mystery in which it was shrouded, the superstitious hatred of the man, which believed the wrath of Heaven to have followed him in the Cathedral where he lay, and to have hurled over his grave the ruins of the central tower, all contribute to invest with peculiar associations this venerable

memorial; to which I have now to add another point of interest,
namely, that an archæological question arises for solution as to the
actual identity of the tomb so recently opened, and the remains it
contained, with the tomb and the remains of the Red King.

REV. JAMES GERALD JOYCE,
paper read to the Society of Antiquaries
of London, 18 February 1869

SUCCESSION

In 1087, twenty-one years after the Norman conquest, William
the Conqueror's son William II (better known as William Rufus)
was crowned king of England after his father died in battle. Rufus
was one of at least nine children – four sons and five or six
daughters – William had with Matilda of Flanders, the daughter
of a wealthy count. The eldest son, Robert, nicknamed Curthose
(apparently because of his short legs, from the Norman French
word *courtheuse*, meaning 'short stockings'), had a tricky relationship with his father and the two had eventually become embroiled
in a contest over the control of Normandy. Richard, the second
son, died young in a hunting incident in the New Forest. The
third son, William, was born sometime between 1056 and 1060.
His nickname Rufus, given to him after his death, may have
referred to either his hair colour or his ruddy complexion, and
one medieval writer referred to him as '*rus rei*' – the Red King.
Henry, the youngest of the four boys, was born after the conquest.

William the Conqueror's death had come about through an
accident. He had travelled from England to Normandy to take
part in an attack on Mantes, a town to the west of Paris that lay

in territory disputed between the Normans and King Philip of France. Even though reportedly seriously overweight, William insisted on riding into the torched town on horseback. But in the chaos of the attack, his horse stumbled while leaping a ditch, sending the king tumbling and causing him serious injury. Though he was taken to a priory outside Rouen for treatment, it quickly became clear that William would not survive. Knowing he lay on his deathbed, the king summoned his two younger sons, but not Robert, his eldest, and named Rufus as his successor, initially intending to disinherit Robert altogether. To seal his decision, he gave Rufus his sword, symbolic of the Norman duchy, and his crown and sceptre, symbolising England. However, under pressure from the nobles surrounding him that day, the Conqueror eventually gave in and left Normandy to Robert.

Keen to assert his claim to the English throne, Rufus deserted his dying father's bedside and rushed straight to Winchester, with the additional motive of making sure he could oversee the distribution of the nation's wealth. Winchester had been home to the English treasury for centuries, something new kings knew to take advantage of. The wealth in question was significant: 'It was impossible for any man to say,' records the *Chronicle*, 'how much was gathered there in gold and in silver and in vessels and in purple cloth and in gems and in many other precious things which are difficult to recount.' According to William of Malmesbury, the citizens of Winchester welcomed Rufus on arrival, and he was promptly given the key to the treasury. Much of the wealth was distributed among churches and counties, something that helped him gather support. Seventeen days later, on Sunday 26 September, Rufus was crowned by the Archbishop of Canterbury in Westminster Abbey.

The England that William Rufus inherited had been transformed in the years since his father's defeat of Harold. The country was now firmly under Norman power, significantly changed from that once co-ruled by Rufus' grandmother once removed, Emma, but a country whose Scandinavian roots ran deep. One testimony to the changes can be seen in Domesday Book, the huge survey of most of England ordered by William the Conqueror in 1085, which was kept in Winchester. Having sent his men into every shire in England in order to find out how many hides there were in each; how many people occupied it; what land and livestock was owned; and how much he was due to receive in taxes, he also wanted to know how much everything was worth and, according to the *Chronicle*, no single hide, yard of land, ox, cow or pig had been left out – shameful though it was, the chronicler lamented, to record such things. The survey typically also contains two entries for each estate, one *tempore regis Willhelmi*, or at the time of King William, that is, 1086, and one *tempore regis Edwardi*, during the time of Edward's rule, that is, before his death in January 1066. This means we can observe how property changed hands and how the country was transformed: for instance who the new landowners were and which towns and villages were allowed to thrive. In many cases land was rearranged and reorganised, with entirely new estate patterns formed by 1086. A significant change could be seen in the drastic reduction of Scandinavian names listed as landowners in the later entries.

CONFLICT AND DEBAUCHERY

Rufus' is the Norman reign we know the least about, but we do know that it was not an easy one. Later he would become known for his death, in an accident (or perhaps murder) while hunting, and for reports of his scandalous and licentious personal behaviour: Henry of Huntingdon called him 'the evil king who indulged unashamedly in unspeakable debauchery'. In reality, he was a colourful and enigmatic figure and a highly effective king. Although Rufus' coronation was generally accepted, his succession would later be contested in a rebellion organised by his half-uncle Odo, Bishop of Bayeux, and several other nobles in support of his brother Robert Curthose. The rebels were quickly quashed, however, and Odo was banished. Yet rivalry between Robert and Rufus would colour the politics of the decades to come. When, in 1095 during the First Crusade, Pope Urban called on men to take part in an armed pilgrimage to Jerusalem, Robert answered the call. But to do so, he needed money and mortgaged Normandy to his brother in return for ten thousand marks. At the time the tensions between Rufus and Robert had escalated dangerously, and Robert's departure for the Holy Land must have solved some problems. In Britain, Rufus also faced threats from the Scots and the Welsh, the former launching numerous violent raids in England. In 1093, he crushed a revolt that led to the death of Malcolm III, king of the Scots. Rufus also had a problematic relationship with the church, both because of disagreements with Anselm, the Archbishop of Canterbury, and because of how he managed bishoprics to maintain an income. For this reason, several medieval narratives present Rufus' reign as an intense struggle between an evil king and a holy archbishop. Others, however, portray him as a model king and capable warrior, who did much good for the country as a strong and generous ruler, keeping the nation at peace. The twelfth-century Geoffrei Gaimar said that 'Never was there a king held in such affection or in such honour by his men.' Others praised Rufus for his general talents and great ideas. Yet ultimately, the negative view of him stuck, not least his reputedly outrageous behaviour. Orderic Vitalis, a monk writing English and Anglo-Norman chronicles in the twelfth century, was explicit about this: 'He never married,' said the chronicler, 'but was insatiably addicted to obscene fornication and frequent adulteries, giving his subjects a damnable example of shameful debauchery.' Rufus' sexuality has been a hot topic for discussion. While no contemporary sources confirm it, it is widely believed that he was homosexual, in part because he had never married nor, as far as we know, had any children. Later sources accuse him of sodomy, which at the time referred more generally to non-procreative sex and was certainly not seen as suitable behaviour for a monarch. Rufus and his followers were also accused of other behaviours that might encourage sodomy, such as wearing their hair long – a fashion among the young men at his court – and sporting effeminate clothing. According to one description, he was not very tall, but strong and squarely built, if a little overweight. He wore his blond locks swept back from his ruddy face, and his sparkling eyes would stare at people with menace, intimidating those he spoke to. Yet in private he could be easy-going, with a keen sense of humour and an ability to laugh at his own mistakes. He spoke in brief and sharp phrases, using peculiar expressions, and is said to have had a particular taste for expensive clothes.

Feasting and banquets at major holidays became a feature of Rufus' court, as they had been for his father William. Both of them wore their crowns and jewels to dazzle at these events. In part to facilitate this feasting on a grand scale, in 1097 Rufus began work on a vast *magna aula*, or Great Hall, at Westminster in London. The palace that Edward the Confessor had built there back in the 1040s likely had a hall already and Rufus chose to build his to the north of it. Completed within two years, just in time for the Pentecost crown-wearing feast on 29 May 1099, the spectacular hall – measuring 73 metres long and nearly 21 metres wide – was comparable in size to the nave of Winchester Cathedral. At the time it was the largest secular building in Western Europe and an immense statement of Rufus' wealth and power. In fact the hall was so large by contemporary standards that his courtiers suggested it was perhaps *too* big, causing Rufus to respond, according to Henry of Huntingdon, that it was only half big enough. From this point on, the Great Hall became the ceremonial centre of the kingship of both the Norman and later the Plantagenet kings of England: it formed a key element of coronations, as Westminster still does today. Later in the Middle Ages, Westminster Hall would take on a role as a home for law courts, something that further marked the shift of the centre of gravity from Winchester to London. In fact, as well as designing it as a party venue, Rufus might have been motivated to create a place to exercise royal justice. After his father's conquest, the *witenagemot*, the meeting of the *witan*, which had been a core element of the political justice system for centuries, had been replaced by the Great Council led by the king and his barons and churchmen. Alongside this there was the Curia or 'Aula' Regis, where a chief justiciar represented the king: this royal court was held in the Great Hall of the king's palace wherever in the country he happened to be, and it administered all of the king's business. From it, later, the Common Law courts, the Chancery and the Parliament would all develop. Westminster wasn't the only part of London's urban landscape that Rufus had an impact on. Around the same time, severe weather damaged London Bridge, with flooding all but washing it away. Rufus arranged for its reconstruction, but with new taxes from Londoners to fund it. The Tower of London was also a part of his building scheme.

DEATH IN THE FOREST

On Thursday 2 August 1100, Rufus was in the New Forest with his brother Henry and a hunting party ready for the 'fat season', prime hunting time for red deer stags. Numerous later accounts describe what happened that day, many with embellishments, but all tell the same story: the king went out to hunt and was struck by an arrow, which went straight through his heart. Rufus' killer was first named by William of Malmesbury as one Walter Tirel, a visiting Norman, described as an important baron and fine soldier. According to William, Rufus and Walter were separated from the rest of the hunting party, and when the sun was low in the sky, the king fired an arrow at a stag that happened to cross the path in front of him. At the same time, a second stag appeared and Walter took his chance, meaning to fire at it but instead hitting the king. In silence, Rufus looked down at the arrow protruding from his chest, but as he reached to break off the shaft, he stumbled forwards, accidentally pushing the lethal arrow further in. Realising the king was dead, Walter leaped onto his horse and rode off at great speed. Orderic Vitalis later said he escaped to France. Nobody pursued him. There is no way of knowing who the real killer was and more recent historians have speculated that it was not an accident at all, but a murder to benefit Rufus' brother Henry.

The king's death, at the height of his reign, was seen as God's judgment, declaring him a fundamentally bad ruler. Numerous stories mention portents and unusual weather phenomena just before Rufus' death, something that further suggests God's wrath. At the end of a tirade about his appalling behaviour and rule, the chronicler of the *Anglo-Saxon Chronicle*'s Peterborough manuscript wrote that 'therefore he was hated by well-nigh all his nation, and abhorrent to God, just as his end showed, because he departed in the midst of his injustice without repentance and any reparation'.

While his death came as a shock, few apparently showed much sympathy. Rufus' body was allegedly thrown onto a horse-drawn wagon by some peasants and dragged back to Winchester, with the corpse bleeding the whole way. There, the following morning, Rufus was buried with minimal ceremony beneath the cathedral's tower. According to Orderic Vitalis, the church bells, which rang even for the poorest in the community, remained silent. Rufus' brother Henry was immediately declared king.

When disaster struck Winchester seven years later, and the tower of the cathedral, only a decade old, collapsed, chroniclers were quick to put the blame firmly on Rufus: it was an outrage, they said, that someone so scandalous and licentious, who had died without being given his last sacraments, had been buried in such a sacred place. In reality, the failure of the structure likely owed something to the haste with which it had been built, as well as to the high water table in Winchester, which can make building anything substantial a structural challenge. William of Malmesbury even admitted that 'the fabric might easily have collapsed through unsound construction, even had he never been buried there'. While Bishop Walkelin's building scheme was an impressive one, the vast scale and speed at which the cathedrals had been built could also have been problematic. Some of them show signs of poor workmanship and others proved disastrous: at Old Sarum (Salisbury), a mere five days after the cathedral had been consecrated in 1092, the bell tower was blown down by a storm. Abingdon, Gloucester, Ely, Evesham and Lincoln all saw their towers collapse but nothing was quite as dramatic as what happened in Winchester.

THE UNMARKED TOMB

In August 1868, the vice-dean of Winchester Cathedral made the decision to open and examine a stone coffin located in a prominent position in the centre of the choir near the foot of the steps up to the altar, before moving it elsewhere. The coffin, which bore no inscription, had for centuries been thought to be the tomb of William Rufus. On the day of its opening, the vice-dean was joined by the cathedral architect, the curator of the local museum, the town clerk, a surgeon and three other 'medical men', all eager to investigate whether the coffin contained any bones at all and if it did, of whom. When the Purbeck marble lid was removed, the tomb was found to contain a large number of bones in a severely disturbed state. This in itself came as a major surprise, because Rufus' bones were thought to have been disturbed in 1642 and subsequently moved to the mortuary chest that bore his name. The bones they discovered, several of which were broken, belonged to the incomplete skeleton of an adult man, measuring five foot eight to five foot ten in height. When they searched through the dusty insides of the coffin, the men also found a number of artefacts: several pieces of fabric, including ribbons and braids with gold thread, and a curious carved ivory animal head. Reporting on the discovery a year later, Reverend James Gerald Joyce noted that the animal, perhaps a dragon, looked to be Norman in style and may have been the handle of a knife or other similar object. Remarkably, an iron blade and several thin sticks of wood were also found inside the coffin, which the observers thought came from a hunting spear. Could this, it was imaginatively suggested at the time, have been a spear that Rufus himself had held onto at the time of his death, seeing as he was out hunting? Unfortunately, the blade was neither kept nor illustrated.

No further conclusions could be drawn from the study of the remains. It's not clear who first suggested that this coffin contained

Rufus' bones because when it was opened in the nineteenth century his name had already been inscribed on one of the chests resting only a few metres above it, on the choir screen. Records make it clear that the coffin was desecrated and opened in the 1642 Parliamentarian attack and this was presumably when the bones were disturbed and partially broken. Yet the record of William's remains ending up in the mortuary chests goes even further back in time than this. If true, it would seem odd that an almost complete skeleton would suddenly find its way into a stone coffin instead. Joyce concluded that surely a king with such a bad reputation as Rufus, so disliked in particular for his relationship with the church, would not have ended up in this prominent position.

Much of this negative view had been created later. Rufus was the only monarch to have been buried in the cathedral immediately, rather than being translated from one of the minsters, so it is not implausible that he would have been given such a prominent burial. However, subsequent analyses show these bones were probably those of someone else entirely, whose story is deeply connected to the chests: Bishop Henry of Blois. Henry was certainly buried in the cathedral, but the location of his grave had been forgotten by the late sixteenth century. However, as has been pointed out, the location, the simple twelfth-century style of the coffin and the artefacts found in it would seem very fitting for Henry. The gold thread and the rest of the textiles – now almost completely deteriorated but when examined in 1951–2 said to have included silk twill of Byzantine, Syrian or Persian origin – would match what one would expect for a bishop. Finally, that curious ivory animal head has a close parallel in an eleventh-century crozier head from Cologne, and rather than a hunting spear, the supposed metal spear could have been the rest of the staff. In the end, then, Henry may well have ended up right in the middle of the chests he himself took such care to curate.

GIRAFFE

*A*s the bones are carefully taken out of the chests, in among them a curious object appears: the carved head and neck of an animal, less than ten centimetres in length. It is beige and white in colour, with a worn surface, probably made of bone. The head, with a long neck, has broken off from the animal's body, making it difficult to identify the species. It resembles a giraffe, or someone suggests maybe an ox; the team can't quite agree.

The animal's presence in one of the chests is a mystery. There are no other objects among the bones; no gravegoods or other deliberately placed artefacts. The most plausible explanation is that it was mistaken for a human bone and that nobody discovered the mistake. Maybe, it was proposed, after the Parliamentarians' rampage through the cathedral in 1642, the animal was picked up in error. Nobody can say where it originally came from. Could it have been part of a nativity scene, arranged in the lead-up to Christmas? Or perhaps from a representation of Noah's Ark, or even from the statue of a saint, torn from its owner in the aftermath of the Reformation?

THE BONE CHESTS

WINCHESTER, 2023

I'm back in Winchester one more time, in the early spring of 2023. I head straight down the eastern aisle until I get to the stairs just before the choir. I stop to look up and catch a glimpse of one of the chests, high up on the screen. I am struck, again, by the thought that unless you know what you are looking at, you would have no idea the role the chests, and the remains within, have had in the shaping of this country over the past 1,300 years. William Rufus was to be the last English monarch to be buried in Winchester. Some claim that this was the location where Rufus' father, the ruler of a new Norman dynasty, intended for his own to lie forever in peace 'among their English and their Danish forebears'. When the cathedral was consecrated in 1093, remains – including those of Emma and Cnut – were buried in highly prestigious locations within the apse near the high altar. After all, towards the end of the eleventh century, these were the recent dead and Emma in particular was key to William the Conqueror's claim to England – something that explains why she, in contrast to all the West Saxon queens before her, was given such unique treatment. Later, too, Emma's significance has been emphasised: in the sixteenth century, the following five lines of verse were painted on the north wall of the presbytery, facing the choir:

> *This chest here contains Emma the Queen.*
> *Ethelred married her and afterwards Cnut.*
> *She bore Edward and Harthacnut.*
> *She saw these four kings hold the sceptre.*
> *Thus was she the mother and wife of kings of the English.*

William would not be buried here. Although two of his sons were, the Conqueror himself died near Rouen and was buried in the abbey founded in Caen. When Rufus' brother Henry I came to the throne in 1100, the royal connections to Winchester were becoming faint. The city's significance began to wane as London's waxed: 1104 saw the last regular crown-wearing at Easter. The town lost its royal appeal as the political focus of the country shifted.

As I look up at the chests, I am reminded that I am yet another link in a chain, writing and rewriting this history; this nesting doll of version upon version of events that have a core of truth somewhere, an unreachable real past that we will never quite grasp. Bede based his version on unknown sources; Alfred and his chroniclers on Bede. Medieval writers like William of Malmesbury added their flourishes; Victorian antiquarians yet more. Each of these had their own political motivations for writing about the past, grounded firmly in their own present. So, of course, do I, and the emphasis in my own work on scientific evidence makes me no more objective than those who have attempted to untangle these stories before me.

Despite knowing how long these things often take, I can't help but feel a sense of disappointment that the work to identify the remains has not yet been finished. Even when it is complete, however, we have to admit that the science will not answer all the lingering questions we have about the bones. But there are things we do know. I walk away from the chests and into the south transept, where a staircase leads me up to an exhibition. Here fragments of the cathedral and the chest's stories are pieced together. Two fifteenth-century chests are on display; as are 3D printed replicas of bones and skulls, along with selected artefacts from the extensive excavations that have taken place here over the years and, crucially, evidence for what we know so far.

THE EVIDENCE

What, then, can we now piece together about the contents of the chests, on the basis of centuries of historical evidence and archaeological investigations? It is clear that the jumbling up of the Winchester remains goes back a very long time. Their movement between and away from the two minsters clearly had an impact, not least in their translation into the current Norman cathedral. Countless generations have made those bones their own and used their power for their own purposes.

The transferral of bones into chests seems a natural solution to the problem of moving bones: as anyone who has ever excavated a grave will tell you, bones invariably get lost in the process, not least the fragile and delicate fingers, toes and vertebrae. Then, of course, there is the problem of keeping track of who was where when all identifying features have rotted away. Thus, Henry of Blois should perhaps be forgiven for jumbling up the bishops and kings, despite his efforts to label the lead chests he created. Still, it was likely the Civil War attack that caused more damage than any other event – yet afterwards the chests lay largely undisturbed until the first real investigation in 1797 by Edmund Cartwright Jr. Cartwright recorded what he found and had his report published, albeit with pretty limited information. The chests would be opened several times more in the nineteenth and early twentieth century, including in 1932, when new inner chests of wood were placed inside each. In 1992, the chests were reopened and their contents photographed but not disturbed.

In their new investigations, the forensic team counted more than 1,300 fragments of bone, which they could separate into twenty-three unique individuals. Of these, one female skeleton was discovered, the woman aged fifty or above, radiocarbon dated to within the Anglo-Saxon period. Only one woman is named on the chests, and that is Emma. The bones are a perfect match for the profile of Emma, but is the body really hers? The only other female ruler who could plausibly have been buried in one of the minsters is Seaxburh, but her death in the late seventh century is likely too early. With the status and significance of Emma in mind, the identification of this body as being hers seems highly plausible.

Two of the skeletons were those of adolescents, aged between eleven and fifteen at the time of death. Preliminary ancient DNA analysis showed they were both male and the publicised radiocarbon dates placed them in the mid-eleventh to late twelfth century. The result narrows down the search for their identity. One particular king's son, in the minsters' story, offers a very likely candidate: Edgar the Peacemaker's son Edmund. But since he died in 971, this date may rule him out. With the lack of royal and noble burials in Winchester after the reign of Rufus, there are two boys from the Norman royal family, direct descendants of William the Conqueror, who are possible candidates. William and Matilda's second son Richard seems to have arrived in England from Normandy around 1068 – there are diplomas witnessed by him that year and the next – and in 1069 he is in Old Minster in Winchester, in 'the monastery of St Swithun', where that year his father celebrated Easter. After that Richard disappears from the records until his death is described quite some time later, the first and perhaps most plausible account being by Orderic Vitalis. While no date for the death is given, Orderic says that he had 'not yet received the belt of knighthood', which probably meant he was under sixteen. One day, Orderic tells us, Richard was out hunting in the New Forest, the woodland created by his father precisely for that purpose. As the young ætheling galloped his horse through the trees an unfortunate accident happened: a large hazel branch got caught on the pommel of his saddle and Richard was badly crushed, leaving him mortally injured. He survived for a week before he died of his wounds. There is a curious similarity to what befell William in 1087, when his horse leaped over a ditch while the king rode through the burning streets of Mantes. A little later, the prior of Winchester provides an account that suggests Richard was killed by an arrow, while William of Malmesbury blames 'the foggy and corrupted air' of the New Forest, information he says he had from an anonymous source. Regardless of how it happened, it seems likely that Richard died when still a teenager. None of the written sources tell us where he was interred. However, in the existing cathedral, beneath a niche in the south screen in the presbytery, a slab of Purbeck marble covering a tomb bears the inscription: 'Here lies Richard son of King William the Elder and Duke Beorn'. The lettering on this slab is very particular and can be dated to the later twelfth century by its style, while the use of Purbeck marble means it would not have been laid before the middle of the twelfth century. In 1887, a local antiquary by the name of Francis Joseph Baigent examined the tomb, finding a lead coffin inside, with an almost identical inscription, but this time in an eleventh-century script. This means that Richard must have first been buried in Old Minster – the Norman cathedral was not yet built at that point – and later translated.

While we can't confirm if Richard and Beorn's bones are both really in this lead coffin today, thirty years after the tomb was opened Canon John Vaughn wrote the following note: 'Mr. F. J. Baigent . . . states that the skull within the leaden coffin was a small one, with a curiously-shaped, narrow jaw-bone, clearly that of a boy no more than 16 years of age.' Baigent believed only one person was buried in this tomb and from the drawing he made of it at the time, it seems only a small corner of the lead coffin was folded back. There is little to no chance that his estimate of the age and sex could be correct from such a small glimpse, and it seems more likely that the enthusiastic amateur jumped to conclusions. It's very possible that Richard still rests in the coffin bearing his name, but equally his bones may have found their way into the chests somewhere along the way.

The second Norman candidate is, confusingly, also called Richard, another descendant of William and victim of a hunting accident in the New Forest. This particular Richard was William's grandson, the illegitimate child of his son Robert Curthose, making him the other Richard's nephew.

Robert Curthose apparently had quite a rebellious youth, which included fighting against his father and raids on the territories around Normandy. He apparently fathered several children. According to Orderic Vitalis, one of these women was the beautiful concubine of a priest, who he fell in love with. Yet he clearly did not stay to bring up his offspring because it wasn't until several years later that the woman came to Robert's court and presented him with two boys, named William and Richard, who she said were his. Robert was doubtful and made the woman prove her claim by undertaking the ordeal of carrying a hot iron. The test was passed, and the sons' positions were secured. Richard's life ended in May 1100 when he was out hunting in the forest, aged no more than about twenty and probably a little younger. Orderic states that a *lugubris eventus* – a 'tragic event' – occurred, in which one of the knights of Richard's uncle William Rufus fired an arrow at a deer but missed: the arrow, instead, flew towards Richard who was defenceless against its sharp point and died instantly. The unfortunate archer fled to a priory and became a monk, presumably to atone for his sin.

There are no records of where this Richard was buried, nor any descriptions bearing his name. The only person to have commented on it is a seventeenth-century historian by the name of John Trussell, who wrote that 'Hee was buried by his unkle [Rufus] in St. Swythins att Winchester', although we have no idea what source Trussell used to support this statement. Nevertheless, considering his uncle's interment in the cathedral, as well as the place of death so close by, it seems plausible that he would also end up there. In fact, the lack of another tomb for him could even be taken to make it more likely that his remains found their way into the gathering of bones in the chests.

Apart from these three, the bones have so far given few further clues as to who they may have belonged to. To get closer to the identities of the remaining individuals, we need to consider who they *could* be. Yet establishing exactly who was buried in the minsters, and who could have ended up in those chests, is not entirely straightforward.

THE BURIALS

Going back over what we know about royal and ecclesiastical burials in Winchester, listing those who were likely buried in New Minster seems most straightforward, as these individuals relate directly to the relatively well recorded foundation of the new royal house by Edward the Elder. This foundation was a priority for Edward, both for its own sake and for that of his father, Alfred the Great, or rather, for the sake of their *souls*. Edward's mother Ealhswith was buried there after she died in December 902, as was his brother Æthelweard two decades later. Edward was interred there himself in 924, along with his son Ælfweard, who died just a few weeks later. Before his death, Edward moved his father Alfred's body from Old Minster to New Minster. Finally, Edward's grandson King Eadwig was buried in New Minster as well. This, then, means that at least six members of Edward's family were interred in New Minster. Yet the church was demolished when the new cathedral was finished, and by this point the monastic community had already moved to its new site, Hyde Abbey. It has been presumed that all the royal remains of New Minster were moved at the same time, even though only those of Alfred, Ealhswith and Edward are specifically referenced in the written records. Could some of them perhaps have ended up in the cathedral – and the chests – after all?

The Old Minster burials are more complex. The royal burials known to have taken place there can be divided into two different groups: first, the early Wessex kings and second, the Anglo-Danish dynasty of Cnut and members of his family. There are only two other kings in between these: Alfred and Eadred; the former is possibly accounted for, while Eadred is recorded in the *Anglo-Saxon Chronicle* as having been moved to Winchester after his death in Frome.

The earliest king named on the chests is Cynegils, but no other early written sources can confirm he was buried in Winchester. Still, it is not implausible: as the first of the West Saxon kings to convert to Christianity, and with the prominence of Winchester at the time, it would have been a likely place of burial for him. What happened to his son Cenwealh, during whose reign Old Minster was founded, is more uncertain, although a fifteenth-century chronicler claims both he and the other seventh-century kings Æscwine and Centwine were buried in Winchester. Moving into the eighth century, another three West Saxon kings are unaccounted for in the records: Æthelheard, Cuthred and Sigeberth. They may well be among the anonymous dead.

Interestingly, while Egbert, Alfred's grandfather, is one of those listed on the chests, his actual place of burial is not recorded in any pre-Conquest sources: the first mention comes from Richard of Devizes' twelfth-century *Winchester Annals*.

The second group, the Anglo-Danish dynasty, is more straightforward. After his death in Shaftesbury, Cnut was buried in Old Minster, probably behind the Great Altar. Soon he was joined by Emma, Harthacnut and his nephew Beorn, until they were perhaps moved into the new cathedral on its consecration. While we have no evidence for this, their remains must at the latest have been removed when Old Minster was demolished to make space for the new Norman cathedral. The excavations of Old Minster in the 1960s revealed at least four stone coffins set around the monument constructed over St Swithun's empty grave on the western side of the church. Another possibility is that these may originally have contained significant people who wanted to be associated closely, in death, with Winchester's saint. Could they have been Cnut and his family? By the later twelfth century, this area, referred to as a 'memorial court', had fallen into disrepair and in 1158, Henry, Lord Bishop of Winchester, brought a number of bones into the new cathedral, quite possibly from that location. A text records that he moved them from 'an unseemly place' – perhaps the court that was now in such poor condition. Excavations during building work in the cathedral also uncovered several blocks of limestone with inscriptions on them that can be dated stylistically to the twelfth century: these include the names Emma, Ælfwine, Edward and Æthelwulf, all of whom are now listed on the mortuary chests, and it seems likely they belonged to the part of the new cathedral that now held St Swithun's shrine.

But what about Harthacnut's remains – did they end up in the mortuary chests? We know that after his death in London, his body was moved the one hundred kilometres to Winchester, where he was buried in Old Minster alongside his father, the last Danish king to be buried there. But after this point we know nothing more for several hundred years. There is an inscription with his name in a fourteenth-century niche, but he is not listed in the late sixteenth-century list of those in Bishop Fox's chests, although, as we have seen, those early lists are not reliable. Other accounts place him in the same chest as his father, but again that cannot be verified. Harthacnut may, however, be elsewhere in the cathedral: in the north screen of the presbytery there is a plaque with an inscription that reads: 'Harthacnut who lies here carried the sceptre of the kingdom, and was himself born of Emma and Cnut. He died AD 1042.'

Like the one on the opposite side of the presbytery that might house Richard, this renaissance plaque may in fact hold a burial behind or beneath it: if so, this might be the earliest surviving burial of any king of England or Denmark. However, to investigate the possibility, archaeologist John Crook used both a metal detector and ground-penetrating radar up against the stonework, either of which should have picked up a signal if there was a burial within. Using the method on the south side, for instance, the metal detector confirmed the presence of a large metal object (the lead coffin of Richard and Beorn). Yet where Harthacnut is meant to lie, both machines remained silent. Could Harthacnut, therefore, have ended up in the chests after all?

Another candidate for the chests is Eorl Beorn, if he is not in the tomb that bears his name. Why Beorn ended up in Winchester in the first place is unusual, but probably testimony to his status as the highest-ranking Dane in England at the time. He was, of course, also the brother and nephew of kings: not only was Beorn Cnut's nephew, but his paternal aunt Gytha was married to Earl Godwin, making him the cousin of the future Queen Edith and King Harold II as well.

Beorn was murdered in 1049. That year he was persuaded by his exiled cousin, Swein Godwinson, to help plead for forgiveness from King Edward. The two set off to Sandwich but on the way Swein had Beorn killed and buried surreptitiously, either at Dartmouth or Axminster. While we don't know the details, the *Anglo-Saxon Chronicle* states that his remains were later translated to Winchester to be interred alongside his uncle Cnut. One of the manuscripts says that this was done by Harold, while another claims it was his anonymous friends and the 'fleet of London'. Others have pointed out that neither of these candidates likely had the necessary connections to order the re-interment, and that instead it may have come from King Edward himself. Winchester had a very large Scandinavian community and with Beorn of such high status, his respectful reburial may have been politically wise.

The final person whose presence in the chests needs explaining is Edmund Ironside. As we have already seen, Edmund appears also to have had a tomb in the cathedral, according to another inscription on the presbytery screens, despite the written records suggesting he was never in Winchester at all. Yet where Edmund's body finally ended up is a mystery. The grave slab is now located in the wall up against the south screen, but it has clearly been moved several times. In 1798, it was on the floor to the north of the Norman apse and further back, in the mid-fifteenth century, it was in the ground at the north side of the cathedral's altar. This was unlikely to have been the original location because his actual bones had been translated, apparently into a sarcophagus and to the east end of the presbytery, by the mid-fifteenth century. With a grave slab moved so many times, it would seem highly likely that the bones – if they really were in Winchester – could have ended up in the mortuary chests.

Finally, alongside the kings and queens, and the two named

bishops Wini and Ælfwine, it seems likely that Stigand also ended his days in Winchester, with other Winchester clergy. And, if John Crook is correct, the mortuary chests may also have – surreptitiously – ended up housing the remains of the city's most sacred saint, Swithun.

EPILOGUE

We may ask ourselves why, even today, we are so concerned with finding and identifying the bones of the distant dead? Why does it matter to us where they are buried and whether we can identify skeletal remains? For the modern dead, the answer seems obvious: to give closure to the mourners and to provide them with a grave to go to, and in the process to give the deceased the respect and dignity we feel they deserve. We may also consider our beliefs about the afterlife, and in some cultures be wary of what the dead's spirits may do to us if we fail to respect them. In the US, repatriation of recent and historic war dead is a major undertaking: the Defense POW/MIA Accounting Agency works on accounting for the approximately 81,500 Americans missing from conflicts going all the way back to the Second World War.

When we go further back in time, these motivations change, as we can rarely trace living descendants. Here, then, the interest is often more in people we *can* trace the descendants of, and that tends to be royals or other individuals who made a significant imprint on history.

The identification in 2012 of Richard III caused a worldwide sensation. The interest in Richard's discovery was manifold: because of the historical impact of this figure – Richard died at the Battle of Bosworth in 1485, where his army fought against that of Henry Tudor, a battle that signified the end of the Wars of the Roses – and his associated starring role in one of Shakespeare's plays, in which he is portrayed as a villainous hunchback plotting to take the throne; but also because it was a demonstration of what modern science could do: it could solve a *mystery*, it could provide an answer to a centuries-old question. More cynically, there were all those who benefited or profited from the publicity, some with wholly commendable motivations, others perhaps less so. For Leicester, the benefits would be significant: annual visitor numbers to Leicester Cathedral increased from 30,000 to 160,000, all of whom contributed in some way to the city's economy. There's an obvious parallel here to the worshipping of saints' and kings' bones. Consider, for instance, Winchester's cult of St Swithun and the huge number of pilgrims it attracted. Incidentally, later in the Middle Ages, the footfall of such pilgrims to monastic institutions would become the catalyst for the creation of inns and, ultimately, the British pub.

The Winchester chests, and those they contain, owe their fame in particular to Wessex's role in the shaping of England as a nation and to Alfred's dynasty, both his ancestors and his descendants. Few early kings are as well known in England as Alfred the Great; fewer still are given such importance in the nation's history. At the time of writing, those who wish to obtain British citizenship have to pass the 'Life in the UK' test: an exam involving questions on topics including government, culture, language and history, taken from an official syllabus issued by the UK government for students to learn and revise. The history chapter contains a section on the Vikings, summarising three hundred years of history in three short paragraphs. Alfred, the coursebook confidently states, was the king who defeated the Vikings. This is one of the reasons why among the English kings, Alfred is the only one to be given the title 'the

Great'. Ironically, in England, as we have seen, the next to have that same honour would be the Danish king Cnut.

Just as 'every age has the Stonehenge it deserves – or desires', so, too, does every age have the Alfred it desires. The real descendants of Alfred used their family's physical remains to assert their claim to power and the two invading dynasties that were to follow, the Danes and the Normans, were to do the same. In the late Middle Ages, Alfred's educational achievements were important to those concerned with the founding of colleges; in the seventeenth and eighteenth centuries, his triumphs at sea and with shipbuilding were seen as especially important for a growing empire with ever increasing ambitions from its outward shores. In fact, 'Rule Britannia' – with its infamous lyrics 'Rule, Britannia! rule the waves / Britons never will be slaves', was composed in 1740 for a masque (a performance blending drama, music and dance) themed around Alfred's achievements in the swineherd's hut in the Somerset marshes. To the Victorians, Alfred became an icon, a true hero in his efforts to save, and build, a nation; he and his fellow 'Anglo-Saxons' were also essential in giving the country an origin story that aligned with the ethos of the British Empire. In Winchester, Edmund Cartwright Jr's first investigation of the mortuary chests coincided with a newfound and intense antiquarian interest in England's past, and especially its origins as a country. The very term 'Anglo-Saxon', which we now use almost indiscriminately to describe the people and period after the fall of Rome and before the arrival of the Normans, was more or less invented in the eighteenth and nineteenth centuries. Although first used by Alfred in the ninth century, and again by the likes of Athelstan in the tenth century, it was rarely if ever used as an ethnic or cultural descriptive until recent times – with the exception, perhaps, of Alfred's time. The early Victorians needed a national origin story for the country and so the 'Anglo-Saxons' were resurrected: this way, those who became the English could be separated from the Celtic-speakers, the Vikings and the Normans. Some of the early nineteenth-century scholars were influenced by contemporary racial thinking and rooted in a colonial world, into which the white, *Anglo-Saxon* past fitted perfectly. In fact, even now, the term is in many spheres used in this same manner, to denote a white and racially superior culture that is not based on actual historical evidence.

But what about today – do human remains still have the same physical and political power as they had in the past? In some places, it seems that they do. In October 2022, with a devastating and senseless war still raging in Ukraine following Vladimir Putin's invasion, a Russian force launched a targeted mission against St Catherine's Cathedral in Kherson. The force had a specific aim: to steal the remains of the eighteenth-century Russian commander Grigory Alexandrovich Potemkin, who annexed Crimea in 1783 and was a lover of Catherine the Great. In his own invasion, Putin had been inspired by Potemkin's vision to create a 'New Russia' stretching across southern Ukraine, making the historic commander something of a hero for Kremlin loyalists and the illegal invaders of the Kherson region. Inside the cathedral, to get to Potemkin's remains, the looters had to climb down a narrow passageway to enter a crypt set beneath a white marble gravestone. There the remains were held inside a simple wooden coffin marked with a cross: his skull and bones, all carefully numbered with indelible ink, were stored in a black fabric bag. The looters removed the bones and took them to an undisclosed location on the eastern bank of the Dnipro river. Where the bones will finally end up is uncertain, but one thing is clear: the physical remains of historical figures, as manifestations of the past, are still being actively manipulated in today's politics.

A month earlier, for five days in September 2022, a remarkable queue snaked its way through central London. Complete with toilet stops, water stations and colour-coded wristbands, 'The Queue', which stretched for more than sixteen kilometres, allowed an estimated 250,000 people to file past the coffin of Queen Elizabeth II as she lay in state in Westminster Hall; a hall built a millennium earlier by William Rufus, son of William the Conqueror. According to official figures, 29.2 million people in the UK tuned in to watch her funeral on TV, as her coffin, adorned with her crown, orb and sceptre, made its way from Westminster Hall to Westminster Abbey. Only days before, the TV cameras had followed the hearse carrying the Queen's mortal remains in a cortege from Scotland, where she died, before she was flown south to London. Never before has a royal funeral been watched by so many even though the impact of the death of a monarch on our society has perhaps never been smaller. In May 2023, the coronation of the next British king, Charles III, took place. The crown he wore was named St Edward's Crown: this crown was made in 1661 to replace an original allegedly from the eleventh century, worn by Edward the Martyr and kept until it was either sold or melted down by Parliamentarians in 1649.

Although now almost homeopathically diluted, elements of the early medieval past still resonate in this present. When you look up at those mortuary chests in Winchester, with their painted names and anonymous bones inside, it is clear that the present also resonates in the stories that we tell about the past. What is so special about those bones, however, is that when we do what we can to add flesh back onto them, they remind us of the human stories within that history: those past lives of people who were a little bit like us, who lived, loved, and left an imprint on the generations that came after them.

NOTES

CHEST I

17   the *Anglo-Saxon Chronicle* A collection of annals chronicling the history of early medieval England, thought to have been originally created in Wessex in the ninth century. There are seven surviving manuscripts of the *Anglo-Saxon Chronicle*, identified by the letters A to G. Manuscript A appears to be a copy of the *Chronicle* more or less as it was soon after it was first compiled in Alfred the Great's court (871–899). Over time new parts and additions were added. In the tenth century, this manuscript was kept in Winchester, where it was used largely by clerics and monks. This makes it no surprise that the manuscript A *Chronicle* has such a focus on Wessex, as even after Alfred's reign, it recorded the rise of the dynasty that led to a united England.

     Manuscript C dates much later, to the 1040s, and was written down somewhere in the Midlands. It contains the earliest version of what has become known as 'The Chronicle of the Reign of Æthelred'. This covers the period between 983 and 1016, and the author specifically focuses on the years between 1012 and 1016 – that is, the time leading up to Cnut's conquest. This detailed account concentrates on what went wrong – and who was to blame – which enabled Cnut's success. Several later manuscripts with additions date, in some cases, to as late as the twelfth century.

17   *well after the production of such crafts* For preliminary details, see https://www.nationaltrust.org.uk/visit/gloucestershire-cotswolds/

chedworth-roman-villa/archaeological-discoveries-at-chedworth-roman-villa

21 *the researchers estimated* S. Leslie, B. Winney, G. Hellenthal et al., 'The Fine-scale Genetic Structure of the British Population', *Nature*, 519.7543, 2015, p. 313

22 *around ten thousand graves* R. Hedges, 'Anglo-Saxon Migration and the Molecular Evidence', p. 80 in H. Hamerow, D. A. Hinton and S. Crawford (eds), *The Oxford Handbook of Anglo-Saxon Archaeology* (Oxford University Press, 2011)

22 *a team published the results* J. Gretzinger, D. Sayer, P. Justeau et al., 'The Anglo-Saxon Migration and the Formation of the Early English Gene Pool', *Nature*, 610, 2022, pp. 112–19, https://doi.org/10.1038/s41586-022-05247-2

24 *A recent large-scale study* Sam Leggett, Susanne Hakenbeck and Tamsin O'Connell, 'Large-scale Isotopic Data Reveal Gendered Migration into Early Medieval England c AD 400–1100', OSF Preprints, 9 June 2022, doi:10.31219/osf.io/jzfv6

24 *slightly lower than in the ancient DNA study* Sam Leggett, 'Isotopes and aDNA: Teasing Apart Ancestry Versus Migration in Early Medieval England', *Current Archaeology*, 5 October 2022, https://the-past.com/feature/isotopes-and-adna-teasing-apart-ancestry-versus-migration-in-early-medieval-england/

25 *'is a great city on the shore'* Caitlin R. Green, 'Britain, the Byzantine Empire, and the Concept of an Anglo-Saxon "Heptarchy": Hārūn ibn Yaḥyā's Ninth-century Arabic Description of Britain', *Global Perspectives on Early Medieval England*, ed. K. L. Jolly and B. Brooks (Woodbridge: Boydell & Brewer, 2022), pp. 98 and 95

29 *'Oldminster . . . became the very heart'* Barbara Carpenter Turner, *Winchester* (Southampton: Paul Cave, 1980)

32 *well maintained over time* T. Pestell (2011) 'Markets, Emporia, *Wics*, and "Productive" Sites: Pre-Viking trade Centres in Anglo-Saxon England', p. 569, in Hamerow, Hinton and Crawford (eds), *The Oxford Handbook of Anglo-Saxon Archaeology*

33 *underneath the high altar* see R. N. Quirk, 'Winchester Cathedral in the Tenth Century', *Archaeological Journal*, 114:1, 1957, pp. 28–68

33 *describing how the king left his marriage* Anne Foerster, 'Female Rulership: The Case of Seaxburh, Queen of Wessex', *Mittelalter. Interdisziplinäre Forschung und Rezeptionsgeschichte* 1, 2018, pp. 164–8, https://mittelalter.

hypotheses.org/12691; Anne Foerster, 'The King's Wife in Wessex: The Tale of Wicked Queen Eadburh', *Mittelalter. Interdisziplinäre Forschung und Rezeptionsgeschichte* 1, 2018, pp. 169–73, http://mittelalter.hypoth-eses.org/12694

35 *'arrange what was needed'* Rudolf of Fulda, *Life of Leoba* (c.836), https://sourcebooks.fordham.edu/basis/leoba.asp

37 *'to be written many of them'* Laws of Alfred Int. 49.9 in D. Whitelock (ed.), *English Historical Documents, Volume 1, c. 500–1042* (London: Eyre & Spottiswoode, 2nd edn, 1979), p. 373

42 *date of the garter-tags pointed* B. Yorke, 'Royal Burial in Winchester: Context and Significance', p. 65 in R. Lavelle, S. Roffey and K. Weikert (eds), *Early Medieval Winchester: Communities, Authority and Power in an Urban Space, c.800–c.1200* (Oxford: Oxbow Books, 2021), p. 65

CHEST II

59 *at the end of the eighth* Clare Downham, 'The Earliest Viking Activity in England?' *English Historical Review*, 132.554, 2017, pp. 1–12

60 *struck in Northumbria between 737 and 758* E. Screen, 'Small Doors on the Viking Age: The Anglo-Saxon Coins in Norway Project', *British Academy Review*, 24, Summer 2014

62 *powerful neighbouring ally* Foerster, 'The King's Wife in Wessex', p. 170

70 *finally reaching Rome* V. Ortenberg, 'Archbishop Sigeric's journey to Rome in 990', *Anglo-Saxon England*, 19, 1990, pp. 197–246, p. 204

71 *'was not customary'* Janet L. Nelson (ed. and trans.), *The Annals of St Bertin* (Manchester University Press, 1991), p. 83

72 *ceremony itself also made a mark* J. A. Smith, 'The Earliest Queen-Making Rites', *Church History*, 66(1), 1997, pp. 18–35, https://doi.org/10.2307/3169630

72 *used when Queen Elizabeth II was crowned* F. Scott, 'Eadgifu: The Queen who Outlasted Five Kings', https://florencehrs.substack.com/p/judith-the-first-crowned-queen-of?s=r#footnote-1

80 *'kings with bishops and bishops with kings'* T. Rudborne, *Historia Maior*, in *Anglia Sacra*, Vol. 1, ed. H. Wharton (London, 1691), pp. 177–286, p. 194

80 *arms of his numerous bishoprics* John Crook, 'Witness from on High', *History Today*, 65 (10), October 2015, https://www.historytoday.com/witness-high

85 *anatomically speaking* Luke John Murphy et al., 'An Anatomy of the Blood Eagle: The Practicalities of Viking Torture', *Speculum*, 97 (1), January 2022, pp. 1–39, https://www.journals.uchicago.edu/doi/10.1086/717332#_i19

97 *two quite different political* S. Ashby and A. Marriott, 'Territorial Division in the Alfred-Guðrum Treaty: A Ninth Century Diplomatic Innovation?', *Apardjon Journal for Scandinavian Studies*, 2020, pp. 22–53, p. 24

104 *rather than hides* J. A. Stattel, 'Legal Culture in the Danelaw: A Study of III Æthelred', *Anglo-Saxon England*, 48, 2019, pp. 163–203

105 *The study set out* Leslie, Winney and Hellenthal et al., 'The Fine-scale Genetic Structure of the British Population', pp. 309–14

106 *in its infancy* Courtnay Konshuh, 'Constructing Early Anglo-Saxon Identity in the *Anglo-Saxon Chronicles*', in Alexander James Langlands and Ryan Lavelle (eds), *The Land of the English Kin* (Leiden: Brill, 2020), https://brill.com/view/book/9789004421899/BP000009.xml

109 *pain in the spleen* G. Craig, 'Alfred the Great: A Diagnosis', *Journal of the Royal Society of Medicine*, 84, 1991, pp. 303–5; but see also D. Pratt, 'The Illnesses of King Alfred the Great', *Anglo-Saxon England*, 30, 2001, pp. 39–90

113 *define the group that ruled against them* Konshuh, 'Constructing Early Anglo-Saxon Identity in the *Anglo-Saxon Chronicles*', p. 158

114 *those of English origin* S. Foot, 'The Making of Angelcynn: English Identity before the Norman Conquest', *Transactions of the Royal Historical Society*, 6, 1996, pp. 25–49

116 *a greedy king* N. Marafioti, 'Seeking Alfred's Body: Royal Tomb as Political Object in the Reign of Edward the Elder', *Early Medieval Europe*, 23(2), 2015, pp. 202–28, p. 208

119 *for stylistic effect* Mark Atherton, *The Battle of Maldon: War and Peace in Tenth-Century England* (London: Bloomsbury, 2021), p. 120

123 *rejected his wife not long afterwards* Scott, 'Eadgifu: The Queen who Outlasted Five Kings'

124 *field near Harrogate in Yorkshire* 'Vale of York Hoard', *Current Archaeology*, 1 October 2010, https://archaeology.co.uk/articles/news/vale-of-york.htm

127 '*This sarcophagus contains the remains*' The reports on Eadgyth await full publication in English, but see e.g. the University of Bristol press release at https://www.bristol.ac.uk/news/2010/7322.html for the key information

131 '*secure and substantial archaeological evidence*' Battlefields Registration Selection Guide, December 2017, Historic England

132 *none of these graves* Tony Pollard, 'These Spots of Excavation Tell: Using Early Visitor Accounts to Map the Missing Graves of Waterloo', *Journal of Conflict Archaeology*, 16:2, 2021, pp. 75–113

135 *weapons that were common* Jo Appleby et al., 'Perimortem Trauma in King Richard III: A Skeletal Analysis', *The Lancet*, 385 (9964), January 2015, pp. 253–9, https://www.sciencedirect.com/science/article/abs/pii/S0140673614608047

135 *year of death between 1456 and 1530* Richard Buckley et al., ' "The King in the Car Park": New Light on the Death and Burial of Richard III in the Grey Friars Church, Leicester, in 1485', *Antiquity*, 87 (336), June 2015, pp. 519–38, https://www.researchgate.net/publication/273293657_

135 *right shoulder that was higher* Jo Appleby et al., 'The Scoliosis of Richard III, Last Plantagenet King of England: Diagnosis and Clinical Significance', *The Lancet*, 383 (9932), 31 May 2014, p. 1944, https://www.thelancet.com/journals/lancet/article/PIIS0140-6736(14)60762-5/fulltext

137 '*our sceptic would be driven*' T. King, G. Fortes, P. Balaresque et al., 'Identification of the Remains of King Richard III', *Nature Communications*, 5 (5631), 2014, https://doi.org/10.1038/ncomms6631

139 *wealthiest woman in England* F. Scott, 'Eadgifu: The Queen who Outlasted Five Kings', https://florencehrs.substack.com/p/eadgifu#details

141 *finest porphyry marble* E. Albert and K. Tucker, *In Search of Alfred the Great: The King, the Grave, the Legend* (Stroud: Amberley Publishing, 2014)

CHEST III

163 *date to the late twelfth century* John Crook, 'King Edgar's Reliquary of St Swithun', *Anglo-Saxon England*, 21, 1992, p. 193

CHEST IV

176 'About three o'clock this Saturday morning' John Crook, 'St Swithun of Winchester', in John Crook (ed.), Winchester Cathedral: Nine Hundred Years 1093–1993 (Phillimore, 1993), p. 66, citing PRO, State Papers, 1.621 printed in W. De Gray Birch (ed.), Letters and Papers of Henry VIII, xiii.ii (London, 1893), p. 155, item 401

176 'St. Swithan and other reliques whereabout' cited in Crook, Winchester Cathedral, p. 66

179 '[Æthelred] is the only ruler' E. A. Freeman, The History of the Norman Conquest of England, its Causes and its Results, 6 vols (1867 to 79); second edition, vols 1–4 (1870–6); third edition vols 1–2 (1877), 1.258–9

189 up to nine such injuries each C. Falys, 'The Human Bone', p. 57 cited in L. Loe, A. Boyle, H. Webb and D. Score, 'Given to the Ground': A Viking Age Mass Grave on Ridgeway Hill, Weymouth (Dorset Natural History and Archaeological Society, 2014), p. 71

189 another was discovered in 2009 see Loe, Boyle, Webb and Score, 'Given to the Ground', p. 71

191 three examples have been found K. Prangsgaard and P. Bennike, 'Tandtatovering', Skalk, No. 3, 2010

191 total of 132 individuals C. Arcini, The Viking Age: A Time with Many Faces (Oxford: Oxbow Books, 2018) p. 80

195 a catalogue of all the Anglo-Saxon coins Screen, 'Small Doors on the Viking Age'

198 'There is an added embellishment' Narratio Metrica de Sancti Swithuno cited in Lapidge (2003), p. 389

198 silver garter hooks at his knees Biddle (2018), p. 23

198 'where heaven and earth met' Roach (2016), p. 168

201 'King Harald commanded this monument' Else Roesdahl, 'The Emergence of Denmark and the Reign of Harald Bluetooth', in Stefan Brink and Neil S. Price (eds), The Viking World (London: Routledge, 2008), p. 658

205 'And Ulfr has taken three payments in England' Runic inscription U 344 in Scandinavian Runic-text Database latest, Department of Scandinavian Languages, Uppsala University, http://kulturarvsdata.se/uu/srdb/f1ad81a4-7f22-4f17-97fc-1cfb6ff294fd

205 'Gunnkell placed this stone' Runic inscription Sm 101 in Scandinavian Runic-text Database latest, Department of Scandinavian Languages, Uppsala University, http://kulturarvsdata.se/uu/srdb/b907d60d-19b8-4223-9c7e-9207997216c7

205 *high-status burial as a stone coffin* 'A Story of Swords', The Baths Bloggers, 17 March 2021, https://bathsbloggers.blogspot.com/2021/

206 *'to the Norsemen of the Seine'* Lesley Abrams, 'Early Normandy', in David Bates (ed.), *Anglo-Norman Studies 35: Proceedings of the Battle Conference 2012* (Woodbridge: Boydell & Brewer, 2013), pp. 45–64, note 3

206 *found in this part of Normandy* Abrams, 'Early Normandy', p. 46

207 *dauðamaðr . . . and flóttamaðr . . . respectively* Jean Renaud, 'The Duchy of Normandy' in Brink and Price (eds), *The Viking World*, p. 455

211 *researchers tried* https://www.medieval.eu/ganger-rolf-rollo/

211 *radiocarbon dates delivered the blow* https://www.vg.no/nyheter/utenriks/i/QLk8R/rollo-mysteriet-dette-fant-de-i-graven

214 *'Yet in the end'* Ann Williams, 'Thorkell the Tall and the Bubble Reputation: The Vicissitudes of Fame', p. 144 in Ryan Lavelle and Simon Roffey (eds), *Danes in Wessex: The Scandinavian Impact on Southern England, c.800–c.1000* (Oxford: Oxbow Books, 2016)

CHEST V

247 *none of the archaeological investigations* Patrick Ottaway et al., *Winchester: St. Swithun's 'City of Happiness and Good Fortune': An Archaeological Assessment* (Oxford: Oxbow Books, 2017)

249 *shows parts of two distinct scenes* Biddle (2018), pp. 26–7

251 *some kind of joint enterprise* J. Jesch, *Ships and Men in the Late Viking Age: The Vocabulary of Runic Inscriptions and Skaldic Verse* (Woodbridge: Boydell & Brewer, 2001), pp. 232–5

252 *date to the 1020s to 1030s* Biddle (2018), p. 24

254 *stereotype of the pagan warrior* C. Ellis, 'Cnut's Ecclesiastical Policy in the Context of his English and Danish Predecessors', pp 355–78, in R. North, E. Goeres and A. Finlay (eds), *Anglo-Danish Empire: A Companion to the Reign of King Cnut the Great* (De Gruyter, 2022)

256 *When and why this changed* Thijs Porck and Jodie E. V. Mann, 'How Cnut Became Canute (and How Harthacnut Became Airdeconut)', *NOWELE: North-Western European Language Evolution*, 67 (2), pp. 237–43

269 *a virgin abbess rather than a queen* Catherine Karkov, *The Ruler Portraits of Anglo-Saxon England* (Woodbridge: Boydell Press, 2004), pp. 119–20

CHEST VI

277 *he opened three prehistoric barrows* R. Gough, *Sepulchral monuments in Great Britain; applied to illustrate the history of families, manners, habits and arts, at the different periods from the Norman conquest to the seventeenth century. With introductory observations* . . . (London, Printed for the author, sold by T. Payne and son [etc.], 1796), p. cccxxxvii

281 *Edward the Confessor* Kathrin Prietzel, 'Treachery and Betrayal in the Anglo-Saxon Chronicle: The Incident of 1051', in Winfried Rudolf (ed.), *Clerks, Wives and Historians: Essays on Medieval English Language and Literature* (Peter Lang, 2008)

282 *somewhere between 7,000 and 14,000 men* L. Roach, *Empires of the Normans: Makers of Europe, Conquerors of Asia* (London: John Murray, 2022), pp. 52–3

282 *a depth of over a metre* Biddle (2018), p. 23

291 '*with the whole contents of his treasury*' *Liber Eliensis: A History of the Isles of Ely from the Seventh Century to the Twelfth*, trans. J. Fairweather (Woodbridge: Boydell Press, 2005), pp. 207–8.

297 *comparable in size to the nave* M. Collins, P. Emery, C. Phillpotts, M. Samuel and C. Thomas, 'The King's High Table at the Palace of Westminster', *Antiquaries Journal*, 92, 2012, p. 205

300 *all had their towers collapse* Roach, *Empires of the Normans*, p. 91

302 *rather than being translated* J. Crook, 'Medieval Royal and Episcopal Burials in Winchester Cathedral', *Antiquaries Journal*, 102, 2022, pp. 134–62

THE BONE CHESTS

307 '*This chest here contains Emma the Queen*' In Biddle and Kjølbye-Biddle (2016), p. 238

311 *dated to the later twelfth century* Crook, 'Medieval Royal and Episcopal Burials in Winchester Cathedral', p. 146

311 '*Mr. F. J. Baigent*' J. Vaughan, *Winchester Cathedral: Its Monuments and Memorials* (Selwyn & Blount, 1919)

313 '*Hee was buried by his unkle*' Manuscript cited in Crook, 'Medieval Royal and Episcopal Burials in Winchester Cathedral', p. 160

315 *in the western part of the church* Crook 1994, p. 173

315 *quite possibly from that location* Crook 1994, p. 181

316 *'Harthacnut who lies here'* Biddle and Kjølbye-Biddle (2016), p. 241

316 *might be the earliest surviving burial* Biddle and Kjølbye-Biddle (2016), p. 229

317 *apparently into a sarcophagus* Biddle and Kjølbye-Biddle (2016), pp. 2–6

EPILOGUE

321 *'Rule, Britannia'* Edward Rimbault Dibdin, 'The Bi-Centenary of "Rule Britannia"', *Music & Letters*, 21 (3), July 1940, pp. 275–90, https://www.jstor.org/stable/728364?seq=11

321 *the 'Anglo-Saxons' were resurrected* Howard Williams, 'The Fight for "Anglo-Saxon"', *Aeon*, 29 May 2020, https://aeon.co/essays/why-we-should-keep-the-term-anglo-saxon-in-archaeology

323 *29.2 million people in the UK* Jim Waterson and Tobi Thomas, 'More Than 29m People in UK Watched Queen's Funeral, TV Data Shows', *Guardian*, 20 September 2022, https://www.theguardian.com/uk-news/2022/sep/20/about-250000-people-queued-to-see-queens-coffin-in-london-says-minister

SELECT BIBLIOGRAPHY

Preliminary results of the Mortuary Chests projects

https://www.bristol.ac.uk/news/2019/may/winchester-cathedral-chests.html

https://archaeology.co.uk/articles/news/unlocking-the-secrets-of-the-winchester-cathedral-mortuary-chests.htm

https://www.winchester.ac.uk/news-and-events/press-centre/media-articles/unlocking-the-history-inside-winchester-cathedrals-mortuary-chests.php

https://www.independent.co.uk/news/uk/home-news/winchester-cathedral-anglo-saxon-bones-queen-emma-king-remains-wessex-a8915861.html

General texts

Some general texts on the Anglo-Saxon period and the Viking Age include:

H. Hamerow, D. A. Hinton and S. Crawford, *The Oxford Handbook of Anglo-Saxon Archaeology* (Oxford: Oxford University Press, 2011)

N. J. Higham and M. J. Ryan, *The Anglo-Saxon World* (New Haven: Yale University Press, 2013)

R. Naismith, *Early Medieval Britain, c. 500–1000* (Cambridge: Cambridge University Press, 2021)

N. S. Price and S. Brink, *The Viking World* (London: Routledge, 2008)

A. A. Somerville and R. A. McDonald, *The Viking Age: A Reader*, 3rd edn (Toronto: University of Toronto Press, 2020)

Michael Wood, *In Search of the Dark Ages: A History of Anglo-Saxon England* (London: BBC Books, 2022)

Online resources

There are many online databases that provide starting points for further research. The following are especially useful for the early medieval period:

The Electronic Sawyer – a searchable online catalogue of Anglo-Saxon Charters – https://esawyer.lib.cam.ac.uk/

Open Domesday – a searchable online copy of Domesday Book, with maps – https://opendomesday.org/

Oxford Dictionary of National Biography – although many entries now need some updating, the ODNB provides helpful starting points for most of the individuals covered in this book, and most entries have good bibliographies for further reading – https://www.oxforddnb.com/

PASE – Proposography of Anglo-Saxon England, a database of records relating to 'all the recorded inhabitants of Anglo-Saxon England from the late sixth to the late eleventh century' – https://pase.ac.uk/

The Portable Antiquities Scheme Database – for more about archaeological objects, either those mentioned in this book or similar examples, the PAS database can be searched at http://www.finds.org.uk. Records often include further reading.

Selected primary sources

Asser, *Life of King Alfred and Other Contemporary Sources*, ed. and trans. S. Keynes and M. Lapidge (London: Penguin Books, 1983)

The Anglo-Saxon Chronicles, ed. and trans. M. Swanton (London: Phoenix, 1996)

Bede, *Ecclesiastical History of the English People with Bede's Letter to Egbert and Cuthbert's Letter on the Death of Bede*, ed. and trans., L. Sherley-Price, R. E. Latham and D. H. Farmer (London: Penguin Classics, 2003)

Encomium Emmae Regina, ed. A. Campbell, with introduction by S. Keynes (Cambridge: Cambridge University Press, 1998)

English Historical Documents, Volume 1, c.550–1042, ed. D. Whitelock (London: Eyre & Spottiswoode, 2nd edn, 1979)

Henry of Huntingdon, *Historia Anglorum: The History of the English People*, ed. and trans. D. Greenway (Oxford: Oxford University Press, 1996)

The Liber Vitae of the New Minster and Hyde Abbey, Winchester, ed. S. D. Keynes, Early English Manuscripts in Facsimile 26 (Copenhagen: Rosenkilde and Bagger, 1996)

Orderic Vitalis, *The Ecclesiastical History of Orderic Vitalis*, Vol. V (Books IX and X) and Vol. VI (Books XI, XII and XIII), ed. and trans. Marjorie Chibnall (Oxford: Clarendon Press, 1975 and 1978)

The Sagas of Icelanders, with a preface by J. Smiley (London: Penguin Books, 2001)

William of Malmesbury, *Gesta Regum Anglorum: The History of the English Kings, Volume 1*, eds R. M. Thomson, M. Winterbottom and R. A. B. Mynors (Oxford: Clarendon Press, 1998)

Selected secondary sources, Winchester

M. Biddle, Excavations at Winchester 1967: Interim Report, *Antiquaries Journal*, 48, 1968, pp. 250–84

M. Biddle, *The Search for Winchester's Anglo-Saxon Minsters* (Archaeopress Publishing Ltd, 2018)

M. Biddle and B. Kjølbye-Biddle, 'Danske kongegrave i Winchester: Knud den Store og hans familie' in Karin Kryger (ed.), *Danske Kongegrave*, Selskabet til Udgivelse af danske Mindesmærker (University of Copenhagen: Museum Tusculanum Press, 2005)

M. Biddle and B. Kjølbye-Biddle, 'Danish Royal Burials in Winchester: Cnut and His Family', in Ryan Lavelle and Simon Roffey (eds), *Danes in Wessex: The Scandinavian Impact on Southern England, c. 800–c. 1100* (Oxford: Oxbow Books, 2016), pp. 212–49

J. Crook, *Winchester Cathedral: Nine Hundred Years, 1093–1993* (Chichester: Phillimore, 1993)

J. Crook, 'The Bones of King Cnut', in A. Rumble (ed.), *The Reign of Cnut: King of England, Denmark and Norway* (Leicester: Leicester University Press, 1994), pp. 165–98

J. Crook, 'The "Rufus Tomb" in Winchester Cathedral', *Antiquaries Journal*, 79, 1999, pp. 187–212

J. Crook, 'Medieval Royal and Episcopal Burials in Winchester Cathedral', *Antiquaries Journal*, 102, 2022, pp. 134–62

B. W. Cunliffe and J. Collis, *Winchester Excavations, 1949–1960* (Winchester: Museums & Libraries Committee, 1978)

M. Lapidge, with contributions by J. Crook, R. Deshman and S. Rankin, *The Cult of St Swithun* (Oxford: Clarendon Press, 2003)

D. McDermott, 'Winchester, Æthelings and Clitones: The Political Significance of the City for Anglo-Saxon Aristocracy and Norman Nobility', in R. Lavelle, S. Roffey and K. Weikert (eds), *Early Medieval Winchester: Communities, Authority and Power in an Urban Space, c. 800–c. 1100* (Oxford: Oxbow Books, 2021), pp. 103–24

P. Ottaway, T. Matthews, K. Qualmann, S. Teague, R. J. B. Whinney and M. Biddle, *Winchester: St. Swithun's 'City of Happiness and Good Fortune': An Archaeological Assessment* (Oxford: Oxbow Books, 2017)

J. Vaughan and D. Collins, *Winchester Cathedral: Its Monuments and Memorials* (London: Selwyn & Blount, 1919)

B. Yorke, 'Royal Burial in Winchester: Context and Significance', in R. Lavelle, S. Roffey and K. Weikert (eds), *Early Medieval Winchester: Communities, Authority and Power in an Urban Space, c.800–c.1000* (Oxford: Oxbow Books, 2021), pp. 59–80

B. A. Yorke, 'The Bishops of Winchester, the Kings of Wessex and the Development of Winchester in the Ninth and Early Tenth Centuries', *Proceedings of the Hampshire Field Club Archaeological Society*, 40, 1984, pp. 61–70

Selected secondary sources, general texts

R. P. Abels, *Alfred the Great: War, Kingship and Culture in Anglo-Saxon England* (London: Longman, 1998)

Frank Barlow, *William Rufus* (London: Methuen, 1983)

T. Bolton, *The Empire of Cnut the Great: Conquest and the Consolidation of Power in Northern Europe in the Early Eleventh Century* (Leiden: Brill, 2009)

T. Bolton, *Cnut the Great* (New Haven: Yale University Press, 2017)

M. Collins, P. Emery, C. Phillpotts, M. Samuel and C. Thomas, 'The King's High Table at the Palace of Westminster', *Antiquaries Journal*, 92, 2012, pp. 197–243

A. Dodson, *The Royal Tombs of Great Britain: An Illustrated History* (London: Duckworth, 2004)

S. Foot, *Monastic Life in Anglo-Saxon England, c. 600–900* (Cambridge: Cambridge University Press, 2006)

S. Foot, *Æthelstan: The First King of England* (New Haven: Yale University Press, 2011)

G. N. Godwin, *The Civil War in Hampshire (1642–45) and the Story of Basing House* (London: E. Stock, 1882)

D. M. Hadley, *The Northern Danelaw. Its Social Structure, c. 800–1100* (London and New York: Leicester University Press, 2000)

D. M. Hadley, *The Vikings in England. Settlement, Society and Culture* (Manchester: Manchester University Press, 2006)

S. Hollis, *Anglo-Saxon Women and the Church: Sharing a Common Fate* (Woodbridge: Boydell Press, 1992)

D. P. Kirby, *The Earliest English Kings* (London: Routledge, 2000)

R. Lavelle, S. Roffey and K. Weikert (eds), *Early Medieval Winchester: Communities, Authority and Power in an Urban Space, c. 800–c.1200* (Oxford: Oxbow Books, 2021)

Ryan Lavelle and Simon Roffey (eds), *Danes in Wessex: The Scandinavian Impact on Southern England, c. 800–c. 1100* (Oxford: Oxbow Books, 2016)

A. J. Langlands and R. Lavelle (eds), *The Land of the English Kin* (Leiden: Brill, 2020)

M. K. Lawson, *Cnut: The Danes in England in the Early Eleventh Century* (London: Longman, 1993)

M. K. Lawson, *Cnut: England's Viking King 1016–35* (Stroud: History Press, 2011)

N. Marafioti, *The King's Body: Burial and Succession in Late Anglo-Saxon England* (Vol. 16) (Buffalo, N.Y.: University of Toronto Press, 2014)

D. McDermott, 'Wessex and the Reign of Edmund II Ironside', in A. J. Langlands and R. Lavelle (eds), *The Land of the English Kin* (Leiden: Brill, 2020), pp. 336–351

D. Musgrove and M. Lewis, *The Story of the Bayeux Tapestry: Unravelling the Norman Conquest* (London: Thames and Hudson, 2021)

Janet L. Nelson, *Charles the Bald* (London: Longman, 1992)

R. North, E. Goeres and A. Finlay, *Anglo-Danish Empire: A Companion to the Reign of King Cnut the Great* (Berlin: De Gruyter, 2022)

S. J. Ridyard, *The Royal Saints of Anglo-Saxon England: A Study of West Saxon and East Anglian Cults* (Cambridge: Cambridge University Press, 1988)

L. Roach, *Kingship and Consent in Anglo-Saxon England, 871–978: Assemblies and the State in the Early Middle Ages* (Cambridge: Cambridge University Press, 2013)

L. Roach, *Æthelred the Unready* (New Haven: Yale University Press, 2016)

L. Roach, *Empires of the Normans: Makers of Europe, Conquerors of Asia* (London: John Murray, 2022)

S. Roffey and R. Lavelle, 'West Saxons and Danes: Negotiating Early Medieval Identities', in Ryan Lavelle and Simon Roffey (eds), *Danes in Wessex: The Scandinavian Impact on Southern England, c.800–c.1000* (Oxford: Oxbow Books, 2016), pp. 20–1

A. R. Rumble, *The Reign of Cnut: King of England, Denmark and Norway* (London: Leicester University Press in association with Manchester Centre for Anglo-Saxon Studies, 1994)

C. Spencer, *The White Ship: Conquest, Anarchy and the Wrecking of Henry I's Dream* (London: William Collins, 2020)

P. Stafford, *Unification and Conquest: A Political and Social History of England in the Tenth and Eleventh Centuries* (London: Edward Arnold, 1989)

P. Stafford, *Queen Emma & Queen Edith. Queenship and Women's Power in Eleventh-Century England* (Oxford: Blackwell, 1997)

I. Strachan, *Emma, the Twice-crowned Queen: England in the Viking Age* (London: Peter Owen, 2004)

M. Townend, *Viking Age Yorkshire* (Pickering: Blackthorn Press, 2014)

A. Whitehead, *Women of Power in Anglo-Saxon England* (Barnsley: Pen & Sword History, 2020)

B. Yorke, *Kings and Kingdoms of Early Anglo-Saxon England* (London: Seaby, 1990)

B. Yorke, *Wessex in the Early Middle Ages* (Leicester University Press, 1995)

B. Yorke, *Nunneries and the Anglo-Saxon Royal Houses* (London: Continuum, 2003)

ACKNOWLEDGEMENTS

The first huge thanks go to Tessa David for helping me shape the idea for *The Bone Chests* into a coherent form and to Bernard Cornwell for his kind encouragement and advice on the initial concept.

I'm really delighted to once again be in the safe hands of my editor Arabella Pike and her fantastic team at HarperCollins, especially Iain Hunt, Nicola Webb and Sam Harding, along with everyone else who helped to turn it into its final shape.

I'm very lucky to have the support of my brilliant agent Caroline Michel and her excellent team at Peters Fraser + Dunlop, who look after me and my books so well both in the UK and internationally, especially Tris Payne, Bea Hartshorn, Lucy Barry, Becky Wearmouth, Laurie Robertson, Kieron Fairweather, Fran Morgan and Sam Brace.

I'm very grateful to Levi Roach for kindly agreeing to fact-check the manuscript and sharing his insights, although any remaining errors are my own!

Countless other colleagues and friends have helped in the years of writing this book, either directly by answering questions and discussing ideas, or indirectly, by inspiring with their own excellent research (many by contributing to one of my podcasts!) – it's impossible to list you all. For this book, I'm especially grateful to Lesley Abrams, Martin Biddle, Jan Bill, Emma Brownlee, Clare Chapman, John Crook, Clare Downham, Octavia Dryden, Caitlin Ellis, Mark Horton, Jane Kershaw, Sam Leggett, Marianne Moen, Peter Reavill, Charles Spencer, Jessica Treacher, Katie Tucker, Ellie Williams. Thank you all!

Finally, the biggest thank you to my wonderful family for their constant support and endless patience.

LIST OF ILLUSTRATIONS

Winchester Cathedral *(Luisa Ricciarini/Bridgeman Images)*
Presbytery *(Author's collection)*
Chests *(Author's collection)*
View of the chests *(Author's collection)*
The stained-glass windows *(Author's collection)*
Coin of Cynetryth *(Classical Numismatic Group, CNG)*
Henry of Blois *(British Library Board/Bridgeman Images)*
Codex Aureus (Public domain)
Richard Fox *(National Portrait Gallery, London)*
Finger-ring *(Trustees of the British Museum)*
Ninth-century 'two emperor' coins *(Portable Antiquities Scheme)*
The Watlington hoard *(Portable Antiquities Scheme)*
The Alfred jewel *(Author's collection)*
Sarcophagus *(LDA Saxony-Anhalt, Juraj Lipták)*
Tenth-century St Peter's coin *(Derby Museums Trust)*
Frances Burney *(National Portrait Gallery, London)*
Illumination of Old Minster (British Library Board)
Eleventh-century 'helmet type' coin *(Portable Antiquities Scheme)*
Human remains *(Oxford Archaeology and Dorset County Council)*
Runestone 241 *(Berig)*
Grave marker *(Author's collection)*

Tomb *(Author's collection)*
Emma receiving the *Encomium (British Library Board)*
Emma and Cnut *(British Library Board)*
Runestone from Jelling *(Niels Quist/Alamy)*
Section of Bayeux Tapestry *(funkyfood London – Paul Williams/Alamy)*
Drawing of tomb *(John Crook)*

INDEX